POMPEIAN HOUSEHOLDS

An Analysis of Material Culture

Penelope M. Allison

Monograph 42
The Cotsen Institute of Archaeology
University of California, Los Angeles
2004

Editorial Board of The Cotsen Institute of Archaeology at UCLA
Jeanne E. Arnold, Marilyn Beaudry-Corbett, Susan Downey, Ernestine S. Elster,
Lothar von Falkenhausen, Charles Stanish, and Jo Anne Van Tilburg

The Cotsen Institute of Archaeology at UCLA
Charles Stanish, Director
Julia L. J. Sanchez, Assistant Director and Director of Publications
Leslie Ellen Jones, Publications Assistant

Edited by Rita Demsetz, Marilyn Gatto, Beverly Godwin,
Pat Hardwick, Brenda Johnson-Grau, Kathy Talley-Jones, and Carol Leyba
Production by Judith Botsai, Erin Carter, Tara Carter, Louise Krasniewicz,
Merlin Ramsey, Ken Stuart, Alice Wang, and Marian Olivas

Library of Congress Cataloging-in-Publication Data

Allison, Penelope Mary.
   Pompeian households: an analysis of the material culture /
Penelope M. Allison.
      p. cm. — (Monograph 42)
   Includes bibliographical references and index.
   ISBN 978-0-917956-96-6
   1. Pompeii (Extinct city)—Social life and customs. 2. Material
culture—Italy—Pompeii (Extinct city) 3. Furniture—Italy—Pompeii
(Extinct city) 4. Architecture, Domestic—Italy—Pompeii (Extinct city)
I. Title. II. Monograph (University of California, Los Angeles.
Institute of Archaeology); 20.
   DG70.P7 A645 2001
   937'.7—dc21   00-065581

Companion website: <*http://www.stoa.org/pompeianhouseholds*>

Cover illustration: Stairway along west wall of room 7, Casa della Venere in Bikini
Title page: East side of courtyard 44, Casa del Menandro

Illustration credits
Accademia Nazionale dei Lincei, Roma: Figure 5.11
Ministero per i Beni e le Attività Culturali—Soprintendenza archeologica di Pompei:
      Figures 1.3, 2.7, 3.1, 5.8, 5.9, 5.18, 5.23, 6.11, 8.4, 8.6, 8.7
Ministero per i Beni e le Attività Culturali—Istituto centrale per il catalogo e la
      documentazione, Roma: Figures 4.6, 5.15, 5.19, 5.20
Joyce Agee: Cover, Title page, Figures 2.1, 2.3, 2.4, 2.5, 2.10, 3.2, 3.3, 4.4, 4.5, 4.8, 4.9, 4.14,
      5.4, 5.5, 5.7, 5.12, 5.13, 5.14, 5.16, 5.21, 5.22, 6.6, 7.1, 8.1, 8.3, 8.10, 9.1
Penelope M. Allison: Figures 1.1, 1.2, 2.2, 2.6, 2.8, 2.9, 3.4, 4.1, 4.2, 4.3, 4.7, 4.10, 4.11, 4.12,
      4.13, 4.15, 4.16, 4.17, 4.18, 4.19, 4.20, 5.1, 5.2, 5.3, 5.6, 5.10, 5.17, 6.1, 6.2, 6.3, 6.4, 6.5, 6.7,
      6.8, 6.9, 6.10, 8.2, 8.5, 8.8, 8.9, A.1–A.30
Judith Botsai: Figures 1.4, A.1–A.30
Jaimie Lovell: Figures A.1–A.30

This book and database are dedicated to all those people who,
over the last two hundred years, have compiled the
Giornali degli Scavi di Pompei *and the*
Pompeian inventories.

Contents

List of Figures

List of Tables

Preface

THE ISSUES THAT THIS STUDY of Pompeian house contents addresses arose from my research into Pompeian wall painting and my skepticism about current chronological and typological approaches to this decoration of domestic space (for example, Allison 1991a, 1989, 1991b, 1992a; Allison and Sear 2002). The present study was first undertaken as a doctoral thesis in the Department of Archaeology at the University of Sydney. Data collection began in 1987 and the thesis was completed in 1992. Publication was first delayed by a spinal injury I suffered in 1994. Since this research was first undertaken and published as a thesis (Allison 1994a), there has been a burgeoning interest in the study of Pompeian domestic space (for example, Moormann 1993; Descœudres et al. 1994, Wallace-Hadrill 1994, Laurence and Wallace-Hadrill 1997, Bon and Jones 1997). In particular, a number of scholars have taken up the issues of spatial functions and artifact distribution in Pompeian houses (for example, Foss 1994; Pirson 1996; Berry 1997). There have also been more sensitive approaches to chronological issues in Pompeii (for example, Fröhlich and Jacobelli 1995). I have attempted to address these more recent studies in this volume. I am grateful to the scholars (for example, Foss 1994; Laurence 1995, 1997; Berry 1997) whose critiques of some of the arguments and methods presented in my preliminary publications of this research have forced me to sharpen the presentation of my arguments here. I hope that these arguments are now more succinct. A major contributing factor to some of the critiques is, however, the difference in approaches between scholars of the Roman world who are trained in documentary research and those trained more in material cultural research (Allison 2001). The archaeological record at Pompeii must be analyzed within rigorous frameworks of archaeological method and theory and the relationships of this archaeological record to ancient textual sources critically investigated.

In addition, to quote Rawson and Weaver, it is "our responsibility to other disciplines to guide them into drawing appropriate conclusions from the evidence" (1997:5).

Since the thesis was first presented, processual and post-processual debates have advanced considerably. I have attempted to update the text accordingly. While this study is grounded in processual method, it is not, however, intended as a comprehensive catalogue of the contents for each house in the sample. The intention is to present an overview of the patterns of spatial distribution of house contents. I have tried to present a summary of all house contents; however, the complexity of the data collection procedures and the volume of material involved mean that there will undoubtedly be errors, important to those looking for a precise catalogue of finds. While such detail is less significant for the aims of this project, I have attempted to keep errors and oversights to a minimum and apologize for any that may have slipped through.

This study has in no way exhausted all the possible analyses to which these databases can be subjected. Rather, it represents only a sampling of the ways in which artifact assemblages can be analyzed to produce a deeper understanding of life in Pompeii; and to compare Pompeian lifeways with those at other Roman sites, and with perspectives presented by literary élite, usually in Rome. Many other questions that may be answerable through this dataset have not yet been answered, and much detail has yet to be explored in depth. These issues will, I hope, be taken up by other scholars who can add to the body of data in more informed ways that are less dictated by textual approaches.

The opportunity to carry out research in Pompeii was first provided to me by the Australian Expedition to Pompeii. I am grateful to its directors, the late Prof. Richard Apperley (University of New South Wales), Prof. Jean-Paul Descœudres (University of Geneva), and Prof.

Frank Sear (University of Melbourne), for inviting me to be a member of this team. For permission to carry out the research I am indebted to Prof. Maria Giuseppina Cerulli Irelli, Prof. Stefano De Caro, Prof. Baldassare Conticello, Prof. Pietro Giovanni Guzzo, and Dr. Antonio Varone of the Soprintendenza Archeologica di Pompei. For their valuable assistance during my fieldwork campaigns, especially for the archival and artifact research, I am grateful to all the staff of the Soprintendenza Archeologica di Pompei, but particularly Dr. Antonio d'Ambrosio, Sg. Luigi Matrone, Sg. Franco Striano, Sg. Ciro Sicigniano, and Sga. Maria Oliva Auricchio. I also thank the Soprintendenza for providing some of the archival photographs and am grateful to Antonio Varone, Sg. Antonio Parlato, and Dssa. Greta Stephanie in this regard.

The British School at Rome and the German Archaeological Institute have been of great assistance in providing me with library facilities. I am also grateful to the library staff for their friendliness and helpfulness, especially Dr. Horst Blanck, Dr. Richard Neudecker, and Valerie Scott. I would also like to thank Mr. Halsted B. Van der Poel for the use of his private library and for access to his reference material.

So many people have provided physical, emotional, intellectual, and logistical support that it is impossible to name them all. Among these, Roland Fletcher was a supportive supervisor for my doctoral thesis and has continued to be a valuable colleague. Gretchen Poiner's mentoring ensured that I kept my mind on the job. The British Pompeii Research Committee and its field director, Prof. Roger Ling (University of Manchester), provided the opportunity to include a detailed study of the finds from the Insula de Menandro in my research. Drs. Tim Potter and Ralph Jackson (Department of Prehistoric and Romano-British Antiquities, the British Museum) provided access to the Department's library and discussions concerning the functions of Roman artifacts. Dr. Stefan Mols (University of Nijmegen) has generously assisted me with the identification of furniture fittings. Mme. Suzanne Tassinari (Musée du Louvre) provided useful information regarding bronze vessels, as well as drafts of her manuscript. Dr. Eric Moormann (University of Amsterdam) has supplied me with published material not available in Australia and advice concerning many details of the history of the Pompeian excavations. Prof. Richard Wright (University of Sydney) assisted with the original design of the databases used for this project, and Dr. Diana Modesto (University of Sydney) assisted with Italian language problems. None of these people can, however, be held responsible for any mistakes in the text of this volume.

For their companionship in Pompeii and for numerous discussions regarding the houses in the German Project, I thank all the members of the German Expedition to Pompeii, especially Prof. Volker M. Strocka, Prof. Wolfgang Ehrhardt (who introduced me to the Giornali degli Scavi in the Pompeii archives), Dr. Florian Seiler, and Dr. Thomas Fröhlich. I am also grateful to Dr. Estelle Lazer (University of Sydney) for her companionship and many useful discussions. The examiners of the doctoral thesis, Prof. Stephen Dyson (New York State University, Buffalo), Dr. Peter Brennan (University of Sydney), and Prof. Andrew Wallace-Hadrill (British School at Rome) provided useful comments that I have attempted to incorporate in this publication. I am also grateful to Peter Brennan, Prof. Eleanor Leach (University of Indiana), and Dr. Ted Robinson (University of Sydney) for reading drafts of various chapters and for their useful comments; to Dr. Svend Helms (University of Sydney) for reading the complete manuscript; and to Dr. Jaimie Lovell, Neel Smith, and Katie Lamberto for their work on the databases and website. Special thanks are owing to friend and photographer Joyce Agee for taking many of the photographs in 1993 and 1995, as well as for her much-needed support and companionship in the field. Among the other numerous friends and colleagues who have provided valuable assistance, encouragement, and enthusiasm I name but a few: Ross Balzaretti, Amanda Claridge, Peter Grave, Stephanie Moser, and Beryl Rawson.

Funds to carry out research and fieldwork were provided by an Australian Postgraduate

Award, a British School at Rome Scholarship in Italian Studies and Grant in Aid of Research, and a grant from the British Federation of University Women. A visiting fellowship in the Department of Prehistory and Archaeology, University of Sheffield, in 1997, and a U2000 Postdoctoral Research Fellowship in the Department of Archaeology at the University of Sydney have provided the opportunity to prepare the manuscript which was submitted for publication in 1999. Last, but not least, I am grateful to Julia Sanchez, Marilyn Beaudry-Corbett, Louise Krasniewicz, Brenda Johnson-Grau, Ken Stuart, Judith Botsai, and Leslie Ellen Jones (Cotsen Institute of Archaeology at UCLA), to Jean Kennedy (Australian National University), and to Carol Leyba (Leyba Associates in New Mexico) for bringing this work to publication.

—*Penelope M. Allison*

Figure 1.1   Objects found in southeast corner of hall 41 (inv. nos 4972–73, 4977–81), Casa del Menandro

1.

Considering Pompeian House Contents

THE EXCAVATIONS OF THE southern Italian town of Pompeii are some of the oldest and most renowned archaeological explorations in the world. For over two centuries, thousands of tourists have visited each year (figure 1.2) in the desire to witness an ancient Roman town "frozen in time." For over two centuries this site has also been continuously reinvestigated by classicists, ancient historians, art historians, and archaeologists. It may come as a surprise to some, therefore, that no comprehensive study of Pompeian house contents, and particularly of the materials removed during those excavations, has ever been carried out. This study undertakes—for the first time since Giuseppi Fiorelli organized lists of artifacts according to function from his excavations of Pompeian houses (1873:168–171)—a systematic collation of household assemblages to produce baseline data for analyzing the spatial distribution of domestic activities in these dwellings. These data also provide a useful body of evidence for a detailed investigation of the state of the town during the period leading up to and including the final abandonment.

One of the main issues facing such a study is the need to reinterpret the excavations carried out during the last 250 years. Questions now being asked were not considered relevant at the time of excavation and therefore were not taken into account in the excavation procedures and recording strategies. In addition, commonly accepted notions of the spatial organization of domestic activity in Pompeii are fraught

Figure 1.2   Tourists in the Via dell'Abbondanza

with assumptions based on unsubstantiated analogical inference, as well as cultural and social prejudices.

According to the mythologies of archaeology (for example, Augusti 1967:15; Will 1979:34), Pompeii ought to be the perfect site to study household assemblages. The so-called New Archaeologists have viewed these remains and their "systemic house floor assemblages" (Schiffer 1985:18) as the archetype against which all less well-preserved sites might be measured (Ascher 1961; Binford 1981). Archaeologists working in other areas have adopted the name "Pompeii" to draw attention to the deposition processes at their own excavations (for example, "Pompeiis in the Pacific," Torrence et al. 1990). Pompeii's quality of preservation and completeness has been assumed to provide a standard from which all other archaeological sites can be seen to diverge—a standard that Robert Ascher termed the "Pompeii Premise" (1961:324). The volcanic covering over Pompeii has been estimated to have reached as high as 8 m (Cerulli Irelli 1975:294). The implications of the Pompeii Premise are that this covering left the town hermetically sealed and in a pristine condition. Schiffer believed, therefore, that the house-floor assemblages could be analyzed as "systemic inventories—unmodified by [the] formation processes" (1985:38) witnessed in the more usual archaeological condition (see Schiffer 1987). For these New Archaeologists, or processualists, it should therefore be a simple task to use Pompeian house contents to understand the living conditions in the town at the time of the eruption. On the other hand, to classicists and ancient historians these excavated remains represent the materialization of ancient texts and provide insights into Roman domestic behavior during the early Empire. The situation, however, is more complicated (Allison 1992b).

The high profile of Pompeii, both in the minds of professional archaeologists and in the public view, has obscured details of the nature, extent, and emphases of previous research. The arguments underlying many interpretations of Pompeii's histories are frequently based on nineteenth- and early twentieth-century scholarship and have seldom been critically reassessed for their continuing validity. Throughout much of Pompeii's excavation history, the predominant emphases have been on unearthing building structures to illustrate textual references to Roman architecture, retrieving works of art for display in museum collections (figure 1.3), and ensuring that the Pompeian excavations remain an economically viable resource for cultural tourism (Allison 2002). Less artistically interesting artifacts have been removed to storerooms for typological studies, and still less intrinsically valuable finds have been left in situ for public display. Broken and fragmentary material of no perceived value has been discarded.

Removal of loose finds from their original contexts has been a widespread practice in the archaeology of complex societies, particularly those with substantial built structures. During the processes of excavation, analysis, and interpretation, these finds have been consistently decontextualized. During excavation, they are often removed from their physical location without the context being precisely documented. Their analyses of these artifacts have been largely typological and their interpretations concerned predominantly with trade and production patterns, rather than with studies of the (often domestic) contexts in which they were discovered (see Allison 1997a). The remaining empty structures then become the primary resource for investigating domestic behavior or, more precisely, domestic architecture. This approach has been common practice for archaeological research in the Mediterranean region for all of the last century (for example, compare Atkinson et al. 1904 with Sackett et al. 1992).

Notions persist that the built structure provides the main key to comprehending the activities carried out therein. The artifacts found there are analyzed as manufactured and traded objects rather than as used or consumed items (compare Ciolek-Torello 1984:129). Although a dominant cultural or social group might dictate the nature of these structures, the activities that occur within them can vary considerably. The

Figure 1.3 Finds being excavated near south end of room EE, Casa di Julius Polybius.
Pompeii photo archive neg. D14453

distribution of artifacts within a building—especially one used for domestic purposes—is governed by the traditions of the local and/or current inhabitants (Rapoport 1990), rather than by either the dominant powers that might have imposed the buildings on them, the previous inhabitants, or the architects of an earlier period (Allison 1999a). Not only have the processes of recording and analyzing settlement sites frequently removed the evidence of activity areas, but the processes of interpretation have also filled the empty spaces with external evidence. In classical archaeology, particularly since the first studies of Greek and Roman material culture, investigators trained in the classics and historical methods have sought clarification of fragmentary textual information through the fragmentary excavated remains. Terms from ancient texts have been applied to empty excavated spaces and to the decontextualized artifacts without rigorous validation. Sites have

been treated as illuminations of the textual record (Finley 1985:7); where they do not conform to this record, the interpretation of the material record has often been adapted to match the written reference (Allison 1992b:52; see figure 5.3). The texts are perceived to present an accurate and more readable record of the past, but the material evidence is viewed as confused and confusing.

Since the days of antiquarian collection, archaeological research at Pompeii has been concerned principally with epigraphy, art, or architecture. Analyses of the chronological developments of painting, building techniques, and architectural styles have been particularly prominent. Interpretations of the fabric of domestic life in Pompeii have combined these structural and decorative data with the epigraphical evidence and with information from external written sources. It has also been widely assumed that the term "archaeological data" applies only to the visible, in situ, and visitable remains at Pompeii. The artifacts removed during excavation, which more precisely constitute the "unique upper layer of the site [that] provides abundant data for the most recent history of the town" (Jongman 1988:56), have been largely neglected. Despite Tania Warscher's observations in the 1930s that "a thorough study of provenance was a necessary beginning for the study of Pompeian art and artifacts" (Dwyer 1982:16), such a study has not been accomplished. As for many other Roman sites, these decontextualized artifacts have been reserved for typological catalogues (for example, Carandini et al. 1977; Scatozza Höricht 1986; De Carolis 1987), with only very generalized provenance information.

Pompeian studies have tended to be segregated into architectural, art historical, or artifact typologies. Studies of chronological or consumption issues have usually drawn on only a limited spectrum of archaeological analytical procedures. In Pompeian research, considerable emphasis has been placed on the ancient written texts to interpret the archaeological remains of this site. Indeed, the excavations have been carried out within an intellectual tradition whereby written remains are given precedence over the material—archaeology being only "a technology for extracting evidence from the past" (Tilley 1998:692). As a result, interpretations have often been provided before excavation, the excavation serving only as embellishment (see Dyson 1981:8). According to Kenneth L. Ames, however, "investigating literature is an inefficient way to learn about artifacts of the past" (1982:210). Mary Douglas and Baron Isherwood also argued that "goods that administer to physical needs . . . are no less carriers of meaning than ballet or poetry" (1979:49). In their attempts to reconstruct Pompeian domestic life, the excavators have often selectively ignored, altered, or even destroyed the material evidence, as well as ignored the lack thereof.

Other branches of the archaeological discipline may be less burdened with large amounts of data than classical archaeology. Nevertheless, they have equally long and rigorous histories of data collection, and their theoretical positions are continuously being reevaluated (Trigger 1989). Classical archaeology, however, has been slow to examine many of its long-held assumptions (Dyson 1989). Nineteenth- and early twentieth-century interpretations of classical sites, frequently based on unrelated written texts, continue to serve as the foundations for current understandings of the classical world. As a consequence, we tend to believe that we are intimately acquainted with life at these sites and that we are well informed about more general concepts of Greek and Roman life.

Approaches to Roman archaeology are changing. Nevertheless, artifact studies are still dominated by a concern for questions relating to production and intersite distribution patterns (for example, Harris 1993). Few studies use provenanced artifact assemblages to better understand the consumption of Roman material remains. A lack of concern for specific artifact contexts in the published finds catalogues from quite recent excavations (for example, Ricci 1985; Sackett et al. 1992) makes such studies extremely difficult to pursue. Consequently, provenanced artifact assemblages have seldom been systematically treated for the information they provide, about either their context or the individual artifacts within the assemblage.

Before we can hope to use Pompeian evidence to write a substantive history of domestic behavior in Roman houses (Andreau 1973a: 214), we must first develop a holistic approach to the Pompeian remains, which includes investigation of the distribution of house contents. To assume that the Pompeian architectural and decorative evidence, combined with the academic treatises of the Roman literary élite, will provide us with a picture of domestic behavior that is representative of the Roman world, over the whole Roman period, simplifies reality and conflates and juxtaposes often unrelated data.

This study used a sample of thirty Pompeian *atrium* houses (figure 1.4). The contents of these houses were collated into a database, and the resulting assemblages were studied room by room and then house by house. The first procedure used the predominant patterns of

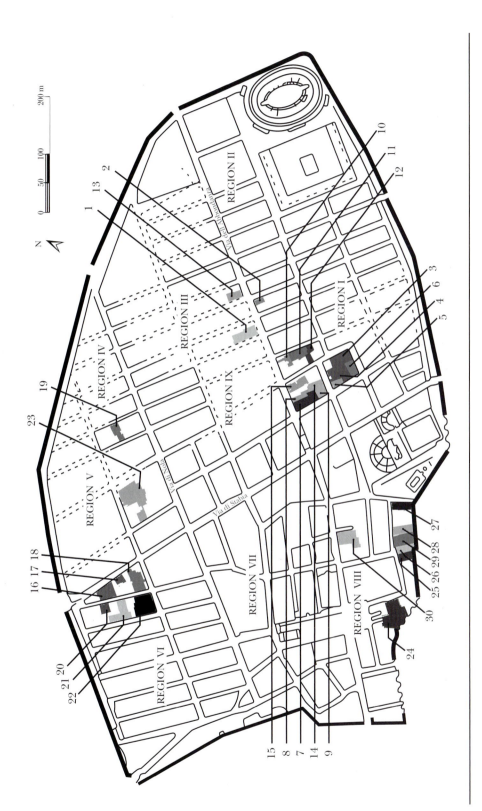

Figure 1.4 Plan of Pompeii showing location of houses studied

1. Casa di Julius Polybius IX 13, 1–3
2. Casa della Venere in Bikini I ii, 6–7
3. Casa del Menandro I 10,4
4. Casa del Fabbro I 10,7
5. House I 10,8
6. Casa degli Amanti I 10,11
7. Casa dei Quadretti Teatrali I 6,11
8. House I 6,8–9

9. Casa di Stallius Eros I 6,13
10. Casa del Sacerdos Amandus I 7,7
11. Casa dell'Efebo I 7, 10–12
12. House I 7,19
13. Casa di Trebius Valens III 2,1
14. Casa dei Ceii I 6,15
15. Casa del Sacello Iliaco I 6,4
16. House VI 16,26

17. Casa della Ara Massima VI 16,15
18. Casa degli Amorini Dorati VI 16,7
19. Casa di M. Lucretius Fronto V 4,a
20. Casa del Principe di Napoli VI, 15, 7–8
21. House VI 15,5
22. Casa dei Vettii VI 15,1
23. Casa delle Nozze d'Argento V 2, i

24. House VIII 2,14–16
25. House VIII 2,26
26. House VIII 2,28
27. Casa di Giuseppe II VIII 2,39
28. House VIII 2,34
29. House VIII 2,29–30
30. House VIII 5,9

assemblages in each room type to systematically test whether the current correlation of room function with room type, based on textual nomenclature and modern analogy, was appropriate. The second tested each house for the accepted model of a single phase of occupation from AD 62 to 79. The results did not always correspond to the traditional concepts of room use in Pompeian houses, nor did they correspond with the ideal model of a single phase of occupation from the earthquake of AD 62 to the final eruption of AD 79. Rather, they showed that a single house floor assemblage, reputedly dating to AD 79, could in fact include layers of deposition indicating various and changing activity within the preceding period (see Smith 1992:29–30).

The assessment of room use through artifact distribution showed that the nomenclature borrowed from the textual evidence was not necessarily a reliable guide to the use of space in these houses. Also, the apparent functions of rooms in Pompeian, and probably Roman, houses did not necessarily conform to the assumptions made about the spatial distribution of domestic activities that tend to be based on analogies with those of the middle classes and the élite of modern Europe.

Using this sample to interpret the living conditions in Pompeii during the period lead-ing up to the final eruption demonstrated that these final years and the abandonment process were more complex and involved more piece-meal changes than had been widely assumed. The period between AD 62 and AD 79 in Pompeii cannot be viewed as a static interim phase between two major events, with all the damage ascribed to one earthquake and all the repair deriving from it. Ordinary domestic change and ongoing disturbance of some kind (possibly low-level seismic activity) leading up to the final eruption have produced varying patterns of damage, repair, changing room use, and deterioration in Pompeian houses.

The methods by which the dataset in this study has been collected and systematized might be classified as *processual*. The analysis of this material involves a comprehensive awareness of the selective processes by which it was deposited, and then excavated and redeposited. Interpretations of the patterning observed in this analysis and its relationships with human activity draw, however, on interdisciplinary approaches to the archaeological and historical record (see Shanks 1997; Parker Pearson 1998). As James Whitley has commented, the study of artifacts provides a "rigorous testing ground . . . for revealing the limits of theory" (1992/1993: 27).

Figure 2.1 Ambulatory l, Casa del Principe di Napoli

2.

Nature of the Evidence

WITH A LONG HISTORY OF investigation by scholars from around the world, the objectives, approaches, outcomes, and interrelationships of various Pompeian research programs are complex and often confusing. The history and development of this research, however, play a major role in the possibilities, limitations, and emphases of the present study. A precise understanding and a critical appraisal of the objectives of the relevant previous research are therefore required. Acquiring such an understanding involves a critique of the investigative procedures employed to assess both the spatial distribution of household activities and the process of events and behavior in Pompeii in the last decades before the eruption and immediately after it. Of particular significance is the overwhelming importance that previous scholarship has accorded to a time horizon between a documented earthquake in AD 62 and the eruption in AD 79.

USE OF SPACE IN POMPEIAN HOUSES

Classically trained scholars investigating houses in Pompeii since the mid-eighteenth century have used analogies with Latin textual remains to interpret the activities that took place in these spatial remains. The writings of Varro (ca. 116–27 BC), Vitruvius (floruit 20–10 BC), and Pliny the Younger (ca. AD 62–110) have been the primary sources for insights into the spatial arrangements of Pompeian domestic practices. From the very first explorations, a similarity was seen between Vitruvius' ideal plan and the plans of many of the houses being unearthed (for example, Mau 1899:239; Boëthius and Ward-Perkins 1970:154–155; figure 2.2). Labels from Varro's language study and Pliny's descriptions of his country villas have also been applied to these plans. It has become common practice to label

rooms with Latin terms as soon as they are excavated (see Wallace-Hadrill 1994:6). As a result, the architectural remains of Pompeii are almost everywhere interpreted in combination with textual nomenclature, and plans of individual Pompeian houses are generally labeled with these terms (for example, Mau 1899: Fig. 110). Often the labels on such plans have been translated into the assumed appropriate modern counterpart (Grant 1971: Figs. 6–11; McKay 1977: Figs. 8, 9, 11). The resulting impression is that we are well informed not only as to the name ascribed to each room in a Pompeian house, but also as to the activities carried out in each (for example, Richardson 1983).

Some of the nomenclature provided by ancient authors was undoubtedly used by Pompeians, but any assignment of such labels to excavated spaces should be treated with the utmost caution. Such an assignment not only assumes a direct and unproblematic relationship between Pompeian houses and the lived worlds of these ancient authors, but also frequently attributes unchanging functions to these excavated spaces. Interpreting, for example, a space labeled a *cubiculum* as a bedroom (Grant 1971: Fig. 8) or one labeled an *oecus* as a dining room (Grant 1971: Figs. 7, 9) makes unvalidated assumptions about relationships between ancient and modern spatial separation of domestic activities. Pompeian architectural remains, textual descriptions from Latin authors, and modern analogy have thus been combined and this combination used to establish a concept of the universal spatial divisions of Roman domestic life.

It has also frequently been argued that room function governed the decorative schemes of Pompeian houses. While undoubtedly valid in broad terms (see Wallace-Hadrill 1994:708), arguments based on the premise of a precise relationship between architectural remains at

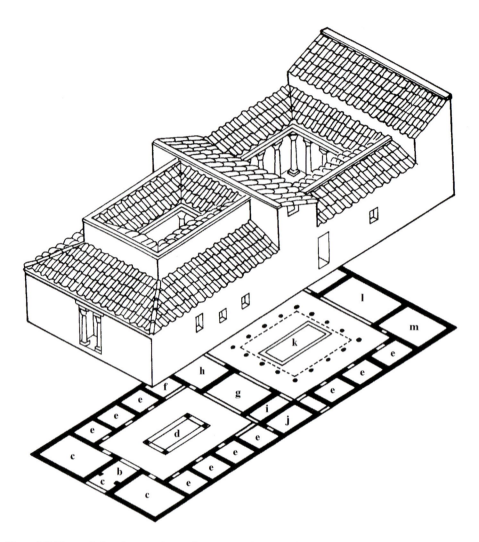

Figure 2.2 Type of plan frequently used as a typical Roman house, with labels from Vitruvius: a, *vestibulum*; b, *fauces*; c, *taberna*; d, *atrium*; e, *cubiculum*; f, *ala*; g, *tablinum*; h, *triclinum*; i, *andron*; j, *culina*; k, *peristylum*; l, *exedra*; m, *triclinium*

Pompeii and textual references to room type and use often become trapped in a circular argument (for example, van Binneke 1991:139–142). A relationship between particular rooms and their decorative schemes is better demonstrated from the standpoint of the architectural rather than the functional type (Corlàita Scagliarini 1974–1976; Barbet 1985:57–58, 123–124; Allison 1992a). These types should not be confused.

Some scholars view the iconographic details of wall paintings, particularly figured panels with mythological scenes, as indicators of room use (figure 2.3). While this may be valid (see

Bryson 1983:39), it is a fairly subjective approach as currently practiced. It draws on analogies with Renaissance and post-Renaissance painting and tends to give the iconography of central panels overriding significance within the overall wall scheme, crediting the ancient viewer with perceptions similar to those of the modern viewer. It also pays little attention to the significant roles that modes of execution and choice of models might have played in selecting certain iconographic schemes, particularly those that appear to be almost randomly repeated across a number of houses and room types (see Allison 1997b).

Figure 2.3 Wall paintings with love scenes used to identify room 12 as a bedroom, Casa dell'Efebo

The current state of research into the use of space in Pompeian houses is the result of an overlay of the textual evidence on architectural and, to a certain extent, decorative evidence. A basic problem in using the Pompeian archaeological record in this manner is that functions and spaces in Pompeian houses are interpreted without studying the actual material left there in the period before the eruption. While it has long been acknowledged that a number of fixtures, such as cooking hearths (Salza Prina Ricotti 1978/1980:239–240), household shrines, water-catchment areas, and garden colonnades, provide evidence of room use, no systematic examination of room contents, fixed or movable, has been made. Because the houses are empty today (except for a few items of furniture placed for display), the general trend has been to treat them as if they had always been so. This approach is comparable to the concept of the "period room" (Shanks and Tilley 1987:76–77), but in the case of Pompeii the room contents have not merely been reordered; many have been ignored completely. George's reference (1998:83)

to "missing evidence" makes a distinction between material left in a display location for cultural tourism and material catalogued and put in storerooms. This comment demonstrates the continuing lack of comprehension among Pompeian researchers of common archaeological practice.

Not all previous research completely ignored the contexts of Pompeian house contents. Studies such as the *Häuser in Pompeji* series (for example, Strocka 1984a; Michel 1990; Seiler 1992) reiterate the lists of excavated finds as they appeared in the earlier *Notizie degli Scavi* publications.[1] These artifacts and their assemblages, viewed in isolation from the contents of other Pompeian houses, have little part in the interpretation of how activities are spatially distributed in the houses unless they correspond with preexisting, text-based ideas on the use of each space. In his study of domestic sculpture, Eugene J. Dwyer (1982) listed the recorded finds from five Pompeian houses according to room. However, in his assessment of room use, he relied on textual nomenclature as a premise for the "correct" furnishings for such rooms (Dwyer 1982:113–120). Thus, the handful of studies that have included any room contents in interpreting room use have begun from the premise that the textual evidence provides the proper and aggregate picture of room furnishings. Archaeological discoveries that do not conform to this model have been interpreted as indications of disruption.

An important factor for an analysis of room use in Pompeian houses is the chronological relationship between the structure and decoration of the room and its contents. Much of the structure and some of the decoration in Pompeian houses obviously long predated the final eruption. If current chronologies for the establishment and growth of the town of Pompeii are reliable (for example, Eschebach and Eschebach 1995; Wallace-Hadrill 1997), some of the buildings may have been in use for some 300 years. While some general relationship is likely to exist, the planned function of a space at the time of construction may have been very different from that associated with its final decoration, and again from its final use. Not only has Dwyer noted (1982:113) that the textual evidence warns us that "the physical and functional organization of Roman houses depended on a model, which was subject to change as certain fashions became obsolete . . ," but there must also have been a general process of domestic change whereby room functions were reallocated and various parts of the house were altered, downgraded, or reorganized (see David 1971:125–126).[2]

Inevitably, the structure of a room, its proportions, shape, size, and location within the plan of the house, and probably its intended function, predate its decoration and thus its decorated function. In turn, the structure certainly, and the decoration probably, predate the contents of the room. The contents provide documentation of the condition of a room during its final state. It is therefore not logical to assume that the simple amalgamation of structure, decoration, and contents will either provide a reliable illustration of room use as indicated in the textual nomenclature or show that the contents are unreliable evidence. Only when a consistent pattern of structure, decoration, and contents is evident across a number of rooms might one start to formulate concepts of generalized Pompeian domestic behavior. Only then can relationships between the textual evidence, generally provided by the élite in the city of Rome, and the archaeological evidence from the Vesuvian towns and other sites of the Roman period be used to investigate any universal concepts of Roman domestic behavior. Any lack of a consistent pattern of structure, decoration, and contents in Pompeian houses need not be seen as a lack of information. It may rather reflect variation within and between their individual histories or, conversely, disruption and abandonment effects in those houses during periods of seismic activity. Before household assemblages can be used as documentation of disruption and abandonment processes, current opinions regarding those processes need to be appraised.

RELATIVE CHRONOLOGY AND DEPOSITIONAL PROCESSES

Much accepted wisdom concerning the sequence of events that affected the lives of Pompeians leading up to and following the AD 79 eruption is based on three main assumptions. The first is that there was only one earthquake in the period between AD 62 and AD 79. The second is that the Pompeians not driven out by the disruption of the AD 62 earthquake, had no concept of the impending threat and so did not start to abandon the town until Mount Vesuvius began to erupt (Thérasse 1979:301; Ward-Perkins and Claridge 1980:13; Sigurdsson et al. 1982:47; Dobbins 1994). The third assumption is that, except for the return of some citizens immediately after the eruption to retrieve their valuables, the site lay undisturbed for the next 1700 years. In all probability, the processes of disruption, repair, and abandonment were much less uniform and spread over the final decades in a complex mosaic of disturbance, alteration, and deterioration. Furthermore, processes of post-abandonment intrusion extended for centuries.

Most scholars appreciate that the Pompeian remains do not represent a "frozen moment," but many assume that, in the Pompeian household, everything should be in its right place within the developmental cycle (Stenning 1969). Even where the Pompeian house floor assemblages represent domestic change, however, it is still misleading to use Pompeii as a default condition (Schiffer 1985: esp. 22). The patterns of deposition at this assumed ideal site also display the diachronic and post-depositional disturbance characteristics (the formation processes that "contribute variability to house floor assemblages") from which it was presumed to have been free. There cannot therefore be a Pompeii Premise in the conventional sense, based on the eponymous ideal that presents an ethnographic picture of past reality. This does not mean that there can be no Pompeii Premise at all, since the site plainly has unusual potential. The site is, in fact, very informative about the nature of archaeological evidence, cultural behavior, and residential social life.

Two major factors, known from the occasions when Pompeii was deemed worthy of comment by Roman authors, are believed responsible for disrupting the archaeological record so that it does not accord with traditional perspectives of the Pompeii Premise, thus making the study of household assemblages more complex. The first is seismic activity prevalent in the area prior to the AD 79 eruption of Mount Vesuvius (Tacitus *Ann.* 15, 22; Seneca *Natur. Quaest.* 6, 1, 2–3). The second is disturbance by salvagers after the eruption (Suetonius *De Vita Caesarum: Titus* 8; Dio Cassius 66, 24), believed to have begun immediately after the volcanic burial of Pompeii and to have had an impact on the deposit. This particular type of salvage is thought to explain the absence of valuable items and materials in the excavated houses.

DEPOSITIONAL PROCESSES PRIOR TO THE AD 79 ERUPTION

It has been widely accepted that textual references indicate that only two seismic events occurred in the Vesuvian region during the 60s and 70s and that all the taphonomic processes in Pompeii can be ascribed to one or other of these events: a single earthquake in AD 62 and an eruption in AD 79. These assumptions and the associated time horizons have had a major effect on past interpretation of the material remains of Pompeii, particularly on the construction of the chronologies of structural and decorative remains which, in turn, have formed the frameworks for assessing living conditions during the final decades.

R. C. Carrington's history of the masonry techniques and styles used in Pompeii (1933) has continued to form a basis for dating Pompeian buildings, despite his own caution (1933:127) concerning its reliability.[3] Some of the earlier phases of Carrington's masonry chronology were identified and dated through pottery deposits from excavations below the AD 79 level. Many of his later phases, more relevant to this study, were based on structural relationships in the AD 79 level, often using covering decoration as a *terminus ante quem*. Subsequent chronologies of wall painting frequently use masonry styles to establish their absolute dates, thereby creating a circular argument.

Amedeo Maiuri's refinement (1942) of Carrington's chronology, to isolate a final building phase between AD 62 and AD 79, stemmed from the assumption that the condition of the material remains of Pompeii can be directly related to two seismic events for which there is dated textual verification. Thus, any evident damage, or even alteration, to the structure, seen as late in the history of the building, was identified as resulting from a single documented earthquake in AD 62. Any incomplete repair or alteration was considered to have been initiated as a result of this earthquake damage and terminated by the final eruption. This so-called final building phase has remained the basis for current perspectives on construction activities in the last years of the town (for example, Richardson 1988a; Adam 1989a:230–231, 471; Eschebach and Eschebach 1995: Fig. 66). While Roger Ling concluded (1989) that a definitive architectural history of Pompeii remains to be written, Carrington's study and, more particularly, Maiuri's concept of a single building phase after AD 62 remain the bases for current chronologies of Pompeian building, with only very recent attempts made to provide critical reevaluations (for example, Fröhlich 1995; Fulford and Wallace-Hadrill 1998).

As with building chronologies, current chronologies of Pompeian wall painting are based on stylistic analyses. August Mau (1882) separated the paintings into different types, largely according to the stylistic treatment of their prevalent architectural arrangements: the so-called Four Pompeian Styles. These styles are believed to have followed each other chronologically, the Fourth Style being the one in vogue at the time of the AD 79 eruption.[4] Still debated, and pertinent to this study, is the date for the commencement of the Fourth Style. Karl Schefold (1952;

1962:99–185) divided it into a Neronian Fourth Style (ca. AD 54–68) and a Vespasianic Fourth Style (ca. AD 68–79), largely on the basis of stylistic differences but also on observed damage and repair to the paintings. His stylistic analyses, however, have been shown to be unreliable (for example, Allison 1991a; Allison and Sear 2002:84), and the chronological development of this most prolific of the Four Pompeian Styles is still problematic (figures 2.4, 2.5). In attempts to fit the development of this style into the frameworks of assumed time horizons, the debate has generally revolved around the association of either damaged, repaired, or altered wall decoration (figure 2.6) with the recorded earthquake of AD 62 or incomplete decoration with the final eruption (see de Vos 1977:38–42; 1982:336–338 n. 50–51; Strocka 1984b:130–131 n. 17; Archer 1990:

Figure 2.4 Wall paintings datable after AD 71 but labeled Neronian by Schefold (1957a:180), room 13, Casa della Caccia Antica

Figure 2.5 Wall paintings datable after AD 71 but labeled Neronian by Schefold (1957a:180), room 11, Casa della Caccia Antica

16

Figure 2.6 Coarsely plastered area of south wall, room k, Casa del Principe di Napoli

113–115 n. 47; Ling 1991:72; Peters et al. 1993: 367–372; compare Strocka 1995).

Major dilemmas continue to arise where the relative chronology of some paintings does not fit these assumptions (see Kockel 1986:558–559). The most notable case is room h in the Casa dei Vettii (Peters 1977:95–98). Schefold attempted to explain this and similar discrepancies with the single earthquake concept by hypothesizing a second earthquake nearer in time to the final eruption (1957b:152; see also Schefold 1995). While Schefold's hypothesis is probably nearer seismological reality than the single earthquake concept, it has frequently been rejected, largely because of a lack of any literary reference to such an event (for example, Strocka 1984a:36). Thus, to date, assumptions about the exclusive significance of a single AD 62 earthquake play a major role in the accepted chronologies of Third- and Fourth-Style wall paintings and therefore in the domestic history of the final years of the town.

In summary, modern scholars have generally attributed the evident damage and repair of both public and private houses in Pompeii to a single earthquake seventeen years prior to the final eruption. The general opinion among Pompeianists is that the town was still in some disarray, recovering from that disaster, when Mount Vesuvius erupted in AD 79 (for example, Maiuri 1942; Andreau 1973b; Adam 1989b; Zanker 1995:133–140). Like the concept of a frozen moment, however, these assumptions and their related interpretations of the archaeological material are oversimplified readings of the texts, seismic activity, and human behavior.

ONE OR MORE EARTHQUAKES?

A one-line reference by Tacitus (*Ann.* 15, 22) indicated that the Campanian town of Pompeii was largely destroyed by an earthquake during the consulship of P. Memmius Regulus (that is, AD 62). Seneca (*Natur. Quaest.* 6, 1, 2) stated that it was actually on the Nones of February in the consulship of C. Memmius Regulus (son or nephew of the above) and L. Verginius Rufus (that is, 5 February AD 63) that an earthquake caused great destruction in Campania. Despite the disparity between the two dates, and yet another given by Seneca (*Natur. Quaest.* 6, 1, 13), scholars have generally accepted that all the dates refer to a single earthquake on 5 February

17

AD 62 (for example, Seneca *Natur. Quaest.* transl. Corcoran 1972:126 n. 2; see Strocka 1995:175).

Even if all these references reported the same event, the possibility that more than one earthquake caused the evident damage to Pompeii in the decades prior to the AD 79 eruption is by no means ruled out. Not only was an earthquake felt in Naples during Nero's reign, in the consulate of Gaius Laecanius and Marcus Licinus (Tacitus *Ann.* 15, 34) and dated to AD 64,[5] but textual evidence also indicates that seismic activity was not unusual in the Campanian region (Seneca *Natur. Quaest.* 6, 1, 2; Pliny *Ep.* 6, 20, 3). Pliny the Younger, in his detailed description of the AD 79 eruption, indicated that there had been earthquakes for several days prior to this eruption but that people were not particularly alarmed because such tremors were frequent in the area. Pliny the Elder's belief (*Nat. Hist.* 2, 198) that earthquakes could continue for up to two years may well have been founded on phenomena observed from his base at Misenum near Naples. Thus, assumptions that a final phase of Pompeii can be identified through damage and repair to its buildings and can be dated from AD 62 represent a misreading of the written documentation.

These misreadings have been hard to correct. Even in recent studies of earthquakes in Italy that treat the problem of relating interpretations of archaeological data to seismic events (for example, see Rapp 1989:398–403 and Ward-Perkins 1989:410), the assumptions underlying this single-earthquake concept, and its identification in the Pompeian material evidence, have remained unquestioned. George Rapp, Jr. (1989: 403) criticized scholars such as Sir Arthur Evans at Knossos who wrote seismic interpretations into their data. In the same volume, however, Paul Arthur (1989:502) attributed archaeological remains both to the effects of an earthquake in Pompeii, traditionally dated to AD 62, and that reported by Tacitus in Naples, traditionally dated to AD 64, without distinguishing between them. Similarly, Jean-Pierre Adam's argument (1989a: esp. 231; 1989b) was based on the premise that not only is earthquake damage easily discernible in Pompeii, but that it is also

datable to that specific earthquake and that the quantity and nature of damage can be used to estimate the intensity of the tremors of AD 62 (Adam 1989b: esp. 473). Thus, two crucial factors—the acknowledged difficulty of assessing earthquake damage in archaeological remains and the textual evidence for possible ongoing seismic activity between the AD 62 earthquake and the eruption of Mount Vesuvius—have had negligible impact on chronologies of the last decades in Pompeii. This situation indicates just how in-built the assumptions of fixed and datable archaeological time horizons in Pompeii have become.

Given current knowledge about volcanic activity, it is timely that these assumptions be more rigorously and thoroughly deconstructed. Russell Blong's study of the effects of volcanic eruptions shows that earthquakes frequently occur prior to the eruptive activity of a volcano even if they are not directly connected (Blong 1984:47–54). For example, at Api Siau, earthquakes were associated with ongoing eruptive activity from January 1972 to October 1976 (Blong 1984:115). The recent volcanic activity at Monserratt consists of pyroclastic flows that have continued for more than five years (*Volcano World*).

Even if the major earthquakes referred to by Seneca and Tacitus are one and the same, we still cannot assume that because only one Campanian earthquake was reported in Rome, there must have been only one (Jacobelli 1995:17). If, as has been argued, the wealthy and the nobility left Pompeii after this earthquake, Rome may well have been little concerned about further economic and social disruption to the town (see Adam 1989b:460 regarding rich families living in Pompeii). While the first earthquake or volcanic activity may be front-page news (for example, Pozzuoli from 1970, Mount Etna from 1989, Pinatubo in the Philippines from 1991, and Monserratt in 1996–1997), the concern of those not directly affected soon dwindles, and they tend to lose interest in any possible subsequent tremors or eruptions, particularly if the incidents are frequent.

Because the assumption that all damage and upheaval is attributable to a single earthquake has so pervaded Pompeian research, it is difficult to break free of its frameworks and implications. For this reason, Schefold's solution, brought in to solve an observed phenomenon that had created a chronological dilemma for him, has been given little credence. Only recently has more notice been taken of Pliny the Younger's reference to the familiarity of the people of Campania with earthquakes to explain the ongoing damage and repair (for example, Schefold 1990:23–24; Pappalardo 1990:207, 209; De Caro 1990:160; Jacobelli 1995:17; De Simone 1995:37). Only in recent years have some archaeologists and vulcanologists paid closer attention to the problems that result from interpreting the Campanian chronologies from the standpoint of these long-held assumptions (for example, Seiler 1992:85, 1995; Guadagno 1995; Jacobelli 1995; Marturano and Rinaldis 1995; Varone 1995). If these assumptions are no longer viewed as verified and fixed points in the chronology, more informed perspectives of the process of events during Pompeii's last decades may be possible.

DEPOSITIONAL PROCESSES DURING THE AD 79 ERUPTION

While the precise date of 24 August for the eruption of Mount Vesuvius that buried Pompeii is debated (for example, Pappalardo 1990:209–210), there seems little reason to dispute Dio Cassius' account (66, 21–23) that this event occurred in AD 79, even though it was written some 150 years later. Assumptions about the sequence of events and the behavior of Pompeians during and immediately after this eruption, however, need to be reappraised.

Many current perspectives of the inhabitants' behavior, both before and during this eruption, stem from the opinion that the Pompeians did not comprehend that Mount Vesuvius was an active volcano and did not heed warnings of impending disaster (Ward-Perkins and Claridge 1980:13). Like Pliny the Younger at Misenum, they reputedly saw little danger during any previous seismic activity or the early phases of the eruption. Many were allegedly undecided whether to remain in their houses or flee (for ex-

ample, Ciprotti 1964:44; Thérasse 1979:302). In general, and by analogy with Pliny the Elder at Stabiae, they are assumed to have started to panic and leave their houses only on the second day, fleeing towards the sea (Ciprotti 1964:48). Population estimates (see Ciprotti 1964:47; Adam 1989a:225) have been used to deduce that, like Pliny the Younger and his mother in Misenum, the majority of inhabitants of Pompeii escaped from the town, if not from the area, during the final eruption (Ciprotti 1964:47; Thérasse 1979:301; Sigurdsson et al. 1982:51).

Volcanoes were not unknown to the Romans at this time. Diodorus (4, 21, 5) and Strabo (*Geography* 5, 4, 8), both writing in the first century BC, knew Mount Vesuvius to have been active, at least in ancient times. Suetonius (*De Vita Caesarum: Caligula* 51) recorded an eruption of Mount Etna around AD 40, and the anonymous Etna Poem has been dated on stylistic grounds to the early empire and prior to AD 62 on the grounds that its author had dismissed the volcanic zone of Campania as inactive (Duff and Duff 1982:351–352, 431–432). This reasoning implies that opinions would have changed after AD 62 (see Jashemski 1979b:606) when such delusions were unlikely to have continued. In other words, the argument assumes that the recorded earthquake of AD 62 had in fact alerted the inhabitants of the region to a potential threat from Mount Vesuvius. Indeed, Pliny the Elder (*Nat. Hist.* 2, 200) indicated that the Romans knew an earthquake to be a premonition of some impending event. Pliny the Younger reported that there had been earth tremors for several days prior to the eruption. Thus, there are no grounds to assume that Pompeians could not have prepared themselves for this eruption. Klaus Neumann has demonstrated (1996:41–42) that inhabitants threatened by the eruptions in Rabaul in 1994 did not wait for the authorities to tell them that their lives were in danger.

Another confusing factor in comprehending the details of the process of abandonment and burial of Pompeii is that considerable emphasis has been placed on the account of the seventeen-year-old Pliny the Younger, who reported secondhand on his uncle's activities in Stabiae (*Ep.*

6, 16) and reputedly gave an eyewitness account of the eruption, but viewed from the other side of the bay (*Ep.* 6, 20). Because these two letters are the fullest written accounts available, they are assumed to be accurate sources concerning the sequence of events and behavior during the eruption. Pliny's own reactions and perceptions are generally assumed to reflect the behavior of all those affected by the eruption.

Pio Ciprotti (1964:45) noted that the situation for Pompeians must have been worse than that for Pliny the Younger at Misenum on the other side of Naples. More important, Renata Copony (1987: 219–220, 227) has thrown doubt on the accuracy of Pliny the Younger's report, and Helmut Wilsdorf argued (1979:40–41) that, being a literary man and not a scientist like his uncle, Pliny had based his account of the eruption on the Etna Poem rather than on actual observation.

Investigations of human behavior in the face of more recent volcanic activity show that victims have varying attitudes regarding the nature of the threat and the need for evacuation (Blong 1984:132–186; see also Neumann 1996: 32–34). Surprisingly, panic, shock, and irrational behavior are rare (Sheets and Grayson 1979:626; although see Neumann 1996:62–65). Rumors, misinformation, and contradictory statements, however, abound during a volcanic eruption and, because of the chaotic conditions, much of the recording may reflect the bias of the reporter (Blong 1984:156, 184). Neumann contrasted the evocative and poetic report of a final-year schoolgirl with the scientific account of the vulcanologists (1996:52–58).

It is feasible that while some Campanians left the area after the AD 62 earthquake (Seneca *Nat. Quaest.* 6, 1, 10), others, subjected to ongoing seismic and volcanic activity, left over the intervening years. At Monserratt, some people left their homes and lived in shelters for more than a year. Others stayed in the danger zone despite official instructions to leave because they had nowhere else to go and had animals to feed. Still others, with mortgages, had difficulty deciding whether or not to leave and start afresh (*Volcano World*). Pliny's reference to empty houses in the

districts (*Ep.* 6, 16, 13) is obscure and could equally refer to departures during the intervening years as to abandonment during the final eruption. The lack of records of victims in the streets and gateways of Pompeii is traditionally taken to indicate that most of the inhabitants had escaped into the surrounding countryside during the eruption. Rather, at least some are likely to have abandoned the town during the preceding decades.

It should be possible to acquire useful information concerning the final abandonment of Pompeii through detailed and specific assessment of the volcanic deposition. A number of recent studies of the volcanic stratigraphy of the Somma Vesuvius eruptions have established a relative chronology of the eruption process by examining the related stratigraphy at Pompeii, Herculaneum, and Oplontis (for example, Lirer et al. 1973, 1993; Delibrias et al. 1979; Sigurdsson et al. 1982; Livadie 1986; Cioni and Vecci 1988; see also Kockel 1986:543). The absolute chronology for the different phases of the eruption, however, has been based on the premise that Pliny's time scales (*Ep.* 6, 16, and 20) are an accurate documentation of the whole event.[6] Thus, no chronology of the volcanic deposit independent of Pliny's letters has been developed. No study has assessed the eruption process, its effect on the population, and its relationship to the literary evidence.

Epigraphers have used the preserved election graffiti on house walls in Pompeii (figure 2.7) to demonstrate a lively political life in the town right up to the eruption (for example, Castrén 1975:124; Franklin 1980:61–69, 124; Mouritsen 1988: esp. 32–33, 106–107; see also Kockel 1986:536–537). They have, however, based their arguments on the assumption that AD 79 is an absolute date for the latest extant electoral programmata, whereas, in fact, it can serve only as a *terminus ante quem.* They support their arguments with the observation that the graffiti appeared to be fresh and that their survival rate was likely to be low; such a line of argument is unsubstantiated. Some of the programmata excavated in the early twentieth century have survived, exposed to the sunlight, for nearly a

Figure 2.7 Façade with electoral graffiti, Casa di Trebius Valens *(Spinazzola 1953: Pl. IX)*

hundred years. Surely they could have survived in good condition for an equally long period prior to the eruption.

It has also been argued that after the AD 62 earthquake, a new building period began in Region VIII of the town (Noack and Lehmann-Hartleben 1936:157; for Regions, see figure 1.4); a new bath complex was being built in Region IX (Mau 1899:202); the Temple of Vespasian, the Comitium in the Forum (Zanker 1988:42), and the Temple of Isis (Maiuri 1942:68–69) were repaired; many commercial institutions, notably those requiring much water (Adam 1986:81), were established (Maiuri 1942:161–162); and many large houses were lavishly refurbished in Fourth-Style decoration (Andreau 1973b:386). Espen B. Andersson noted that a great number of summer *triclinia* with water displays were installed after AD 62 (1990:232) and that Casa del Torello was remodeled at least once after that date (1990:217).

All this appears to contradict assumptions that after the AD 62 earthquake, the town was in a state of devastation and civic disorder, lacked an adequate water supply, and was abandoned by the wealthier citizens. In contrast, at the time of the AD 79 eruption, many of the buildings were considered to be still in ruins, reputedly

from this particular earthquake (Cerulli Irelli 1990:234). Important families are assumed to have departed after this earthquake, leaving the town to the merchant and lower classes (Andreau 1973b:370, 386; Zanker 1988:42). Parts of many luxury houses are assumed to have been converted for industrial or commercial use (Andreau 1973b:370 passim), shops abandoned (Andreau 1973b:385), and the traditional public center, the Forum, defunct as the commercial center (Andreau 1973b:389; Zanker 1988:4, 28). The aqueduct was also reputedly damaged by this recorded earthquake, such that there was only a provisional municipal water system during the final seventeen years (Maiuri 1942:90–91; Dybkjaer-Larsen 1982:42; Adam 1986:80; see Kockel 1986:467, 504). As Parslow noted (1990), such inconsistencies can only be resolved by more careful review of the precise relationship between this recorded earthquake and the archaeological remains.

DEPOSITIONAL PROCESSES AFTER THE AD 79 ERUPTION

While Schiffer emphasized the significance of redeposition and post-abandonment uses of settlement sites, the New Archaeologists conventionally treated Pompeii as the epitome of a pristine site (Schiffer 1985:29, 38). Not only is the condition of the Pompeian archaeological record prior to AD 79 more complex and interesting than generally presumed, but post-eruption disturbance of the Pompeian remains has also rendered the archaeological record a less than perfectly preserved document of everyday Roman life (compare Sigurdsson et al. 1982:39; Schiffer 1985:18).

The excavators of Pompeii frequently reported that the supposedly sealed volcanic deposit was disturbed. They have also attributed the many holes in the walls of the houses (for example, figure 2.8) to post-eruption disturbance (Cerulli Irelli 1975:295). However, because of the excavation methods, aims, and recording procedures (see chapter 3), little stratigraphic information is available for this disturbance or for

any that might have resulted from natural causes. Textual evidence, as well as accepted perspectives on human behavior in the aftermath of a volcanic eruption, also suggest that post-depositional human disturbance was likely. It is an oversimplification, however, to assume, as many do (for example, Bechi 1834:2), that all observed disturbances to the volcanic deposit and the lack of certain classes of valued artifacts are attributable to Pompeians returning to collect their possessions immediately after the eruption.

Dio Cassius' description (66, 24) of the aftermath of the eruption indicated that Emperor Titus went to Campania himself and sent two ex-consuls to the region to supervise restoration and grant to survivors the land of those who had perished in the catastrophe and left no heirs (see also Suetonius *De Vita Caesarum: Titus* 8). It

Figure 2.8 LEFT: North wall of room 12 showing holes and burning of painted plaster during eruption, Casa degli Amanti. RIGHT: East wall of room 17 showing hole, Casa del Menandro

is widely accepted that this reference indicates that the Roman delegates visited Pompeii.

It is important to note that much of the textual evidence on the situation during and after the eruption, particularly the accounts of Dio Cassius and Pliny the Younger, did not refer to Pompeii specifically but rather to the Campanian region in general. Both Pliny the Younger (*Ep.* 6, 16, 9–10) and Strabo (*Geography* 5, 4, 8) indicated that the stretch of coast affected by the eruption had been thickly populated. It is therefore equally possible that authors such as Dio Cassius and Suetonius were as concerned with the villas and houses in the surrounding area as with the population of a specific market town within the region (compare Jongman 1988:28–29). The emperor in Rome might also have been more concerned for the villas in the area, many of which belonged to prominent Romans, than for the townspeople of Pompeii. The proposed cleanup operations mentioned by Dio Cassius and Suetonius referred to the Campanian region in general and did not name Pompeii or Herculaneum at all. Rolfe's translation (1924:333) of Suetonius's reference to *"afflictarum civitatium"* (*De Vita Caesarum: Titus* 8, 4) as "the buried cities" would seem to be prejudiced by the modern reputation of these renowned excavations. Thus, there is no precise evidence that an imperial commission visited Pompeii immediately after this eruption, or that such a visit might explain the absence of valuables at the site.

Scholars have also surmised that Pompeian survivors returned to salvage their possessions (for example, Maiuri 1927:63; Dexter 1975:165, 248; Cerulli Irelli 1975:292; Dybkjaer-Larsen 1982:42). The tops of the buildings are thought to have been visible after the eruption (Ward-Perkins and Claridge 1980:14; Cerulli Irelli 1975:292), allowing the salvagers to locate their dwellings and remove their own possessions. These scholars have assumed that a lack of valuables, statuary, marble revetment, and even lead piping in many of the houses can be attributed to salvaging. In her study of Casa di Caecilius Iucundus, Caroline E. Dexter (1975:165) surmised that the returning inhabitants left behind only articles that could easily be replaced, such

as utensils, tools, personal items, and a few decorative pieces, mostly broken. Dexter's view of what was valuable might be rather subjective, and her interpretation is based on the assumption that inhabitants had indeed returned. Nevertheless, certain classes of material that might be anticipated in Campanian houses are notably lacking. For example, although two large hoards of silver vessels were discovered in the region—one in the Casa del Menandro in Pompeii (Maiuri 1933:241–403) and one in the Villa at Boscoreale (Scarfoglio 1988)—all the remaining finds of silver vessels from all other Pompeian houses together would barely equal the size of either one of these two collections.

The theory that any evident post-eruption disturbance was carried out by the house owners themselves assumes that they were able to locate their own dwellings after the eruption. Plutarch (*Moralia*, 398E) believed that it was not even possible to identify where the cities had been, let alone individual houses. While Guiseppina Cerulli Irelli (1975:295) cited skeletons with a Roman lantern and a pick in room 19 of Casa del Menandro, late Roman lamps in the Villa dei Misteri, and a reputedly Christian lamp in the Villa di Julia Felix as evidence for intrusion dating to the Roman period, she also attributed some of the evident disturbance to the arbitrary, undocumented diggings of the Bourbon period (Cerulli Irelli 1975:292).

The original depth of deposit over Pompeii was undoubtedly considerably greater than is visible today (figure 2.9). Blong (1984:343) noted that tephra or *lapilli* compact to about half their thickness in the first two weeks after an eruption. To my knowledge, there are no figures for the amount of compaction that would have occurred over nearly two thousand years. It cannot therefore be assumed on the basis of the depth of the deposit today that the tops of houses were visible, permitting the survivors and salvagers to locate them and to identify their own. Although it might be argued that such identification was not an issue because the removal of material was more clandestine immediately after the eruption, analogies with more recent volcanic eruptions suggest clandestine removal is

Figure 2.9 View of volcanic deposit beside one of the tombs in the
Necropolis of the Porta di Nocera

not necessarily a major concern. Payson Sheets
and Donald Grayson (1979:626) concluded that
crime and looting do not necessarily increase after a volcanic disaster. Klaus Neumann (1996:
79–88) is more circumspect, but he notes that at
Rabaul most of the looting seems to have occurred in the search for food and shelter, although it also included household goods. He
points out, however, that the image portrayed
by the media "of a tranquil and innocent pre-
eruption Rabaul does not hold" (1996:88).

An examination of Pompeian house contents
must take into account the fact that the house
floor assemblages were not all hermetically
sealed on 24 August AD 79. There is a high probability that deposits in rooms and houses were
disturbed, in some cases quite severely, prior to
their documented excavation. For this study, it
matters little whether this disturbance was the
work of Romans, Bourbons, or the occupants of
the area in the intervening centuries. It is also invalid to assume that all the holes through the
walls of Pompeian houses were made after the
eruption (see chapter 8). The skeletons from corridor L and room 19 in Casa del Menandro,
found on either side of a hole in the west wall of
room 19 (figure 2.10) and assumed by Cerulli
Irelli to have been intruders, were believed by

Maiuri (1933:13) to have been fugitives. Estelle
Lazer has identified some of these as juveniles
under the age of five (1997:342). It is improbable
that such infants were in a party of post-eruption salvagers. The presence of children seems
more likely to indicate a party of fugitives attempting to escape the eruption. If so, then the
hole in the wall was more probably made by the
fugitives rather than by later intruders. This sur-
mise could apply equally to comparable holes in
other houses, in particular those with associated
victims in the second entranceway of Casa di
Obellius Firmus (Della Corte 1911:350; Spano
1911:372–373; Trevelyan 1976: Fig. 70).

Similarly, it is not necessarily justifiable to
attribute the lack of any anticipated finds to
post-eruption intrusion. Reuse, relocation, or
abandonment in the preceding years are other
possible reasons why these assemblages differ
from a supposed concept of normality. Nevertheless, the possibility of post-eruption intrusion must be part of any artifact assemblage
analyses. A careful assessment of the relationships between disturbed stratigraphy and evident holes in the walls and the location and
composition of the assemblages is necessary if
conclusions are to be made based on the absence of material.

Figure 2.10 Room 19 from northeast corner, showing open hole in west wall and patched hole in south wall. Skeletons from this room and corridor L are in the modern case, Casa del Menandro

CONCLUSIONS

Traditional Pompeian studies have combined textual, architectural, and decorative evidence to reconstruct the conditions in Pompeian houses in the AD 60s and 70s. The actual contents of these houses have been largely excluded from these reconstructions. Before these household assemblages can be investigated for the information they can provide on domestic behavior, however, an understanding of the possible living conditions in Pompeii prior to the final eruption is needed. The earthquake recorded by Tacitus and Seneca and dated 5 February AD 62 has been widely taken as the main fixed point; it is assumed to have caused all the visible damage and to have necessitated the repair to both the structure and decoration of public and private buildings in Pompeii. This earthquake has also been assumed to have been the turning point in the social and economic fortunes of the town (Maiuri 1942; Eschebach 1970:57; Andreau 1973b; Kockel 1986:543; Zanker 1988:41–43). From Pliny's two letters, Dio Cassius' account,

and the number and state of the victims excavated in Pompeii, it has also been surmised that the Pompeians had no concept of a volcanic eruption and that when Vesuvius started to erupt they were completely taken by surprise.

A reappraisal of the textual references in the light of current knowledge of earthquake and volcanic activity suggests that the sequence of events and the conditions during these final years were not so straightforward. Seismic activity between AD 62 and 79, including the period immediately preceding the eruption, may well have caused ongoing damage and subsequent repair to buildings and their decoration, or the abandonment of such repair, as well as social and economic deterioration. Far from going unheeded, the AD 62 earthquake and subsequent activity may have made the Pompeians only too conscious of imminent danger. The geological likelihood that a major impending eruption would be accompanied by such seismic activity highlights the dubiousness of relating all disruption to the two recorded events.

A study of Pompeian house contents is therefore not bounded by a moment that begins and ends on 24 August AD 79. Rather, it provides a substantial body of material for analyzing the period leading up to the eruption, but which has also been affected by subsequent cultural and environmental disturbance. When integrated with the structural and decorative evidence, this study is a rich and complex source of information documenting the changes experienced in the houses before and after the eruption in AD 79.

NOTES

1. This *Notizie degli Scavi* format has also been adopted by Berry (1997).

2. Cross-cultural studies show that, except in situations where there is a significant injection of funds for recycling (for example, the current conversions of nineteenth-century terrace houses), downgrading rather than upgrading tends to be the norm.

3. This includes its use by others who have also stressed its unreliability (for example, Franklin 1990:47 n.1).

4. For a recent description of the stylistic and chronological divisions of Roman wall painting, see Ling 1991:1–100.

5. Eschebach and Eschebach (1995:90) provide a date of AD 59 for what would appear to have been the same earthquake.

6. For an argument that Pliny had actually documented the third phase of the volcanic activity, see Jashemski (1979b:609–610).

Figure 3.1 Excavations in front hall b, Casa dei Ceii. *Pompeii photo archive neg. C754*

3.

Data Collection and

Interpretative Procedures

CENTRAL TO POMPEII'S LONG HISTORY of research is its equally long history of excavation and recording. In this chapter, methodological frameworks and interpretative procedures are set up to accommodate the varying quality of the evidence resulting from these records, and the availability of the data for the study of Pompeian household assemblages.

At the core of this study are linked databases containing information on the spaces and contents of a sample of Pompeian houses. Pompeii rather than Herculaneum was chosen because data on these assemblages are more readily available and come from several different sources that can be cross-checked. For excavations carried out in Pompeii between the 1870s and 1970s, it was possible to collect the relevant data from both published and unpublished excavation reports and from separate finds inventories. For each period, the excavation techniques have a bearing on the usefulness and reliability of the data. Until Giuseppe Fiorelli became director of the excavations in 1860, the reports on completely disinterred houses are generally not very useful for the study of artifact distribution, except for isolated instances of antiquarian interest in particular artifacts.

THE SAMPLE

The choice of individual Pompeian houses in the sample was dictated by the availability of documentation. Throughout the nineteenth century and until the 1950s, the excavators tended to concentrate their efforts on larger houses, ascribed to the upper-middle to upper classes, believing that houses such as these

might produce more artworks and finds of precious materials and that they could serve as illustrations of the types of Roman houses mentioned in the textual evidence. These were invariably the so-called *atrium* houses. Consequently, the archaeological context and finds provenances in such houses have generally been more carefully described than those in smaller dwellings and commercial buildings. The excavators also concentrated on houses that had the most complete assemblages and the best-preserved paintings. As a result, the best-documented houses were those likely to have been fully functioning as residential and workplace establishments at the time of the eruption. The data used for this study will therefore tend to bias the outcome towards indications that Pompeii was a fully functioning town at the time of the eruption, rather than might a more random sample. The corollary, however, is that any demonstration to the contrary—that domestic conditions in these houses were varied, unstable, or had deteriorated—is likely to be of greater significance.

All the houses selected for this study were *atrium* houses and tended to be the larger of this type, belonging to Wallace-Hadrill's Quartiles 3 and 4 (1994:81, table 4.2). They ranged in ground-floor area from approximately 200 m² for the Casa della Venere in Bikini to approximately 2000 m² for the Casa del Menandro (see plans on page 205). Because of the types of houses selected, there was considerable architectural conformity within the sample. This conformity made it possible to identify a set of room types that had a relatively consistent relationship to the overall plan of each house across the sample. Each house, as identified, had its own street entrance and can be seen as an architectural, and potentially functional, entity. For example, Houses I 6,8–9 (see plan on page 208), and I 7,19 (see plan on page 210) are treated as separate houses, whereas House I 10,16 is considered part of the Casa del Menandro complex. With the exception of the Casa della Ara Massima (see plan on page 213), each house has a garden courtyard, usually with colonnades on one or more sides. If the open rooms on the street front of a house (the so-called shops) were not connected to the complex behind by an existing doorway, they are not included in the study. Most types of *atrium* houses are included (see Evans 1984).

Thirty *atrium* houses covering three geographical areas of the city and three different excavation phases between the late nineteenth century and the 1970s were selected (figure 1.4). Fifteen houses were selected from Regions I, III, and IX along the Via dell'Abbondanza in the eastern area of the town (excavated mainly between the 1920s and 1970s), eight from Regions V and VI in the central northern area (excavated between 1890 and 1915), and seven from Region VIII in the southwest (excavated mainly between 1880 and 1890). More houses were selected from Regions I, III, and IX because these areas are more recently excavated and tend to be more extensively documented.

Many of the houses in the sample have also been studied recently for their architecture and decoration (for example, the Casa di M. Lucretius Fronto [Peters et al. 1993], the Casa del Principe di Napoli [Strocka 1984a], and the houses in the Insula del Menandro [Ling 1997]). Up-to-date information on other aspects of these houses, such as building and decorative histories, was therefore available.

THE SOURCES

Three main documentary sources provide data for investigating the distribution of artifacts in Pompeian houses: the excavation reports published in the *Notizie degli Scavi di Antichità*; the unpublished *Giornali degli Scavi di Pompei*, held in the Pompeii archives; and the separate inventories of the finds that were brought from the excavation to the Pompeii storerooms, also held in the archives.

Notizie degli Scavi di Antichità

The earliest reports published in the *Notizie degli Scavi di Antichità* date from 1876 and consist of direct publication of the reports in the *Giornali degli Scavi*. Consequently, the day-to-day notebooks of these excavations, while admittedly brief, are available in published form, although not always accurately copied. By the early twentieth century, with the excavations of Giuseppe Spano and Vittorio Spinazzola, these notes were often accompanied by the synthesis and interpretation of observed architectural and decorative aspects of the house. By the 1920s, Amedeo Maiuri and Olga Elia were publishing only synthesis and interpretation. Any information concerning the finds was relegated to a list at the end of the report for each house, catalogued according to fabric type rather than immediate association and generally copied from the inventories of the finds rather than from the original *Giornali degli Scavi*. The provenances of these finds were usually provided, so that room and house numbers, sometimes omitted in the original *Giornali degli Scavi*, could often be correctly allocated. Mistakes with room numbers had often been made in the inventories and subsequently transferred to these publications, however. Inaccurate inventory numbers were also frequently transferred to the published reports. The precise find spot or its height above floor level, which was crucial to its actual association with the room, was not usually provided in these reports. The distribution of the finds was also generally ignored in the interpretations of room use or house occupancy. The publications concentrate on the extant and in situ material, its structure and decoration, often after it had been restored. The excavated, and therefore now decontextualized, material was given little emphasis. Although sporadic reports on the excavations of public buildings, sondages into the pre-AD 79 levels, and graffiti appear until 1951, the excavations of Pompeian houses were no longer published in the *Notizie degli Scavi* after 1934. Spinazzola's publication (1953) of his excavations in the Via dell'Abbondanza between 1910 and 1923 concentrated on the reconstruction of the architecture; again, the removed finds received no mention. Prior to the series *Häuser in Pompeji* (see Strocka 1984a:9–11), individual houses had rarely been published in special monographs (although see Maiuri 1933).

Giornali degli Scavi di Pompei
In the initial stages of this study, the published reports were of great help in selecting a well-documented sample. For more detailed information, a study of the *Giornali degli Scavi* (figure 3.2) was necessary. These handwritten notebooks follow the day-to-day process of the excavations and are therefore the most original resource. They also provide the best evidence for the varying techniques and objectives of the excavators. Even in the period after 1860, reputedly the beginning of scientific exploration at Pompeii, these records indicate that the excavations followed a traditional procedure. This procedure would appear to be symptomatic of ongoing excavation at a site with an excavation history of more than 250 years, using an established system, and a workforce with family continuity over successive generations. These procedures are therefore unlike those at other sites with excavation histories of comparable length, but each site excavated by multiple expeditions, each with new methods and objectives.

Figure 3.2 Giornali degli Scavi di Pompei, Volume VII

Generally, for material removed during excavation—volcanic deposit and loose finds, as opposed to the architecture and decoration left in situ—the recording was, at best, particularly schematic. The deposit was not mentioned in the earliest excavations. Over time attention to the volcanic stratigraphy increased. Initially, the concern was whether or not it had been disturbed after deposition. Only in excavations since the 1960s has the deposition of the volcanic layers itself been documented. The standard procedure of excavation has been to clear the street first, locate the entranceways of houses, and then excavate horizontally inside the house (figure 3.1). References to sporadic finds made after the initial excavation of a room or house, notably of coins and small pieces of jewelry, indicate that each room or space was not necessarily systematically cleared of the volcanic deposit.

On reading these reports, it became apparent that the primary purpose of recording the excavated finds was administrative control of the material removed. The provenance of the finds was documented largely to inventory the extant material and to record the progress of the excavations. Only in the more recent excavations was the precise context regularly documented: indications of post-eruption disturbance; location of finds within a room; and height above ground level at which the finds were made.

The writers of the *Giornali degli Scavi* did not always state explicitly in which room or space objects were found. In some instances the initial room numbering, for which correspondingly numbered maps no longer exist, differs from later publications. There are also instances where gaps were left in the report to be filled in later with room and house numbers, but this was never done. In the earlier excavations, a room or space was identified as to whether, for example, it was on the left or the right of the *atrium* rather than by a room number. In such cases, relatively specific provenances could be reconstructed only by carefully reading the reports and following the daily process of the excavations.

The excavators, especially the earlier ones, were primarily interested in objects considered to be works of art, objects made of a valuable material (silver and gold), or objects with inscriptions. A near obsession with metal objects is evident in the greater attention paid to bronze, but also iron, fittings (hinges, chains, or nails) rather than ceramic or glass vessels. Although interest in the latter, nonmetallic objects has increased over time, fragmentary glass and pottery were largely ignored prior to the 1930s. Stamped roof tiles have often been removed from their architectural context, as inscriptional evidence. Except in the latest excavations, amphorae were recorded only if they bore inscriptions. Fiorelli introduced the method of making plaster casts of organic material in the 1860s, this method does not seem to have been employed for furniture prior to 1910. This practice also appears to have been abandoned by Maiuri in the 1920s–1950s, to be taken up again by Alfonso de Franciscis in the 1960s–1970s. The following entry from the *Giornali degli Scavi* on 29 November 1886 exemplifies the prevailing interests at the time: *"il restauratore dei bronzi nel lavorare alla sistemazione degli scheletri umani gia scavati in Pompei, fra essi ha rinvenuto e consegnato: Argento = un anello* [during the work of systematizing the human skeletons already excavated in Pompeii the bronze restorers discovered and handed over a silver ring]." No further mention was made of the skeletons.

Inventories

The inventories of finds currently held in Pompeii began on 1 January 1890, with a new numbering system introduced on 2 January 1906. There is no useful inventory of the artifacts excavated from the sampled houses in Region VIII before 1890 and taken to the Naples National Museum. The inventories kept in Pompeii were written up after the *Giornali degli Scavi* and the information usually copied from the *Giornali*. Finds provenances, as documented in the inventories, consist of the house and normally, but not invariably, the room. Inventory numbers were either already assigned to objects in the *Giornale degli Scavi* and transferred to the inventory or introduced into the inventory at this time. Only the finds to be housed in the

storerooms, and some large objects or door fittings left in situ, were so inventoried. In the earlier excavations, this did not include pottery and glass or organic material unless it was particularly notable. In later excavations, these classes of material were also stored but not if they were fragmentary or undecorated. At the stage when finds details were being transferred to the inventories, mistakes with room numbers were frequently made. By paying careful attention to the process by which the *Giornale degli Scavi* and the inventories had been compiled, it was, however, possible to trace the origin of the mistakes and rectify them before including them in the databases.

Other Documentary Sources

Further documentary sources consist of Fiorelli's compilation of the excavation notes from exploration prior to 1860 in *Pompeianarum Antiquitatum Historia* (Fiorelli 1860–1864) and the independent, usually first-hand, reports of the excavations in the 1880s and 1890s made by August Mau (in the *Bulletino dell'Instituto di Corrispondenza Archeologica* and the *Mitteilungen des Deutschen Archäologischen Instituts*, Römische Abteilung). Given the date of his work, Mau can be seen to have paid close attention to excavation details, and his reports often provide a good check on the *Notizie degli Scavi*. He indicated when he witnessed the excavations himself, in which cases he offered his own interpretations. On other occasions, he appears to have been using the *Giornali degli Scavi* as his source of information.[1]

The Houses

The extant houses themselves were a further source of data, particularly for fixtures, but also for artifacts not removed to the storerooms but left in situ (for example, uninscribed amphorae, building material, stone furniture, and plaster casts). While the current locations of such artifacts are recorded in the databases, they were used in the analysis only if it could be shown that they were definitely in situ. Comparisons with the documentation in the *Giornali degli Scavi* demonstrated that many artifacts left in the houses today, particularly pottery and broken furniture, have been moved around by the authorities.

Heavy foliage or an extensive state of disrepair made access dangerous to parts of some houses exposed in the older excavations, particularly below ground level in Region VIII. Damaged during an earthquake in 1980, this region was subsequently closed to the public and its upkeep abandoned (figure 3.3).[2] As a result, information on wall paintings, pavements, and fixtures in these areas could not always be collected or checked. The only house with a currently accessible upper floor was the Casa di Julius Polybius (see plan on page 204). Where no information is given in the excavation reports, evidence of upper stories is normally provided by the presence and location of stairways, whether the upper stories were connected to the lower house or constituted separate apartments.

Figure 3.3 House VIII 2,34 overgrown with vegetation

***

This is a brief overview of the variety and reliability of the excavation and recording techniques in Pompeii from which data for this study were retrieved. More specific information concerning the excavation and recording of individual houses is provided on the associated website *(http://www.stoa.org/pompeianhouseholds)*. A major difficulty with such a study is that its concerns, questions, and methodologies were not those of the original excavators and recorders. For example, a great deal of material is likely to have gone unrecorded, particularly fragmentary glass and pottery, originally considered to be of little intrinsic value, and organic material. Also, archaeological techniques and inquiries at Pompeii have not always kept pace with more thorough information-gathering techniques employed at other, less "complete" archaeological sites. This is, perhaps, the dilemma for a purportedly "perfectly preserved" site. With such an overwhelming volume of material, the problems of recording and conserving everything within the limitations of the available resources have been insurmountable (see Conticello et al. 1990:2–25). For this reason, since Maiuri's excavations in the 1950s, excavation has been kept to a minimum, has involved re-excavation with different research objectives, or excavation below the AD 79 levels.[3]

The data collection for this study has therefore been an exercise in gleaning information from far-from-perfect resources. However, this is not in itself a reason for not attempting it. It is precisely the situation at any archaeological site (Schiffer 1985:24). Although the Pompeian remains and their recording do not constitute the mythical time capsule of a single instant (Allison 1992b), this does not mean that the evidence of the Pompeian finds is unusable or that investigators should rely on the textual, architectural, and decorative evidence to interpret living conditions in the town. A more reliable archaeological practice is to use a large sample of the archaeological data available, taking into account its limitations and imperfections, rather than to reject it out of hand. Even with its limitations, Pompeii still provides an exceptional wealth of material remains.

Database Formats

Given the amount and complexity of material, it was obvious that data from these household assemblages should be compiled electronically. Initially, the data were collected on manual datasheets from information in the *Notizie degli Scavi*. These were then checked and adjusted according to the fuller and more accurate information from the *Giornali degli Scavi* and in the extant houses, as well as from Mau's reports and *Pompeianarum Antiquitatum Historia* (Fiorelli 1860–1864), where applicable. Only then were the data transferred to electronic databases and re-checked against the inventories. If discrepancies were found among the sources, the origin of the mistake was determined and the data corrected accordingly. The systematic nature of compiling this database necessarily required the resolution of as many ambiguities as possible. If the documented provenance of an artifact was too vague to establish a precise location, the artifact was provenanced to the house in general. On the rare occasions when even the house provenance was not discernible, the artifact was omitted from the study.

Initially, two databases were designed for this study: one with a room or space as its principal field and the other with an artifact or group of artifacts. These two databases were subsequently linked to a third database that consists of house-by-house descriptions and analyses. This information is now all provided on the website. Some 863 rooms are described, and there are 6300 artifact entries. The number of entries does not indicate the actual number of artifacts in the study, as some entries include more than one artifact. The artifact database includes finds that have been removed from their context or were documented at the time of the excavation (for example, traces of organic material). It also includes fixtures (for example, benches or holes for shelf supports) that throw light on room use, changing room use, or house aban-

donment. In general, water systems (for example, cisterns and cistern heads) are excluded unless they indicate specific room use or change of room use that can be shown to be a late adaptation. Wall graffiti have not been included. Finds of structural origin (for example, architectural decoration or bricks) have been included only if the find spots provide information on repair or destruction of the house. Door fittings were included because they are not always distinguishable from furniture fittings. Holes cut into the walls have also been documented (see chapter 8).

Terminology

Because this study is based on an examination of the archaeological evidence in Pompeii, Latin or Greek nomenclature for the rooms and spaces in Pompeian houses has been avoided. Rather, for most of the study, labels based on the following have been used: location relative to the front-hall/garden complex; size, relative to house size; through-routes; and functions defined by fixtures (see table 5a). Textual nomenclature is used only in the interpretative sections of the house-by-house analyses, where interpretations of past scholars are reiterated, and in chapter 7 where the appropriateness of such labeling is assessed in light of the artifact assemblages. The term *room* is often used when it may not seem strictly appropriate to the space being discussed. This usage indicates that a specific space is being discussed and not a more generalized concept of an area or space. The room numbers used in this study follow those of the *Pitture e Pavimenti di Pompei, Repertorio della fotografie de Gabinetto Fotografico Nazionale* (Bragantini et al. 1980; 1983; 1986), which in turn usually follow those of the original excavation reports. Sometimes the excavators used multiple room numbers for a space that seems to have been one entity, particularly for gardens with ambulatories. Hence it is not always logical that some gardens in this sample are split between the garden proper and ambulatories. Artifacts from the upper floors have usually been analyzed as a group, because it is invariably impossible to distinguish separate rooms in the upper floors.

I could not hope to examine physically each individual artifact in this sample, particularly because many of them are no longer extant. One of the basic difficulties with this method of data collection was identifying artifacts from written descriptions, invariably without illustrations. I have relied on the individual recorders for the identification and descriptions of artifacts. These identifications are often interpretative and imply function, either from the subjective view of what the artifact most closely resembles in the contemporary experience of the recorder or from terminology borrowed from the ancient texts (for example, a *guardispigolo* or a *fritillus*; see chapter 4). The functions of artifacts and their state at the time of their discovery have also been frequently interpreted according to preconceived perspectives concerning domestic activities and living conditions in Pompeian houses. In addition, because of the diversity of reporters, there is often a diversity of terms for the same artifact or, vice versa, the same term for a diversity of artifacts. For example, the terms *tegame* or *casseruole* are used for a saucepan-shaped bronze pot with a long handle (see figure 4.17), the terms *tegame* or *patera* for a shallower pan with a handle, and the term *patera* for a shallow, handleless dish. Overcriticism of the excavators' judgment in interpreting artifact function is, however, not warranted. Excavators have handled more such material and, prior to the 1950s at least, were generally identifying it from a perspective that was likely to have been less influenced by modern urbanism and mass production than my own.

To familiarize myself with the range of artifacts in Pompeian houses, I made a separate study of the actual finds from the Insula del Menandro, instead of using excavators' descriptions in the reports (Allison, n.d.). This study entailed compiling a catalogue and analyzing the contents of the buildings in this *insula*, including a full description of the extant finds according to their context (see Allison 1997a). Because the Insula del Menandro is one of the more recently excavated *insulae* in Pompeii, the houses in it

(Casa del Menandro; Casa del Fabbro; House I 10,8; and Casa degli Amanti; see appendix A for house plans) offer a fairly comprehensive range of the possible artifacts to be found in a Pompeian domestic context, as well as the range of Latin and Italian terminology used in the excavation reports. This study has also offered a more firm basis from which to assess the validity of either any Latin terminology or general functional interpretations applied to Pompeian artifacts (see Allison 1992b:53, 1996:103–104, 1997a, 1999b).

Because I did not directly analyze the bulk of the artifacts in this study and because of the interpretative nature of any translation, the terms used by the original recorders are retained in the database unless the identification is obvious (for example, stairway) or does not make unwarranted assumptions about the function of an artifact (for example, statuette). Where possible, the terminology moves towards a less interpretative description than that of the original recorders. For example, the term *focolare* is replaced with "bench," a descriptive rather than interpretative label, because this fixture's use as a hearth is not always evident. This policy guards against the artifact database becoming more interpretative than the original archives. In general, the descriptions and labels of artifacts in the *Giornali degli Scavi* are less interpretative than in the *Notizie degli Scavi* and other publications. Hence, they have usually been used in the database unless a number of artifacts (for example, hinges and bosses) have been convincingly assembled into one identifiable object after excavation (for example, a chest).

There is generally a tendency among archaeologists to lack rigor in dealing with terms for household material, particularly vessels and utensils. Here in particular, the Italian terms are kept because the direct translation is often misleading. Thus, the interpretative, often functional terminology (for example, *forma di pasticceria*) remains in the database until the specific artifact and its context can be more closely studied and a more convincing identification offered. For this reason, many Italian and Latin terms are found in the database and in this study. The glossary attempts to give the most likely English equivalent for non-English terms used in this study. It should not, however, be taken as the prescription of current meanings to words from the past or of British meanings to Italian usage (see Miller 1985:51–55; Allison 1999b). Also, as the artifacts themselves have not been studied, it is not necessarily guaranteed that the translations in the glossary are exactly appropriate for each so-identified artifact. The analyses deal mainly with gross functional patterning.

Interpretative Procedures

The information in the original room and artifact databases has been summarized and integrated with the house-by-house analyses to form the relational databases provided on the website and forms the basis for the results in chapters 4 to 8. The house-by-house analyses include analyses of artifact assemblages relative to both their physical settings and past discussions regarding the individual rooms in the houses. They are not strictly a catalogue as they include much interpretative material. Nevertheless, in order to treat each room separately, there is a certain amount of repetition, as in a catalogue.

Each house is analyzed separately, with an assessment of the proficiency of the excavation and its recording. The houses are analyzed in reverse sequence to that of their sequence of excavation, except where a group of houses was excavated together, as in the Insula del Menandro. The first house analyzed is the Casa di Julius Polybius, excavated between 1966 and 1978, and the last is House VIII 5,9, excavated between 1881 and 1882. Thus, the analysis commences with the most rigorously documented houses— that is, those in Regions I, III, and IX. The information gleaned from these houses is then used in the appraisal of artifact assemblages in the less well-documented houses from the earlier excavations. For example, if wooden cupboards with bone hinges are found to be prevalent in the front halls in more recently excavated houses, then the recording of bone hinges in the

older excavations is seen to indicate a similar presence of wooden cupboards. Thus, this sequential house-by-house analysis is a direct consequence of the possibilities and limitations of the available data.

Each space in each house is given an architectural room type, as defined in chapter 5, and the analysis of each space is treated in four parts: a description of the room, including its decoration; an assessment of the possible post-depositional disturbance; a summary of the contents of each room or space in each house; and an interpretation of the room's function and state of occupancy assessed in light of prior research into the specific room or house. The order of the rooms in each house as presented is not numerical or alphabetical. The aim is to take the reader through each room as if one were to progress from the main entrance through the house.

Description

This section briefly outlines the structural and decorative characteristics of the room. It includes location and access information and brief descriptions of any wall paintings or pavement. Where the decoration is no longer extant but was described by previous scholars, that description is included. The aim is to give a view of the space and the salient points relevant to the analysis of the finds. The description is in the past tense to give a general sense of how the rooms would have seemed to an ancient observer rather than how they appear to the modern visitor. Many features described in the past tense are still extant. Because both the nature of the recording and the state of preservation of the decoration are patchy across the sample, the quality and detail of the descriptions vary.[4]

Condition of the AD 79 Volcanic Deposit

This section includes available information on the composition and condition of the AD 79 volcanic deposit at the time of excavation, and an assessment of any evidence of the volcanic depositional processes or post-eruption disturbance. The presence and position of holes penetrating the walls is discussed and their chronologies evaluated.

Fixtures and Finds Distribution

Information from the room and artifact databases is used to summarize the room's contents. The data was sorted by provenance (that is, house, room, and location within the room) and by potential mobility (that is, furniture to coins). Any evidence the assemblage offers on individual artifact use is also discussed.

Interpretation

Any indications for the chronology of the decoration are discussed here, particularly evidence of repair, downgrading, or changing room use. Previous interpretations, which have employed traditional nomenclature and decorative and structural evidence to identify the use of each room or its state at the time of the eruption, particularly concerning its relationship to the AD 62 earthquake, are summarized. These interpretations are then reassessed in the additional light of the room contents. Hypotheses are proposed that, alternatively, fit the artifact assemblages with established interpretations and offer new perspectives on the state of the room and its changes during the period AD 62 to 79.

Whole House

For each house, interpretations of significant rooms are summarized, and the living conditions in each complete house at the time of the eruption assessed. Given the complexity and bulk of the data, the body of prior research, and the absence of comparable studies,[5] the decision was made not to set up a predefined model prior to the analysis, as this would impose an unrealistic rigidity. Therefore the analysis uses, as a point of departure, the traditional interpretations of Pompeian living conditions which are largely based on textual and comparative modern analogies. As the analysis progresses and more houses are assessed, these external analogies are reappraised in the light of the archaeological evidence and gradually broken down, to

be replaced with contextual analogies produced within the study. Thus the study uses sequential analogy to develop a dynamic model through the successional interrelationships of the examples.

***

Some elements of the traditional model were able to be dispensed with before the study began. In the light of the reassessment of the depositional processes discussed in chapter 2, the assumption was discarded that damage and repair to wall structure and decoration are datable only to a recorded earthquake of AD 62 or to the final eruption. The states of the structure, the decoration, and the room contents are all assessed using the premise that such alteration and damage could have been caused at any time during the intervening years, if not before AD 62. The presence of, or repair to, Fourth-Style decoration plays a significant role in the conclusions. Because of current debates on whether the commencement of the Fourth Style can be dated before or after the AD 62 earthquake, the study frequently presents alternative conclusions, drawing attention to the subjectivity of such dating.[6]

Other aspects of the traditional model cannot be so easily dismissed and are important to the sequential move from external analogy to internal cross-comparisons. Most important is the concept of dislocation, which cannot be assessed without some assumptions about where the material ought to have been. For this reason, the traditional, largely text-based perspectives of room function in Pompeian houses are used initially to assess whether the evidence from the room contents supports a habitual, traditional room use or deviates from it. Conformity would suggest that textual analogy is a reliable approach for assessing room use in Pompeii. Nonconformity is evidence either, that the textual analogy is inappropriate, or that the textual evidence correctly specifies the original intended use but the contents indicate a change from that use. Such change may be related to behavior during disruption, disturbance, or alteration. At issue is an awareness of various changes that must have occurred during the last decades of Pompeian occupancy.

Distinctions between the two types of non-conformity can be made only by assessing how consistent the nonconformity is across the sample for particular architectural room types. If nonconformity of the textual and archaeological relationship but conformity of archaeological assemblage in similar room types occurs in a significant number of houses, then this indicates habitual behavior and therefore the possible inappropriateness of the textual analogy. While the patterns of what constitutes habitual behavior should have some consistency, considerable variability is likely to exist from house to house, particularly considering the range of house sizes and the number of rooms or internal spaces. This variability may be related both to the social status of the household and to the cycle of domestic change.

Lack of a pattern of conformity of assemblage within a specific room type might be interpreted as evidence of deviation both from textual specifications and any previously ordered and functionally coherent state. Such deviation suggests that some disruption caused the room contents to be misplaced from their usual location, recombined, or selectively disturbed. Patterns of dislocation, particularly across a number of rooms in the same house, are likely to be attributable to altered living conditions brought about by changed occupancy, altered economic situation, or damage and subsequent repair to the structure of the house. Terms such as "haphazard," "makeshift," "salvaging," "downgrading," and "deterioration" are used to explain this nonconformity.

To allow assessment of patterns of "normality," a number of assumptions must be made. First, it is not always possible to determine the precise functions of particular artifacts or assemblages. Similarly, it is not always possible to replace the traditional classification of artifacts by fabric (for example, ceramic, glass, metal) without more detailed artifact study. A general distinction was made, therefore, between luxury (for example, decorated bronze vessels) and utilitarian domestic material (for example, many ceramic vessels), and between utilitarian domestic material and commercial or industrial material (for example, building material, agricultural equipment). Distinctions between domestic, agricultural, commercial, and industrial implements may seem inappropriate in a pre-industrial context, but these terms are used to distinguish between material whose function may relate to the immediate requirements of the household members (for example, food preparation and consumption, sleeping, or ablutions) and what is likely to have been produced either to store for future use or to distribute outside the household.

A broad functional distinction has been made between formal and utilitarian rooms. "Formal" suggests that a principal function of the room furbishings is that they be aesthetically pleasing to the occupant or visitor. "Utilitarian" is used for rooms where furbishing appears to have had no such intent. For example, the formal category can include rooms where sleeping and some ablution activities are carried out, while the category utilitarian is likely to include food storage and food-preparation areas. It is assumed that rooms with painted wall decoration were normally intended for a formal rather than utilitarian function (see Wallace-Hadrill 1994: 155–160). Generally, a decorated room would not be expected to be designed for commercial/industrial activities or for storing construction or utilitarian materials. Therefore, when a utilitarian, repair, or commercial/industrial assemblage is found in a decorated room, it is considered evidence of change of use, possibly downgrading after the room was so decorated. Given the time and the amount of work and materials needed to decorate a room in the fresco technique (see Barbet and Allag 1972; Davey and Ling 1982; Allison 1991b; 1997b:19), we would not normally expect room contents to be replaced in a partially decorated or partially refurbished room unless the decoration plan was altered or aborted. It is also assumed that a room with a type of pink socle, made with the inclusion of crushed ceramic or tile, with white plaster above or completely furbished in white plaster, was a utilitarian space (see Davey and Ling 1982: 47; Allison 1991a:123–125). It is not always clear, however, whether report references to coarsely decorated and undecorated rooms meant the walls were furbished with this pink and white plaster or with only a coarse, grey base plaster and, therefore, their decoration was unfinished. Shelving may indicate a storeroom, although the lack of evidence for shelving does not mean that an undecorated room was not a storeroom.

Certain furnishings (for example, cupboards and large chests) are less likely to be relocated in periods of abrupt disruption and are therefore more useful for assessing patterns of normal room use than are smaller, more movable finds. Any dislocation of such furnishings indicates disruption to "normal" living conditions prior to the final eruption. On the other hand, small objects (for example, coins, buttons, and beads) are easily moved even during the deposition of volcanic material. Thus, they cannot be taken, individually, as indications of activity immediately preceding an eruption, although in larger groups (for example, coin hoards) they may be more significant. During an eruption, valuables are likely to be moved from locations considered dangerous or to be taken by fugitives. Utilitarian or large, broken artifacts might not be expected to be moved under those conditions. The frequent finds of broken statuary and furniture in unexpected places are unlikely to be attributable to hoarding during a final eruption. While it is not impossible, given the length of the eruption, that such material was moved around at that time, in many examples, the combination of this material and the extent of dislocation imply such was not the case. Thus, unless their provenances were the result of post-eruption disturbance, they are presumed to be evidence of pre-eruption dislocation and disturbance.

Absence of material is especially problematic for this study. While it is well known that the volcanic deposit in which Pompeii was buried preserved most types of material, including some organic, and left cavities to indicate the existence of other organic artifacts, much may have gone unrecorded or even may have been removed after the eruption. Of particular importance is the absence of traces of wooden furniture. The excavators in all periods, however, were biased towards recording metal remains over less intrinsically valuable material. The remains reported in room HH in the Casa di Julius Polybius indicate that even beds of simple wooden slats were joined with metal nails (Oliva Auricchio 1966–1978 VIII:58, 69), the presence of which was unlikely to have gone unrecorded in other houses. Further, the fact that the excavators of the Casa dei Ceii in 1912 had the ability and interest to reconstruct the evidence of a wooden cupboard in the front hall in a plaster impression (figure 3.4) indicates that if any such wooden remains were present, particularly in houses excavated in the twentieth century, they would have been noted. It does not therefore seem valid to assume that much wooden furniture went unrecorded. Because rooms that show evidence of post-eruption disturbance tended not to be completely devoid of finds (see chapter 8), and looters had little interest in metal fragments, pottery, or glass, the consistent patterns of absence can be regarded as significant (see Ross 1982 on absence of evidence as evidence of absence). In other words, any lack of recording of wooden material may well indicate its absence at the time of the eruption.

A lack of detailed attention to organic remains, however, has prevented an assessment of whether containers were full or empty at the time of the eruption. There are only a few recorded instances of organic contents in vessels that can be used as evidence of whether these containers were in use. In general, the presence of the containers themselves, rather than organic contents, has been employed as evidence of use.

It is possible that material originating from a ground-floor room had been moved by post-eruption intruders to higher levels in the volcanic deposit. This interpretation is sometimes given in the reports. It is also conceivable that post-eruption disturbance could have caused material from one ground-floor room to have been carried through to another. Each circumstance in

Figure 3.4 Plaster cast of cupboard in southeast corner of front hall, Casa dei Ceii

which this type of disturbance could have occurred is discussed and evaluated in the house-by-house analysis.

Although analogies with our own and other societies can help in the comprehension of anticipated or accepted "normality" or dislocation, this approach needs to be treated with caution (see Kent 1990:5–6). Nevertheless, it might be assumed that certain assemblages are "normally" related while others are not. Attempts are made to break free of the assumption that a pre-industrial house with servants would be more orderly than a modern urban dwelling. Such an assumption, which has pervaded studies of Pompeian living conditions, is an inheritance from the nineteenth- and early twentieth-century, largely upper-middle-class excavators who appear to have perceived Pompeian houses as comparable to their own serviced dwellings. The fact that it has always been possible for modern visitors to enter actual Pompeian houses, but that these houses are now devoid of all but a few selected contents, may have contributed to this perspective. Investigators have been able to visit the empty shell of a Pompeian house, but have had to draw on their imagination, perhaps inspired by literary texts, to conceptualize its contents and functioning. Traces of a late-twentieth-century model unavoidably pervade my own work,

but I have attempted to be cognizant of my own prejudices and to be less ethnocentric in making assumptions about living standards.

By examining a sample of thirty houses, and commencing with those most recently excavated, similarities and variations can be systematically appraised to develop a concept of the overall patterns of room use and general living conditions in Pompeii, as well as the range of differences within and between room types. This study seeks to address these questions with emphasis on the archaeological evidence in this provincial Roman town rather than on the writings of ancient authors or on modern analogical inference. An understanding of the data collecting and processing methods is crucial to comprehending the possibilities and limitations of this study. The solutions often offer alternative explanations from current perspectives. It cannot be claimed that these solutions are the "truth"; rather, they show that the traditional perspectives are no less valid.

NOTES

1. A potential source of information concerning finds distribution is the Consorzio Neapolis, funded by the Fiat-IBM Project (see Ministero per i Beni Culturali e Ambientali 1989:51; Conticello et al. 1990). This project aimed to set up a computerized data-

processing center for all the extant remains in Pompeii, including both published and unpublished reports, with priority given to the remains "most at risk" (for example, paintings and mosaics; see Conticello et al. 1990:19). This project has been compiled primarily as an information and education resource rather than as a research tool (Conticello et al. 1990:11, 115, 121; see Allison 1992c). Much interpretation, notably of the functions of buildings and rooms in houses, has been built into the database (Conticello et al. 1990:21, 75). This project began in March 1987, but data collection ended in April 1989 after funding ran out. Given the speed with which the data was collected, the various and inexperienced archaeologists collecting the data, and the inconsistencies among the sources as discussed here, use of this database as a primary resource should be cautious.

2. In the last few years the Soprintendenza archeologica di Pompei has commenced restoration within this area (Pompei Vesuvius AD 79, Fall–Winter 1999/2000:6).

3. Since 1987 the Casa degli Casti Amanti (I 12, 6-7) is the only freshly excavated house (see Varone 1988, 1989, 1995). For excavations below the AD 79 level of previously excavated houses, see Carandini et al. 1996; Bon et al. 1997; Fulford and Wallace-Hadrill 1998.

4. The very generalized descriptions of pavements and wall paintings are based on those in *Pitture e Pavimenti di Pompei, Pompei: Pitture e Mosaici* (Bragantini et al. 1980; 1983; 1986), Ling (1997), and my own observations. While they may be somewhat repetitive of other descriptions of Pompeian houses, they are useful here in illuminating some of the contexts of the finds in this study.

5. A number of recent studies, which have appeared since this project was initiated, in this and other areas of archaeology show similar approaches and concerns of contextualization of house contents (for example, Roaf 1989; Daviau 1993; Ault 1994; Ault and Nevett 1999; Berry 1997; Nevett 1999; Cahill 2002).

6. Many of the papers at a specialist conference held in Boscoreale in November 1993 (Fröhlich and Jacobelli 1995) were concerned with this specific chronological problem.

41

Figure 4.1 High, narrow recess in southeast corner of room 2, Casa del Fabbro

4.

Functions of Finds and Fixtures

A STUDY THAT USES ARTIFACT distribution as a basis for understanding the spatial distribution of activities must also consider the state of knowledge on the artifacts' functions. The most comprehensive work on the functions of Roman artifacts was carried out by Charles V. Daremberg and Edmond Saglio (1877–1919). At the core of their method was the comparison of particular artifacts from excavated contexts with descriptions of Greek and Roman objects in ancient texts. By this process, which is similar to that used for labeling Pompeian room types (see chapter 7), Latin and Greek terms were assigned to excavated artifacts, and this assigned nomenclature was used to ascribe a function to each artifact. This methodology is still employed. For example, Maria Annecchino claimed to demonstrate the functions of ceramic vessels from the kitchen by providing each individual vessel type with a Latin name (1977a). While some of these vessels do appear similar to those referred to in the textual descriptions, her main criteria were determined by a "common-sense" perception of how these excavated vessels might have been used. Artifact function has also often been identified through parallels between pictorial representations and found objects (see, for example, Bishop 1988; Annecchino 1977a:112). However, vital aspects of archaeological evidence that are missing from artifact function studies are amply supplied by the excavations of Pompeii—the assemblages and provenances of such items. The danger of establishing artifact function through textual, pictorial, or nineteenth- and twentieth-century analogies is that the archaeological evidence becomes merely the illustration, devoid of its own context.

Although there is evident need for a fundamental review of the processes by which functions have been ascribed to Roman artifacts, it is not a central issue for this study, which uses broad functional categories (for example, luxury, utilitarian, industrial, personal) to elucidate the distribution of household activities. As mentioned in chapter 3, it was not possible to physically examine every artifact used in this study. Therefore, a fully critical approach to attributions of artifact function by previous scholars cannot be taken here (see Allison 1999b, n.d.). Nevertheless, for a number of artifacts and artifact types, their traditionally ascribed functions seem either inappropriate or unsupported by the findings of this study. Such cases are discussed below.

FIXTURES

Recesses

A fixture whose traditionally ascribed function is not substantiated by this study but which is important to an assessment of room use is the so-called bed recess or bed niche (table 4.1). A number of the rooms and spaces in Pompeian houses had a ground-level recess built into one of the walls. While these recesses vary considerably in shape and size, they have been widely identified as recesses for beds and are therefore assumed to be diagnostic of bedrooms (see, for example, Maiuri 1933:52; Strocka 1984a:46; Adam 1989a:237; Wallace-Hadrill 1994:96–97, 113–114; Ling 1997:24, 49, 55, 152, 154). Such recesses did not usually occur in rooms with First- and Second-Style decoration that designated an alcove and antechamber, rooms that have therefore also been identified as bedrooms. For this reason Elia concluded that these fixtures were a late addition, postdating the Second Style, and had been cut into the wall to accommodate a bed after the original construction of the room (1932:394). Maiuri even argued that room 7 in the Casa del Menandro was a

Table 4.1 Recesses

House	Room	Room type	High, narrow	Long, low	Low, narrow	Associated fixtures and finds
Casa di Julius Polybius	UU	4			•	Bed fittings
	BB	12	•			Utilitarian domestic
	CC	9	•			Utilitarian domestic
	II	12	• (pair, painted)			Furniture fittings
Casa della Venere in Bikini	3	4			•	No finds
	5	4			• (pair)	No finds
Casa del Menandro	6	4			•	No finds
	A	16			•	Mixed domestic
Casa del Fabbro	2	2	• (painted)			Furniture fittings/ablutions
	4	4			•	Furniture fittings
	5	4			•	Needlework/ablutions
	9	11			•	Bed fittings nearby
House I 10,8	5	18	•			No finds
	13	16			•	Utilitarian pottery
	14	8			•	No finds
Casa dei Quadretti Teatrali	10	12	•			Ablutions
Casa di Stallius Eros	2	4			•	No finds
Casa del Sacerdos Amandus	c	4	•		•	Needlework/lighting
	f	4			•	No finds
Casa dell'Efebo	2	2			•	Fixed masonry block in center/luxury
	7	14		• (pair)		No finds
	9	4			•	Utilitarian pottery
	10	6			•	Utilitarian pottery
	17	11		• (pair)		Bed fittings
House I 7,19	d	4			• (pair)	
	f	12			•	No finds
Casa di Trebius Valens	p	11			•	No finds
House VI 16,26	C	4			•	Luxury domestic/ablutions
	K	8			• (pair)	Luxury domestic/ablutions
Casa di M. Lucretius Fronto	4	6		• (pair)		Chest fittings?
	9	4			•	No finds
	17	12			• ?	Utilitarian pottery?
Casa del Principe di Napoli	c	4			•	Mixed domestic
House VI 15,5	e	6			•	Fixed masonry block in center
	k	11			•	No finds
Casa dei Vettii	x'	16	• (painted)			
Casa delle Nozze d'Argento	h	4			•	Shelving
House VIII 2,26	6	11		• (pair)		No finds
Casa di Giuseppe II	p	10			•	??
	2	16			•	No finds
House VIII 2,34	l	4	•			Shelving
	q	8			•	Shelving?
	a'	12			•	Shelving
	z'	10	•			Shelving
House VIII 5,9	m	11			•	Mixed domestic/industrial

cubiculum of higher distinction than room 6 because the former did not have a recess (1933:53). These interpretations highlight the predominating AD hoc approach to the function of the recesses.

The number, variety, distribution, location, and associations of these recesses in the sample can be used to assess whether this identification is justified. There were three main types of recesses:

1. Relatively high, narrow recesses, varying from approximately 1 to 2.1 m in height, from 0.6 to 0.95 m in width, and from 0.12 to 0.5 m in depth (figure 4.1).

2. Long, low recesses, varying from 0.45 to 1.2 m in height, from 2.2 to 4.2 m in length, and from 0.07 to 0.2 m (figure 4.2) in depth.

3. Low, narrow recesses, varying from 0.35 to 1.35 m in height, from 0.73 to 1.47 m in width, and from approximately 0.07 to 0.2 m (figure 4.3) in depth.

There were eleven high, narrow recesses in the sample: one in room type 2, two in room type 4, one in room type 9, one in room type 10, four in room type 12, one in room type 16, and one in room type 18 (see chapter 5 for room types). They thus occurred in a range of room types, with over half in small closed rooms off the front hall or garden area. The pair of recesses in room II of the Casa di Julius Polybius (3.52 m high and 1.2 m wide) were outside the main size range and also much more elaborately painted than the others (figure 4.4). More commonly, any decoration consisted of a simple red border painted on a white background (for example, in the Casa del Fabbro and the Casa dei Vettii).

Recesses of this type are assumed to have been cupboards (Maiuri 1929:414), and this assumption seems logical for most of them. Two in

Figure 4.2 Long, low recess in west wall of room 6, House VIII 2, 26

this sample were associated with shelving, and two had possible evidence of furniture fittings. Assemblages found in association with recesses of this type, which may have been stored in such areas, included items associated with utilitarian domestic activities, ablutions, needlework, and lighting materials. It seems improbable that the recess in area 5 of House I 10,8, only 0.12 m deep and apparently open to the sky, had served as a cupboard. It seems equally improbable that elaborately painted recesses would form closed cupboards. In summary, it is likely that recesses of this type may have been used as cupboards but not necessarily.

There were eight examples of long, low recesses in this sample, all in pairs. All except one pair (in room 7 of the Casa dell'Efebo) were lo-

cated in room types 6 and 11: medium/large rooms off the front hall or garden area or overlooking the waterfront. The finds associated with the recesses in room 17 of the Casa dell'Efebo imply that they were indeed used for dining couches, allowing more space in the center of the room. Also, one end of each recess in room 6 of House VIII 2,26 was shaped to take the end of a couch (figure 4.2). However, those in room 7 of the Casa dell'Efebo were not of similar proportions, nor in a room type traditionally associated with dining on couches. Further, the finds from room 4 of the Casa di M. Lucretius Fronto seem more likely to have been from a chest than from couches.

There were thirty-four examples of low, narrow recesses in the sample, sometimes two op-

Figure 4.3 Low, narrow recesses in east and west walls of corridor K, House VI 16,26 (view from south)

Figure 4.4 High, decorated recess in east wall of room II, Casa di Julius Polybius

posite each other in one room. Of these, one occurred in a small closed room off the front entrance (room type 2), seventeen in small closed rooms off the front hall (room type 4), three in small closed rooms in the garden area (room type 12), two in room type 6, four in corridors, five in room type 10 or 11, and three in room type 16. Thus, more than two-thirds occurred in small closed rooms, predominantly off the front hall; however, they also occurred in underground, probably service, rooms and in corridors, two opposite each other in the same corridor (corridor K in House VI 16,26; figure 4.3).

This particular type of recess is assumed to have been used for a bed; however, actual remains of beds or couches were recorded in only two: in one type 4 room (room UU in the Casa di Julius Polybius) and in one type 11 room (room 9 in the Casa del Fabbro). This limited occurrence contrasts markedly with the total number of occasions across the sample (twenty-two, possibly twenty-five, rooms) in which bed fittings were reported in other contexts (see chapters 5 and 6). Fourteen rooms with this type of recess had no recorded associated finds. When fixtures or finds were recorded, they consisted of shelving in three rooms; other furniture fittings or fine-quality domestic material in six (for example, sculpture, bronze vessels, or ablution, lighting, or needlework materials); utilitarian pottery in five; and a more mixed domestic and industrial assemblage, sometimes including fragmentary sculpture or tools, in three. Two of this type of recess had a fixed masonry block in the center. Thus, only six cases, besides room UU in the Casa di Julius Polybius and room 9 in the Casa del Fabbro, had assemblages indicating personal activities possibly associated with a bed recess, although these lacked evidence for actual bed fittings. One of these cases was in a corridor (corridor K in House VI 16,26). In addition, the finds associated with the recesses in this corridor and in rooms 4 and 5 in the Casa del Fabbro suggest rather that there may have been cupboards or chests there. The discovery of artifacts related to washing, heating, and lighting in or near the

recess in underground room A of the Casa del Menandro hints at its function as a utility recess.

It is conceivable that corridor q in House VIII 2,34 was constructed by adapting one of the closed rooms off the front hall and that the recess had therefore once been part of a room. It is also possible that the entrance from the front hall to room k in House VI 15,5 had been changed after the inclusion of a recess in the east end of the north wall, but the height of this recess (0.35 m) would make it an improbable bed recess. In any event, these supposed alterations would contradict Elia's conclusion that the recesses were a late adaptation. The form and construction of the entrance from corridor K to front hall B in House VI 16,26 and corridor 14 in House I 10,8 do not allow late alteration as an explanation for the recesses. Although room A in the Casa del Menandro, room 13 in House I 10,8, and room 2 in the Casa di Giuseppe II have recesses of this type, they are improbable places for sleeping.

There was a considerable range of height for this last type of recess. The tallest low recess differed from the shortest high recess only in that it was wider and therefore proportionately shorter. The lowest recess, in room k of House VI 15,5, measured 0.35 m in height above the pavement. This merging of measurements, and hence of the two types, suggests that there may not have been a clear distinction in function. Similar assemblages were found with both. It is problematic to assume, however (for example, Maiuri 1927:25–26), that these recesses had either been of the type that served as a cupboard or of the two types that served as bed or couch recesses, and that in either case they indicated the function of the room. From their distribution and artifact associations, any one type, or indeed any one recess, could have served a number of purposes. It is not a straightforward task to categorize them typologically and hence functionally. It is likely that such recesses provided additional space for various types of furniture and other material.

Thus recesses alone are not sufficient to identify a specific room function. Conversely, if one still wished to argue that these recesses were for beds and couches, then the finds distribution would indicate that many of them had gone out of use in the final occupation phase of the city (for example, room m in House VIII 5,9). If, as Elia (1932) believed, the recesses had been a late adaptation, this adaptation phase cannot be equated with a final occupation phase in many of the houses.

Niches

A frequent fixture in Pompeian houses was a small niche built into the wall, usually located approximately 1 to 1.5 m above ground level (figure 4.5). These niches were either semicircular or almost square. Because many were decorated with *lararium* paintings or were closely associated with such paintings (for example, Orr 1988: Fig. 2; Fröhlich 1991: Pls. 2.2, 4.1, 9.1, 25.2–3 passim), it has been assumed that all such fixtures were household shrines or served a religious function (see Dwyer 1982:114; Orr 1988:295; Foss 1997:216, Fig. 24). Table 4.2 lists examples of niches recorded during this study. It does not include niches under stairways that were usually at ground level and were often semicircular or arched and probably served as cupboards (for example, in room 2 of the Casa del Menandro, stairway h in the Casa di Trebius Valens, corridor 3 in the Casa dei Vettii, and room 2 in House VIII 2,26).[1] Nor does the table include niches in bath complexes that seem to have been for seating (for example, room 8 in the Casa di Giuseppe II). Most of the examples included in table 4.2 were smaller niches. While some were more than 1 m in height, dimensions generally range from 0.3 to 0.6 m. Those with no visible traces of painted decoration today and not recorded as painted were likely to have been unpainted originally. The excavators and subsequent investigators had been reasonably meticulous in recording and preserving painted niches, because of the niches' assumed association with household religion.

Of the fifty such niches recorded in this study, thirty-one were in front halls, gardens, and kitchens. The rest covered nearly the full range of room types, including corridors. Only fifteen either had evidence of painting or were associated with *lararium* paintings. Of these, three were part of the same *lararium* aedicula (House VI 15,5; figure 4.6); one had traces of paint that were not identifiable as a *lararium* painting; another was painted with peacocks, not necessarily a *lararium* subject; and another was associated with paintings of animals. Two others were associated with statuary in an apparent display situation that suggests a religious significance, and a third had statuary stored in a box. Thus, the majority of the niches in this sample did not have evidence to establish any religious function.

Of the thirty-four examples not associated with *lararium* paintings, *lararium* aediculae, or statuary display, twenty-one had no associated finds or fixtures. Of the remaining thirteen, eight were associated with cooking or dining fixtures. It is generally assumed that many of the niches associated with cooking hearths served as shrines in the kitchen; however, none in this sample actually had any evidence of associated *lararium* paintings. The niche in room g in the Casa del Principe di Napoli was covered in coarse red plaster and was unlikely to have been further painted. Those in the garden of the Casa di Trebius Valens seem to have been directly associated with the dining area and were probably used for material associated with dining (for example, food, drink, and utensils: see Spano 1916: 231) (figure 4.7).

Loose finds associated with these niches consisted of utilitarian domestic material (mainly glassware and pottery), animal bones, and lamps. Lamps and utilitarian pottery could conceivably have been associated with religious offerings; however, there was no correspondence between such assemblages and *lararium* paintings in this sample. Of the forty-one niches whose forms were identifiable, twenty-five to twenty-six were semicircular. Only one of the rectangular niches was associated with a *lararium* painting (in front hall B in the Casa della Ara Massima; figure 4.8). However, two of the rectangular niches were associated with semi-

CLOCKWISE, FROM ABOVE LEFT:

Figure 4.5 Niche at west end of ambulatory g, view of north branch, House I 7,19

Figure 4.6 Lararium in front hall, House VI 15,5. *ICCD - Ministero per i beni e le attività culturali, Roma, gabinetto fotografico neg. N59575*

Figure 4.7 View of garden x, from southeast corner, showing niches in west wall, Casa di Trebius Valens

RIGHT: Figure 4.8 View of front hall, looking north, Casa della Ara Massima

Table 4.2 Niches

House	Room	Type	Painting	Shape	Other details	Measurements	Associations
Casa di Julius Polybius	Q	5	No	Rectangular		1.27 m x 0.53 m	Shelves, pottery, bird bones
	O	3	No	Rectangular		H = 1.35 m	Glass, pottery, animal bones
	O	3	No	Semicircular		0.34 m x 0.32 m	In rectangular recess
	O	3	No	Semicircular		0.4 m x 0.4 m	Above rectangular
Casa della Venere in Bikini	8	9	Yes	Unknown		0.4 m x 0.36 m	None
	9	14	No	Unknown		0.6 m x 0.31 m	None
	I 11,7	20	No	Rectangular		0.5 m x0.48 m	None
Casa del Menandro	25	13	Yes	Semicircular	Imitation marbling	0.63 m x 0.90 m	Statues, painted bench
	53	8	No	Unknown		0.25 m x 0.23 m	None
	41	3	No	Semicircular		0.49 m x 0.36 m	Lamps
	45	14	No	Semicircular		0.27 m x 0.19 m	None
Casa del Fabbro	9	11	Yes	Rectangular	Cut into wall painting	0.52 m x 0.42 m	None
	12	9	No	Arched?		W = 0.25m	Herm
House I 10,8	11	9	Traces	Semicircular		0.55 m x 0.47 m	None
Casa degli Amanti	16	14	No	Semicircular		0.57 m x 0.37 m	*Lararium* painting
Casa di Stallius Eros	3	20	No	Semicircular	Nos. inscribed beside	0.5 m x 0.4 m	Utilitarian domestic
	13	9	No	Unknown		Small	None
Casa del Sacerdos Amandus	m	9	Unknown	Unknown		0.57 m x 0.37 m	None
Casa dell'Efebo	A'	3	Yes	Semicircular?		0.5 m x 0.4 m	*Lararium* painting
	19	9	No	Semicircular		1.13 m x 0.8 m	*Lararium* painting
House I 7,19	g	9	No	Rectangular	White-plastered	1.1 m x 0.6 m	Statues in container
	g	9	No	Semicircular		1.1 m x 1.4 m	Other niche
	g	9	Yes	Semicircular	Animals painted beside	0.39 m x 0.5 m	None
Casa di Trebius Valens	i	14	No	Semicircular		Not available	Near cooking hearth
	s	12	No	Rectangular		0.45 m x 0.5 m	None
	x	9	No	Semicircular		0.6 m x 0.5 m	Masonry dining couch
	x	9	No	Rectangular		0.65 m x 0.65 m	Masonry dining couch
Casa del Sacello Iliaco	r	8	No	Rectangular		Not available	None
House VI 16,26	Y	16	No	Semicircular		Not available	None
Casa della Ara Massima	B	3	Yes	Rectangular		0.54 m x 0.54 m	*Lararium* painting
Casa di M. Lucretius Fronto	17	12	No	Semicircular		0.4 m x 0.44 m	None
Casa del Principe di Napoli	g	14	No	Semicircular	Red, unpainted plaster	0.5 m x 0.34 m	Above cooking hearth
	n	9	No	Semicircular		1.2 m x 1.2 m	In *lararium* aedicula

Continued on next page

Table 4.2 Niches (continued)

House	Room	Type	Painting	Shape	Other details	Measurements	Associations
House VI 15,5	b	3	No	Semicircular	Red, unpainted plaster	Small	In *lararium* aedicula
	b	3	No	Semicircular	Red, unpainted plaster	Small	In *lararium* aedicula
	b	3	No	Semicircular	Red, unpainted plaster	Small	In *lararium* aedicula
	b	3	No	Semicircular	Red, unpainted plaster	Small	In *lararium* aedicula
Casa dei Vettii	z	16	No	Rectangular		0.27 m x 0.38 m	None
Casa delle Nozze d'Argento	b	2	No	Semicircular		0.3 m x 0.37 m	None
House VIII 2, 14–16	a	6	No	Rectangular		0.38 m x 0.5 m	None
	f	6	No	Rectangular		0.32 m x 0.35 m	None
	o'	16	No	Rectangular		0.46 m x 0.4 m	None
Casa di Giuseppe II	c	4	Yes	Semicircular		0.38 m x 0.26 m	Nails attached to wall
	f	4	Yes	Rectangular	Painted with peacocks	0.26 m x 0.26 m	None
		4	16	No	Rectangular		0.7 m x 0.75 m	None
House VIII 2, 29–30	p	11	No	Semicircular		1.6 m x 1.1 m	None
	10	14	No	Unknown		Small	Above cooking hearth
	10	14	No	Unknown		Small	Above cooking hearth
	10	14	No	Unknown		Small	Above cooking hearth
House VIII 5,9	n	12	No	Semicircular		0.34 m x 0.34 m	None
	o	14	No	Semicircular		0.63 m x 0.45 m	Near cooking hearth

circular ones; so, there would seem to be no clear functional distinction based on shape.

In summary, it is seemingly invalid to assume either that all niches, or that only semicircular ones, had a religious function. This conclusion is particularly relevant for kitchen areas where the presence of niches has been used to demonstrate that household shrines were characteristic of such areas (for example, Dwyer 1982:114; Salza Prina Ricotti 1978/1980; Orr 1988:295). Without the necessary identifiers for a religious function, it seems highly likely that such niches often served as convenient storage places.

LOOSE FINDS

This study also highlights the unsuitability of certain labels for particular loose finds in Pompeian houses. In addition, it demonstrates how the function or the potential range of functions of certain fittings found in these houses may elucidate the types of furniture from which they originate or, conversely, warn us that precise identification of furnishings is not possible from the recorded remains.

Furniture Fittings

A large number of bone hinges were found in the houses in this study. They occurred as two types: approximately 0.1 m in length and 35 mm in diameter; and 35 mm in length and 35 mm in diameter. They often occurred together, sometimes more than thirty hinges in a single find spot (for example, in front hall 2 in the Casa della Venere in Bikini and in front hall 3 in the Casa del Fabbro; figure 4.9). Generally only two to four large ones were in an assemblage with a greater quantity of smaller ones. Such a group appears to have formed the hinges for upright wooden doors suitable for cupboards. The larger ones had been the end pieces of a hinge band, reinforcing the two ends of a hinge for an upright door, with an alignment of the smaller hinges between. Such rows of hinges appear in plaster casts of cupboards in the ambulatory of garden CC in the Casa di Julius Polybius (figure 4.10).[2] Finds of the larger hinges can therefore be taken to indicate the presence of cupboards (for further examples: Fremersdorf 1940:327, Figs. 8–9; Frere 1972:149; Ricci 1985:54; and for further bibliography Mols 1999:107–109, Fig. 29).

A number of bronze bosses or studs were also found. These bosses, generally found in association with metal hinges (for example, room B in the Casa del Menandro; figure 4.11), were probably fittings for wooden or metal chests. Some can still be seen on the bronze chests in the front hall of the Casa dei Vettii (figure 4.12), as well as on two other metal chests in Pompeii, one in the front hall of the Casa di Obellius Firmus, and another now stored in the Granaio storeroom, beside the Forum. The presence of such hinges with no bronze chest in evidence may indicate the presence of a wooden chest (see Mols 1999:104–105).

Another group of furniture fittings consists of bronze ring handles. These handles were frequently found both with bone hinges, indicating the presence of wooden cupboards (for example, front hall of the Casa del Fabbro), and with bosses and bronze hinges that suggest the presence of chests (for example, room B in the Casa del Menandro; figure 4.13). They can be seen in situ on the plaster casts of cupboards in the Casa

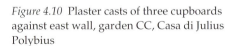

Figure 4.9 Bone hinges (inv. no. 5412, both sizes), front hall, Casa del Fabbro

Figure 4.10 Plaster casts of three cupboards against east wall, garden CC, Casa di Julius Polybius

di Julius Polybius, indicating that they were used as handles for sliding drawers (see figure 4.10).

So-called *guardispigoli* (U- or L-shaped bronze fittings) were also frequently found in the houses of this study (figure 4.14); their precise function is unclear. It has been assumed that they were corner guards for furniture. If so, their shape and the location of nail holes for attachment indicate they were attached around a void or socket. The association of a *guardispigolo* with chest fittings in the front hall of the Casa dei

CLOCKWISE FROM ABOVE LEFT:

Figure 4.11 Chest fittings (inv. nos 4703bis, 4706–08, 4710–12, 4719, 4721), room B, Casa del Menandro

Figure 4.12 Bronze chest against south wall of front hall, Casa dei Vettii

Figure 4.13 Ring handles (inv. nos 4697–99) from room B, Casa del Menandro

Figure 4.14 L- and U-shaped *guardispigoli* (inv. nos 4297A–C) from upper levels in Casa del Fabbro

Quadretti Teatrali suggests that they had been fittings for furniture; however, those found in corridor 16 of the Casa del Menandro and on the threshold of room 11 in the Casa dei Quadretti Teatrali seem to have been associated with door or door-frame fittings. Without a better understanding of their use, these fittings alone cannot therefore provide evidence for furniture.

Forme di pasticceria

Scholars have assigned the label *forma di pasticceria* (pastry or confectionery mold) to two different types of bronze vessels, suggesting that they had a known culinary function. One type was elliptical, often approximately 70 mm high and 200 mm long, with straight flaring sides and a plain rim (figure 4.15). The other was in the form of a shell, often approximately 50 mm high and approximately 100 to 150 mm in diameter (figure 4.16), sometimes with a low

base and a suspension or loop handle (for example, Borriello et al. 1986:178, Nos. 38–39; Conticello et al. 1990:188, No. 86).

Seventeen such vessels were recorded in this study (table 4.3). Five were shell shaped; the rest were elliptical.[3] At least six appear to have been found in a storage situation. Otherwise, there seems to be a more pronounced pattern of both shapes being found in association with material related to ablutions and toilet activities rather than with food preparation. They were frequently found with large bronze basins but also with strigils, probes, tweezers, amphorae (possibly as water containers), and small glass vessels. Suzanne Tassinari recently suggested that the elliptical vessel forms were more likely used for toilet activities than for food preparation or serving but might have had a number of other uses (1993, I:233). Tassinari also suggested that the types of bronze basins with which they were frequently

Figure 4.15 Elliptical *forma di pasticceria* and basin (inv. nos 4932–33) from room 38, Casa del Menandro

Figure 4.16 Shell-shaped *forma di pasticceria* (inv. no. 8582), House I 9,5

Table 4.3 *Forme di pasticceria*

House	Room	Room type	Shape	Associations
Casa di Julius Polybius	EE	11	Shell	Bronze containers and pouring vessels, lampstands, statuary, ceramic vessels
	EE	11	Shell	Bronze containers and pouring vessels, lampstands, statuary, ceramic vessels
Casa della Venere in Bikini	2	3	Elliptical	Bronze basin, bronze and glass vessels, toiletries, jewelry, in storage
Casa del Menandro	38	16	Elliptical	Bronze basin, amphora, ceramic jug
Casa del Fabbro	UF(10)	22	Elliptical	Tools, ceramic cup, amphora
Casa degli Amanti	9	9	Elliptical	Ceramic vessels, tools, tweezers, spindle, lamp, in storage
Casa di Trebius Valens	u	12	Elliptical	Bronze basin, knife, statuettes
Casa dei Ceii	f	4	Elliptical	Silver shell, bronze basin, spinning implements
Casa di Sacello Iliaco	l	4	Elliptical	Bed, patera
House VI 16, 26	C	4	Elliptical	Bronze jug, *casseruole*, ceramic jug, tableware, gaming, weight
Casa del Principe di Napoli	d	3	Elliptical	Bronze basins and buckets, *casseruola*, glass vessels
	k	11	Elliptical	Bronze basin, *fruttiera*, lamps, spindles
	m	13	Shell	Bronze bottle, glass amphora, probes, spindle, ceramic jars
House VI 15,5	b	3	Shell	Bronze jug, bronze and glass vessels, strigil, in storage
	n or o	4	Elliptical	Bronze bowl, bronze *casseruole*, glass vessels, strigil, pestle, spindle, spoon
	n or o	4	Elliptical	Bronze bowl, bronze *casseruole*, glass vessels, strigil, pestle, spindle, spoon
	u	9	Shell	Tweezers, glass bottle, lampstand

found were used in ablutions (1993, I:231). The basins in the Casa del Menandro, the Casa dei Ceii, and the Casa di Trebius Valens were of a particular large sub-hemispherical type with two small vertical handles attached to the body. The terminals of these basins were often in the form of fishtails, which suggests water-related activities.

In 1900, Erich Pernice pointed out that many of the shell-shaped *forma di pasticceria* had a foot, ring handle, uneven rim, and embossed base inverse to that necessary to turn out molded foods, and argued that the label for this vessel type was inappropriate (1900:185–187). Despite his observations, scholars have continued using the term for this vessel type (for example, Borriello et al. 1986:178, Nos. 38–39; Conticello et al. 1990:188, No. 86). Its shell shape rather suggests a function associated with water. Its scoop-like form is suitable for pouring water over oneself, like the women bathers in the wall painting in the bath complex of the Casa del Menandro (Maiuri 1933:154, Fig. 73). Some of these vessels had a small suspension handle that would make a vessel portable when empty. As Pernice noted, this handle is an improbable attachment for a pastry mold but is more useful on a vessel for ablutions.

It is therefore not appropriate to assume that the presence of these vessels indicated dining or food preparation. The label *forma di pasticceria* alludes to molds used by European pastry makers in the recent past (for example, Tannahill 1968: Fig. 52) or to the types of molds used for delicacies such as jelly for a Victorian dinner table (Brett 1968:100). Such analogical inference attempts to equate Pompeian dining behavior with modern western behavior. While these two vessel types did not necessarily have the same function, an association with water seems likely for both (see Allison 1999b:66–67).

Casseruole

Another metal vessel frequently found in Pompeian houses was a deep bowl (often approximately 150 mm in diameter) with a long handle (often approximately 130 mm in length) (figure 4.17). It is frequently labeled a *casseruola* (casserole) or *tegame* (frying pan) (for example, Tassinari 1975:25–36; Borriello et al. 1986:176, Nos. 22–25). Both terms imply that it served as a cooking vessel.

Table 4.4 lists all the vessels that have been labeled *casseruole*. Those that are less deep have also sometimes been labeled *paterae*. In this sample, there were forty-six such vessels from identifiable provenances. Another four (two from the Casa della Venere in Bikini and two from the Casa di Giuseppe II) were without provenance and are therefore not included in the table. Of those in the table, fifteen were found in front halls and ten in type 4 rooms. Others were scattered through a range of room types. Notably, only three were reported in rooms of type 14, identified as kitchen areas, two from the same room, in association with a decorated amphora but not with cooking equipment. Of those found in the front hall, one had no associated material

and six had been stored in cupboards, in association with material more closely related to serving and storage than to cooking. Only three of the forty-six examples were associated with material identifiable as cooking equipment, one in a room with a range of domestic materials (room 12 in House I 10,8). More often these vessels were associated with finer-quality household vessels.

Tassinari noted (1993, I:232) that, of the 190 vessels of this type now stored in the Pompeii Collection and the hundreds stored in the Naples National Museum, none showed any traces of fire blackening, which might have verified that they had been used in cooking. White believed that this vessel type was called a *trulla*, a ladle or dipper (1975:192–193, Fig. 53). One of the uses for a *trulla* was at the table, particularly to take wine out of a larger receptacle (see also den Boersterd 1956:xxi). Three of the vessels in this sample were made of silver. This vessel type has also been found elsewhere made of silver with gold inlay (for example, de la Bédoyère 1989:78, Fig. 46). The occurrence of this type in precious metals implies that it was more appropriately designed for serving or for table use than for cooking.

Figure 4.17 Casseruole and shells (inv. nos 4947–49, 4951) found near northwest corner of hall 41, Casa del Menandro

Table 4.4 *Casseruole*

House	Room	Type	Metal	Shape	Associations
Casa del Menandro	1	4	Bronze		(Provenance insecure)
	b	3	Bronze		Amphora, lamps, bronze *labrum*
	A	16	Bronze		Bronze jug, plate, lampstand, lamps
	B	16	Silver	*Patera*	Silver tableware, jewelry, coins, in storage
	B	16	Bronze	*Patera*	Mixed bronze and glass vessels, in storage
	35	16	Bronze		Ceramic bowl, amphora, jug, glass bottle, weights, lamps
	41	3	Bronze		On table with bronze jugs
	41	3	Bronze		On shelf?, with shells, ceramic jugs
	41	3	Bronze		On shelf?, with shells, ceramic jugs
	41	3	Bronze		On shelf?, with shells, ceramic jugs
	43	4	Bronze	*Patera*	Bronze washing and serving vessels
Casa del Fabbro	1	2	Bronze		Ceramic jugs, tools, buckle
	3	3	Bronze	*Patera*	Bronze basins, weights, in storage
	3	3	Bronze		Storage and drinking vessels
	UF(7)	22	Bronze		Collection of luxury bronze and glass vessels, jewelry, coins
	UF(7)	22	Bronze		Collection of luxury bronze and glass vessels, jewelry, coins
House I 10,8	12	12	Bronze*		Mixed domestic, including cooking pot
Casa dei Quadretti Teatrali	b	3	Bronze	*Scodella*	Mixed domestic, in storage (excluding cooking and toilet)
	b	3	Bronze		Mixed domestic, in storage (excluding cooking and toilet)
Casa dell'Efebo	A'	3	Bronze		Amphora, *patera*, and storage container
	8	14	Bronze		Decorated bronze amphora, ceramic vase
	8	14	Bronze		Decorated bronze amphora, ceramic vase
	13	7	Bronze		Mixed domestic/tools, in storage (excluding cooking)
House I 7,19	a	4	Silver		Jewelry and glass bottle
	a	4	Silver		Jewelry and glass bottle
Casa di Trebius Valens	a	3	Bronze	*Patera*	None
	u	12	Bronze		Luxury glass and bronze vessels, lamps, statuary
Casa del Sacello Iliaco	1	4	Bronze	*Patera*	*Forma di pasticceria* and bed
House VI 16,26	C	4	Bronze		Bronze and ceramic serving and tableware, toilet
	C	4	Bronze		Bronze and ceramic serving and tableware, toilet
Casa della Ara Massima	G	6	Bronze	*Patera*	Serving and storage vessels, mixed domestic/industrial
	N	4	Bronze		Bronze vessels, incl. decorated krater and cooking vessel
Casa degli Amorini Dorati	F	9	Bronze	*Patera*	None
Casa del Principe di Napoli	d	3	Bronze		Bronze, glass and ceramic storage and table vessels
	h	14	Bronze		Bronze, glass and ceramic vessels, faunal remains
	n	9	Bronze	*Patera*	Spouted bronze vase
	UF	22	Bronze	*Patera*	Personal, toilet, gaming
	UF	22	Bronze	*Patera*	Personal, toilet, gaming
House VI 15,5	b	3	Bronze	*Patera*	Bronze and glass serving/storage, toilet materials, in storage
	b	3	Bronze	*Patera*	Bronze and glass serving/storage, toilet materials, in storage
	n or o	4	Bronze		Glass and bronze vessels, toilet, gaming
	n or o	4	Bronze		Glass and bronze vessels, toilet, gaming
	1	10	Bronze	*Patera*	Cooking pot and furniture fittings
Casa delle Nozze d'Argento	d	3	Bronze		Bone vase, ornate ceramic lamp
House VIII 2,26	VIII 2,27	19	Bronze		Mixed domestic assemblage
Casa di Giuseppe II	z'	21	Bronze	*Patera*	Washing equipment, container

* Silver decorated

Fourteen of these vessels were also labeled *paterae*, often taken to assume some religious significance; however, Nuber argued that the flatter vessels of this type were probably for washing hands before dining (1972:83–90, 117–118, Pls. 18, 20.2, 29; see also Tassinari 1993, I:223). As the actual vessels in the sample have not been physically studied, it is difficult to ascertain their precise form. In any event, all these *"casseruole"* were more likely to have been associated with dining and entertainment than with cooking and food preparation.

Pendants

Nine bronze pendants were recorded in this sample and identified as having belonged to horse harness, largely because they were of a type frequently found in military contexts and are considered decoration for horse harness (table 4.5; see Bishop 1988: Figs. 44–47). Ulbert (1969:21) used their presence at the early Roman Kastell Rheingönheim in Germany to conclude that the troop stationed there had been mounted, despite the fact that many of the associated metal finds were buckles and pins from human apparel. Indeed, in 1897 Louis Jacobi identified similar enameled pendants from the Roman military camp of Saalburg as pieces of human adornment (1897:500, Pls. 68–69).

For four of the pendants in this sample, an identification as horse harness ornaments seems justified; however, such identification is not verifiable for the other five. The latter were sometimes found in storage containers with other more personal luxury material (figure 4.18). Such pendants could have been for either animal or human adornment. Thus, their mere presence is not an indication of horse harness.

Figure 4.18 Pendants and other objects (inv. nos 4907–10) found in casket in room 35, Casa del Menandro

Fritilli

The label *fritillus* has been used for two similar types of small ceramic vessels found in Pompeii (table 4.6). Daremberg and Saglio (1892:1341)

Table 4.5 Bronze pendants

House	Room	Type	Shape	Associations
Casa della Venere in Bikini	2	3	Circular	Bronze vessels, jewelry, coins, toilet, and gaming items, in storage
Casa del Menandro	34	19	Shield	Cart and harness
	34	19	Shield	Cart and harness
	35	16	Leaf	Statuettes, small scales, luxury lamp, in box
	35	16	Shield	Statuettes, small scales, luxury lamp, in box
Casa dei Vettii	3	8	Rhomboid	In cupboard with harness
	3	8	Shield	In cupboard with harness
House VI 16,26	UF(H)	22	Shield	Leather, statuette, small ceramic pot
Casa delle Nozze d'Argento	UF(7)	22	Shield	Buckles, statuette, bronze ornaments, lamp

Table 4.6 *Fritilli*

House	Room	Type	Contents	Associations
Casa del Menandro	UF(b)	22		Pottery bowl, lamp
	UF(b)	22		Pottery bowl, lamp
Casa del Fabbro	3	3		Bronze vase, *abbeveratoi*, in storage
	UF(7)	22		Glass and ceramic vessels, glass tubes, shells
Casa dei Quadretti Teatrali	b	3	Traces of paint?	Bronze vessels, knives, clothing, jewelry, gaming counters, in storage
	b	3	Traces of paint?	Bronze vessels, knives, clothing, jewelry, gaming counters, in storage
	b	3		Luxury drinking and serving vessels, statuette, jewelry, in storage
House 6,8–9	b	20		Coins, shop counter
Casa dei Ceii	b	3		Lamps, scales, lantern, knife, in storage

identified this term as meaning dice thrower. Therefore, these so-named Pompeian vessels are identified as gaming implements (see Annecchino 1977b:198–199). One of these vessel types ranged from approximately 70 to 150 mm high, had an oval body with a wide flaring mouth, and a small flattened knob base, such that it stands more securely on its mouth than on its base (Annecchino 1977b: Figs. 1, 3). The other vessel is similar in size and shape but with a more cylindrical body, smaller mouth, and low foot on which it stood securely (figure 4.19; Annecchino 1977b: Figs. 2, 4). Annecchino actually argued that only the first type was a *fritillus* and that the second was a drinking vessel. Her argument is based largely on the discovery of die and astragali in two Pompeian houses, in which examples of the first type of vessel were also found although not in direct association, and on the depiction of similar vessels in painting and relief sculpture, sometimes in gaming scenes.

Nine vessels in this sample were given this label by the excavators. It was not possible to determine to which of Annecchino's two types each belonged. Only two, found together in the front hall of the Casa dei Quadretti Teatrali, could conceivably be associated with gaming equipment; however, these two had traces of color or paint inside and were found in storage with a range of domestic and personal material.

To my knowledge, no such vessels have been found in direct association with artifacts that can be definitely identified as gaming objects (for example, gaming boards or die). Daremberg and Saglio illustrated a very different object as a *fritillus*. Even if evidence can be found to demonstrate that this vessel type could have been used in gaming activities, it was of a very simple form and not very different from the second type, which Annecchino dismissed from having such a function because it was less well designed for dice throwing. The presence alone of such a vessel should not be taken as indicating any specific activity (see Allison 1999b:62–63).

Figure 4.19 Fritillus (inv. no. 409) from House VI 6,22

59

Abbeveratoi

A small ceramic vessel, approximately 50 mm in height with a ring handle, biconical body, and narrow mouth, was frequently found in Pompeian houses (table 4.7). It has been labeled an *abbeveratoio*, often *abbeveratoio d'uccello* (figure 4.20), suggesting that it had a specific and known function as a very small drinking vessel for birds. One might therefore expect them to have been found in gardens and open spaces.

Eighteen vessels in this sample were referred to as *abbeveratoi* by the excavators. Of these, eleven were from room 2 and the front hall (in the Casa del Fabbro), probably in storage. The material with which they were associated indicates food preparation and eating, lighting, or personal activities. Two others were found together in the garden area of the Casa degli Amanti but were stored in a cupboard in the ambulatory with a range of other ceramic vessels and personal material. Other examples were found in predominantly closed rooms (see

also room 14 in the Casa della Caccia Antica: Allison and Sear 2002:87) and in assemblages comparable to those in the front hall of the Casa del Fabbro. The one from room 12 of House I 10,8 was found in association with tools, but not gardening or agricultural tools. It is therefore inappropriate to consider that this label identifies the functions of this vessel type.

Figure 4.20 Abbeveratoio (inv. no. 6298B) from House VIII 2,5

Table 4.7 *Abbeveratoi*

House	Room	Type	Associations
Casa del Menandro	43	4	Bronze serving/tableware, marble strips, lamp, scales
Casa del Fabbro	2	2	Ceramic jug, glass bottle, bone spoon, hoe
	2	2	Bronze basin, glass bottles, lamp, lampstand
	3	3	Bronze vase, *fritillus*, in storage
	3	3	Bronze vase, *fritillus*, in storage
	3	3	Glass vessels, ceramic jugs, scales, knife, tweezers, tongs, in storage
	3	3	Glass vessels, ceramic jugs, scales, knife, tweezers, tongs, in storage
	3	3	Glass vessels, ceramic jugs, scales, knife, tweezers, tongs, in storage
	3	3	Glass vessels, ceramic jugs, scales, knife, tweezers, tongs, in storage
	3	3	Glass vessels, ceramic jugs, scales, knife, tweezers, tongs, in storage
	3	3	Glass vessels, ceramic jugs, scales, knife, tweezers, tongs, in storage
	3	3	Glass vessels, ceramic jugs, scales, knife, tweezers, tongs, in storage
House I 10,8	12	12	Mixed domestic/industrial storage, including 13 ceramic vessels
Casa degli Amanti	9	9	Ceramic jugs, pot and *amphoretta*; tweezers, lamp, tools, *forma di pasticceria*, in storage
	9	9	Ceramic jugs, pot and *amphoretta*; tweezers, lamp, tools, *forma di pasticceria*, in storage
Casa dei Quadretti Teatrali	UF(b)	22	None
Casa della Nozze d'Argento	n	11	Glass bottle, glass rod, jewelry
House VIII 2,26	VIII 2,27	19	Mixed domestic assemblage

CONCLUSIONS

It is clear from the sample of artifacts discussed here that analyses using the data compiled for this study can throw new light on the functions of many of the contents and fixtures, as well as on the spatial distribution of household activities. This discussion indicates that we are not well informed on such issues; indeed, the study serves to highlight that functions traditionally ascribed to Pompeian material are not necessarily universal or even valid. Rather it appears rather that assumptions of specific functions for specific artifact types, consistent throughout the Roman world, need to be replaced with new concepts that concede the possibility of considerable variability. Thorough analyses of artifact form and contents, together with detailed studies of the associations, can lead to better comprehension of the functioning of Pompeian households.

NOTES

1. Ling (1997:266) identified an altar in the larger of the two niches under the stairway in room 2 of the Casa del Menandro. The only difference between the two niches is that one is raised above ground level and has moldings in its base, comparable to the structure in room M in the Casa di Julius Polybius. The assemblages found in these niches suggest that both niches had been used for domestic storage.

2. Stephan Mols has drawn to my attention that these hinges were not preserved precisely in situ but were reconstructed during the making of the plaster casts.

3. Not included here are four small silver vessels found with other silver vessels stored in room B in the Casa del Menandro which were referred to by Maiuri as "*calathiscoi (forme di pasticceria)*" (1933: 371). These four would appear to have been small cups that are functionally distinct from the two types discussed here.

Figure 5.1 Façade showing one remaining seat, Casa dei Ceii

5.

Room Use according to Architectural Type

IN DEFINING THE USE OF SPACE in Pompeian houses, scholars have generally used textual and modern analogy. Textual analogy has first been employed to identify excavated spaces as the architectural types described in ancient literature. Then the functions or activities associated with the room nomenclature in the texts have been ascribed to the so-labeled rooms in Pompeian houses. Finally, modern analogy is often used to separate these activities so that so-named rooms appear to correspond to modern counterparts or to those of the more recent past. For example, certain architectural room types in Pompeii have been designated *cubicula* and then assumed to have functions similar to modern concepts of bedrooms (see, for example, Grant 1971: Figs. 6–11; McKay 1977: Figs. 8, 9, 11; Wallace-Hadrill 1994:57). Thus the spatial division of activities in Roman, not to mention Pompeian, houses was assumed to be equivalent to modern spatial divisions of domestic practices. Pliny the Younger (*Ep.* 2, 17.10), however, indicated that the function of at least one room in his house was interchangeable between a *cubiculum* and a *cenatio*.

The use of Latin and Greek textual nomenclature to ascribe function to spaces in Pompeian houses pays little heed to possible regional and social variation, or to changes over time. The final use of a space may be reflected in neither its architectural design nor its decoration.[1] Although changing relationships might be expected among room type, decoration, and contents during the life of the house, the use of some room types must always have been governed to some extent by their design and location within the house. That is, some rooms (for example, small closed rooms off the front hall) might be more readily adapted to a variety of functions during their life cycle, while others (for example, the front hall itself) might not.

This chapter puts aside textual nomenclature and defines room type in terms of relationship to the front-hall/garden complex; size relative to house size; through-routes; and functions defined by specific fixtures (for example, hearths, water-catchment pools). It focuses on artifact assemblages as evidence for patterns of room use in Pompeian houses, at least during their final occupancy. Because this study is based on a sample chosen for its architectural conformity—the so-called *atrium* house—certain architectural room types occur in most, if not all, of the houses. The rooms are divided into twenty-two types (table 5a). These types are fairly subjective. Some rooms fall between two categories (for example, closed and open, small and medium/large). Others belong to one architectural type but have a fixture that places them in another type. For example, room i in the Casa dei Ceii belongs to architectural type 4 but has a hearth, making it type 14. Others should perhaps have categories all their own (for example, room 10 in the Casa del Menandro, room 3 in the Casa degli Amorini Dorati, and room a' in House VIII 2,29–30). Categories for rooms outside the main front-hall/garden complex are less distinctive, as consistent patterns of architectural conformity were less evident in these areas. As noted in chapter 3, the houses chosen for this sample were among the largest in Pompeii and had the greatest number of rooms. William H. Adams commented that the number of monofunctional activity areas in a house was directly proportional to the size of the structure, with more multifunctional spaces likely to have been found in smaller houses (1987:106). If there was any spatial separation of household activities in Pompeian houses, then this sample is suitably chosen to illustrate it.

The following discussion assesses the assemblages in each room type for patterns that may indicate habitual activities in these areas. Finds that would have been the least easily moved are the most useful for such an assessment. Extensive collections of more easily lost or mobile items are also more relevant than isolated finds of small objects. Artifact assemblages indicate final room use preceding the AD 79 eruption. Predominant patterns of more permanent items or of particular collections across the sample ought to provide information concerning the habitual use of particular room types. Finds of coins and skeletons have not been included in this discussion, as they undoubtedly relate to loss and abandonment processes and are discussed in chapter 8. No room assemblages are precisely the same; hence, they have been divided into categories. The presence and significance of each category is discussed, as well as the overall room assemblage. The selection of these categories and concepts of normality were discussed in chapter 3. It must also be noted that the specific uses of each room type would have been affected by house size. Chapter 7 discusses the degree of correspondence between those activities identified through these assemblages and those which, through the application of textual analogy, purport to have been the activities that took place in these rooms. Rooms lacking both fixtures and contents are generally not included in the tables.

Table 5.a Room types

Type	Section	Location/description	Latin term commonly used
1	Front hall area	Main entranceway	*Fauces, vestibula*
2		Room leading directly off front entranceway	*Cella ostiaria*
3		Front hall, usually with central opening and pool	*Atrium*
4		Small closed room off side of front hall	*Cubiculum*
5		Open-fronted area off side of front hall	*Ala*
6		Large/medium room off corner of front hall	*Triclinium*
7		Open-sided room opposite main entrance or leading to garden	*Tablinum*
8		Long, narrow internal corridor	*Fauces, andrones*
9	Main garden area	Main garden, colonnaded garden and ambulatories, or terrace	*Peristylum, ambulatio, viridarium*
10		Large/medium closed room off garden/terrace but with no view	*Triclinium*
11		Large/medium open-fronted room off garden/terrace with window or wide entranceway giving view of garden or lower floor	*Oecus, exedra, triclinium*
12		Small closed room off garden/terrace or lower floor	*Cubiculum*
13		Small open-fronted area off garden/terrace or lower floor	*Exedra*
14	Other areas	Room with cooking hearth or associated room (kitchen area)	*Culina*
15		Latrine as entire room	*Latrina*
16		Other room outside main front-hall/garden complex	*Repositorium, cubiculum, stabulum, praefurnium*
17		Stairway	
18		Secondary internal garden or court, usually not colonnaded	*Hortus, xystus, atrium, vestibulum*
19		Secondary entrance or entrance courtyard	*Fauces, posticum, stabulum*
20		Room at front of house open to street (shop)	*Tabernae*
21		Bath area	*Balneae, atriolum, apodyterium, tepidarium, caldarium, frigidarium, laconicum*
22		Upper floor rooms and material in upper-level deposits	*Cenaculum*

TYPE 1: MAIN ENTRANCEWAYS

The usually narrow corridors by which one entered from the street, invariably directly to the front-hall area, were a standard room type for all houses in the sample except House I 6,8–9. Three houses had two such entranceways: the Casa di Julius Polybius; House VIII 2,14–16; and House VIII 2,29–30. The Casa dell'Efebo had three. In these four houses, these entranceways are distinguished from type 19 in that they were all on the same side of the complex, leading to front halls. None can therefore be assumed to have been the principal entrance.

These entranceways were all largely devoid of fixtures and movable contents, with the exception of door fittings (table 5.1). Fixed seating (figure 5.1)—either in the entranceway itself, immediately outside the entranceway, or in an adjoining room (that is, in room c in House VIII 2,28)—occurred in nine of the thirty houses sampled. A stairway was found in one entranceway. The other notable finds were cupboards and their contents, which were recorded in two entranceways. If the latter had indeed been from the entranceways and had not fallen from the upper floor, then this situation would suggest activity divergent from what might be expected for a relatively narrow main access route. Under normal conditions, these entranceways would probably have been devoid of contents, permitting easy access in and out of the house.

TYPE 2: ROOMS LEADING DIRECTLY OFF MAIN ENTRANCEWAYS

Only six houses in the sample have rooms of this type (table 5.2), three with two each. Room 1 in the Casa del Fabbro and rooms b and c in the Casa delle Nozze d'Argento appear to have had utilitarian, possibly industrial/commercial uses, whereas room 2 in the former house, room p in House VI 15,5, and room v in House VIII 2,29–30 had more domestic assemblages, comparable to the small rooms around the front hall. Shelving indicates that room c of House VIII 2,26 had been a storeroom. The few examples of this room type had a variety of uses, most of them fairly utilitarian, with little attempt made to impress the visitor. Only room 2 of the Casa del Fabbro, which was a little further into the house, had painted wall decoration. The masonry seating in room c of House VIII 2,28 is included in table 5.1.

TYPE 3: FRONT HALLS

These courts or halls[2] (tables 5.3a–c; figure 5.2) were usually entered directly from the street through the main entranceway and often had rooms on all four sides. Some were set further

Table 5.1 Main entranceways

House	Entranceway	Fixed seating	Stairways	Cupboard with contents
Casa del Menandro	a	•		
Casa del Fabbro	F	•		
House 1 10,8	a	•		
Casa dei Quadretti Teatrali	a			•
Casa dell'Efebo	1'	•		•
Casa dei Ceii	a	•		
Casa degli Amorini Dorati	A	•		
Casa della Ara Massima	A	•		
House VIII 2,14–16	aa		•	
House VIII 2,28	room c	•		
House VIII 2,34	a	•		

Table 5.2 Rooms leading directly off main entranceway

House	Room	Utilitarian assemblages*	Domestic assemblages	No movable finds
Casa del Fabbro	1	•		
	2		•	
Casa delle Nozze d'Argento	b	•		
	c	•		
House VI 15,5	p		•	
House VIII 2,26	c	•		
House VIII 2,28	c			•
House 2,29–30	v		•	
	w			•

* Includes industrial and commercial assemblages and fixtures

Table 5.3a Front halls: ritual fixtures and luxury furniture

House	Front hall	*Lararium* paintings and aediculae	Niches	Tables/ supports*	Statuary/ tables/basins	Puteals/ cistern covers
Casa di Julius Polybius	N	•	•			•
	O					•
Casa della Venere in Bikini	2			•		
Casa del Menandro	b	•			•	
	41		•			
Casa del Fabbro	3			•		
Casa dell'Efebo	A'	•				
	A"				•	
House I 7,19	p				•	
Casa di Trebius Valens	a				•	
Casa dei Ceii	b				•	•
Casa del Sacello Iliaco	b					•
House VI 16,26	B	•			•	•
Casa di M. Lucretius Fronto	2				•	
Casa del Principe di Napoli	d				•	
House VI 15,5	b	•				
Casa delle Nozze d'Argento	d				•	•
House VIII 2,14–16	bb				• ?	
House VIII 2,28	d	•				
Casa di Giuseppe II	b				•	
House VIII 2,29–30	k'	•				

* Includes statue supports and fountain fittings

Table 5.3b Front halls: domestic and utilitarian fixtures and furniture

House	Front hall	Cupboards/ chests*	Weaving	Bulk storage	No movable finds	Utilitarian fixtures
Casa di Julius Polybius	N			•		
	O			•		
Casa della Venere in Bikini	2	•				
Casa del Menandro	b	• ?			• ?	
	41	•				•
Casa del Fabbro	3	•	•			
House I 10,8	1	•	•			
Casa degli Amanti	1				•	
Casa dei Quadretti Teatrali	b	•	•			
House I 6,8–9	c			•		•
Casa di Stallius Eros	b	• ?				•
Casa del Sacerdos Amandus	1	•	•			
Casa dell'Efebo	A'	•				
House I 7,19	p					•
Casa di Trebius Valens	a	•				
Casa dei Ceii	b	•	•			
Casa del Sacello Iliaco	b	•	•	•		
House VI 16,26	B	•		•		•
Casa di M. Lucretius Fronto	2	•				
Casa del Principe di Napoli	d	• ?		•		•
House VI 15,5	b	•				
Casa dei Vettii	c	•		•		
Casa della Ara Massima	B				•	
Casa delle Nozze d'Argento	d	•				
House VIII 2,14–16	bb	• ?				
	b'				•	
House VIII 2,26	d				•	
House VIII 2,28	d			•		
Casa di Giuseppe II	b	•		•		
House VIII 2,34	c	•				
House VIII 2,29–30	k'		•			
	m'		•			
House VIII 5,9	2				•	

*Includes domestic contents

back into the house (for example, in the Casa di Julius Polybius and House I 6,8–9) or to one side (for example, hall 41 in the Casa del Menandro). They generally had an opening to the sky at the center of the roof, with a catchment pool for rainwater under it. Because of the nature of the sample chosen for this study, each house had at least one front hall or courtyard; five houses had two, making a total of thirty-five in the sample. Apart from the central water-catchment pool (*impluvium*), the most frequent fixtures were so-called *lararia*. These were in the form of an aedicula, a

Table 5.3c Front halls: wall furbishing

House	Front hall	Wall painting	Painted socles*	Coarsely plastered/ undecorated
Casa di Julius Polybius	N		•	
	O			•
Casa della Venere in Bikini	2			•
Casa del Menandro	b	•		
	41			•
Casa del Fabbro	3			•
House I 10,8	1			•
Casa degli Amanti	1	•		
Casa dei Quadretti Teatrali	b	•		
House I 6,8–9	c		• ?	
Casa di Stallius Eros	b			•
Casa del Sacerdos Amandus	1		• ?	
Casa dell'Efebo	A'	•		
	A"			•
House I 7,19	p	•		
Casa di Trebius Valens	a			•
Casa del Ceii	b	•		
Casa del Sacello Iliaco	b		•	•
House VI 16,26	B		•	
Casa della Ara Massima	B		•	
Casa degli Amorini Dorati	B	•		
Casa di M. Lucretius Fronto	2	•		
Casa del Principe di Napoli	d	• (simple)		
House VI 15,5	b			•
Casa dei Vettii	c	•		
Casa delle Nozze d'Argento	d	•		
House VIII 2,14–16	bb			•
	b'			•
House VIII 2,26	d	•		
House VIII 2,28	d		•	
Casa di Giuseppe II	b			•
House VIII 2,34	c			•
House VIII 2,29–30	k'	•		
	m'			• ?
House VIII 5,9	2			• ?

* With white plaster above

Figure 5.2 View through front hall from entrance, Casa delle Nozze d'Argento

painting of household deities on the wall, or a combination of these. Such fixtures were recorded in seven front halls (table 5.3a), a comparatively small proportion of the total, possibly supporting Salza Prina Ricotti's proposal that *lararia* had been moved from the front hall to the kitchen in about the second century BC (1978/1980:247–249). Most of the examples recorded here, however, were either built or decorated during the period of the Fourth Style, in the second half of the first century AD, and occurred in some of the largest houses in the sample (see also Foss 1997:202 n.19). Two niches (in front hall O of the Casa di Julius Polybius and hall 41 of the Casa del Menandro) are also referred to as *lararia*. As discussed in chapter 4, such niches occurred in a variety of locations throughout Pompeian houses and Pompeii in general. It has not been demonstrated that they all had a religious purpose.

Fixed bases in or near the central pool and reputedly for supporting display furnishings (for example, statuary or fountain fittings) were found in the front halls of only two houses. Although these bases and *lararia* were present in some front halls, they were not essential furnishings for this room type, which was generally devoid of fixtures beyond the central pool. If these fixtures are considered in combination with display furnishings (marble statuary, tables, basins) from ten, possibly eleven, houses, then display seems to have been commonplace for this area, but such furnishings were not a prerequisite. It would be illogical to ascribe the combined lack of marble furniture in front halls and the presence of a plethora of other finds (for example, the Casa del Sacello Iliaco, the Casa dei Quadretti Teatrali; and House VI 15,5) to post-eruption disturbance. The latter house, in particular, was a substantial establishment that might well be expected to have had such display furnishings.

Of the thirty-one puteals and cistern-head covers recorded in this sample, only six were found in front halls. Thus, like marble furnishings, they were found less often in the front halls than in other parts of the house. The most frequent furnishings in these front halls were wooden cupboards and chests; at least four were found in one front hall (the Casa dei Quadretti Teatrali). Evidence of such furniture was reported in the front halls of at least seventeen houses and possibly another four (table 5.3b). Most of this storage furniture can be shown to have been cupboards with upright doors or small wooden chests (as in the Casa di Julius Polybius, garden CC; see figure 4.10). Strongboxes, such as those in the Casa dei Vettii, seem to have been a rarity (see figure 4.12). These cupboards were mainly used for domestic storage of fairly utilitarian items. A few (for example, in the Casa della Venere in Bikini and the Casa dei Quadretti Teatrali) contained luxury items, and some seemed to contain both domestic and industrial/commercial material (for example, in the Casa del Fabbro and House I 10,8).

Weaving seems to be an activity associated with these front halls. Evidence, predominantly in the form of loomweights, was found in eight of the front halls. Bulk storage, indicated particularly by the remains of amphorae, were found in nine. Vessels for bulk storage were sometimes found in front halls otherwise lacking a record of domestic storage. It has been argued that many such front halls were used for more commercial/industrial than domestic activities at the time of the eruption (for example, Berry 1997:193). Without evidence for the former use, such a change in function is difficult to verify.

In addition to niches mentioned earlier, utilitarian fixtures were found in six front halls: stairways in the Casa dell'Efebo, House VI 16,26, and the Casa del Principe di Napoli; a platform of unknown function in hall 41 of the Casa del Menandro; and cooking hearths in House I 6,8-9 and the Casa di Stallius Eros.

Six front halls were largely devoid of movable finds. Three were in houses with the earliest excavation dates, and so this absence may not be significant. The front halls must therefore have usually been furnished. The most pronounced pattern demonstrates they were packed with domestic storage in wooden cupboards, with little evidence of elaborate chests for household valuables. A smaller proportion contained display furniture in the central area. Such furnishings might have been attractive to post-eruption intruders. The complete lack of any trace in more than 60 percent of the sample, many substantially undisturbed after the eruption, indicates that the front hall in Pompeian houses generally had a fairly utilitarian function. This function could be combined with display activities. The area acted as a service court around which the activities of many, or all, members of the household revolved.

If service areas can be identified by unpainted, plastered walls, the above conclusion is also borne out by the decoration of some of the front halls in this sample. At the time of excavation, about 30 percent of these front halls had remains of painted wall decoration. The others were decorated with a simple red socle and white upper zone, were coarsely plastered, or undecorated, or were furbished with a combination (for example, the Casa del Sacerdos Amandus and the Casa del Sacello Iliaco). The fourteen to sixteen coarsely plastered and un-

decorated front halls might conceivably have been in the process of redecoration. It has been observed, however, that at least eleven also contained cupboards and quantities of domestic apparatus, implying that they functioned as part of a domestic establishment in this condition. Some front halls seem to have been used for industrial/commercial activities rather than being in the process of refurbishing. The general impression is that they had been used for utilitarian and domestic activities, at least in their final phase of occupation.

According to Eugene Dwyer, the front halls were usually unfurnished except for an *impluvium*, a *lararium*, a puteal to take water from the cistern for daily use, a marble offering table (*cartibulum*), and a strongbox (*arca*; 1982:113–115). For this reason, the excavators of the Casa dei Quadretti Teatrali and House I 6,8-9 moved the remains of a marble table from the garden of the latter house and put it at the head of the central pool in the front hall of the former (Allison 1992b:52; figure 5.3). Dwyer also argued that these areas were largely unfurnished because ample room was needed for the circulation of guests. The observed pattern of domestic and utilitarian material in front halls might be seen to constitute a downgrading of formal display areas to utilitarian spaces as a result of conditions following the AD 62 earthquake. However, this pattern proliferated across a sample that includes both decorated and undecorated and some of the most impressive front halls in Pompeii (for example, the Casa delle Nozze d'Argento). While conceivable that some front halls may have been disrupted, this pattern shows that these furnishings had played a part in the normal functioning of Pompeian households. Front halls were a principal circulation area for all household members, and they would have been the first part of the house most people would have entered from the street. Nevertheless, Pompeians did not feel that household storage was out of place there. In fact, the halls undoubtedly were very convenient locations for keeping the necessities of daily life.[3]

Figure 5.3 Central pool with puteal from garden 16 and marble table legs from garden of House I 6,8-9, in front hall, Casa dei Quadretti Teatrali

TYPE 4: SMALL CLOSED ROOMS OFF FRONT HALLS

The small narrow rooms usually located on either side of the front hall are probably the most numerous of Pompeian room types. A total of 128 occurred in this sample, in all houses except the Casa dei Ceii.[4] Because of their number, this type has been divided into two groups: those with painted decoration and those without. In six rooms in the sample, decoration was not documented; these are categorized as decorated. The assemblages of each group were assessed and then the two groups were compared.

Decorated

There were a possible eighty-four decorated or painted rooms of this type, including six whose wall furbishing was indeterminate (tables 5.4a–b). The walls of two others were coarsely plastered over earlier painted decoration (room 3 in the Casa di M. Lucretius Fronto and room k in House VIII 2,34) and are categorized as undecorated. Of the seventy-eight whose painted decoration could be determined as its final furbishing, fixtures or contents were recorded in forty-four to forty-seven, thirty-eight of which had loose contents. More than two-thirds of the decorated rooms from the fifteen most

recently excavated houses had at least some contents. Nine of the nineteen rooms in houses from Regions V and VI had recorded contents but only five of the seventeen rooms from the older excavations in Region VIII. It is probable that the lack of material in the latter two groups was due to poor recording and that decorated rooms of this type would normally have had some contents. The exceptions are those in the more recently excavated Casa dei Quadretti Teatrali where four out of five were empty, despite the wealth of finds from the front hall and despite the fact that the latter had more evidence of post-eruption disturbance than the surrounding rooms.

Thirteen (less than 15 percent) of all the decorated rooms of this type had recesses, and up to eight of them had no other recorded contents (table 5.4a). Of the thirteen recesses, two (in room M in the Casa di Julius Polybius and in room D in House VI 16,26) were high and narrow (see chapter 4). Two other rooms with recesses (room c in the Casa del Sacerdos Amandus and room 9 in the Casa di M. Lucretius Fronto) also had built-in cupboards. Only six of the decorated rooms (some 16 percent of those with recorded finds) contained identifiable evidence of bedding. In only one, room UU in the Casa di Julius Polybius, was such evidence actually associated with a recess. Another room

(room g in the Casa dei Vettii) had a platform that could conceivably have served as a bed. While potential evidence of bedding may have gone unrecorded in the earliest excavations, ten of the thirteen rooms with recesses and no recorded evidence of bedding were excavated during the twentieth century, when such evidence was unlikely to have gone unrecorded (see chapter 3). Two others were excavated late last century (the Casa del Principe di Napoli and the Casa di M. Lucretius Fronto); no loose finds were recorded in the latter, and those recorded in the former were unrelated to bedding. Both houses had substantial assemblages in other rooms. Thus, no direct relationship between evidence of bedding and recesses can be established, as concluded in chapter 4. While a small number of these rooms had convincing evidence of sleeping activities during the final occupation phase, the vast majority did not.

Freestanding cupboards or large chests with a range of domestic contents, both utilitarian and of finer quality, were found in only two to three rooms of this type, which suggests that the types of domestic storage and activity recorded in the front hall were not usual in the surrounding closed and decorated rooms. Storage of this kind, in this type of room, may therefore have been related to altered or deteriorated conditions rather than to habitual use. More common were assemblages consisting variously of the remains of small chests and caskets; a variety of bronze serving, pouring, and storage vessels; ceramic vessels that were usually small and of fine quality, but occasionally included large amphorae; and items related to dress, toiletries, needlework, and lighting. These were found, generally in small quantities, in thirteen to eighteen decorated rooms of this type (35 to 48 percent of those with recorded finds). Three, possibly four, of this group also had evidence of beds or couches (room 6 of House I 10,8; room a of House I 7,19; room l of the Casa del Sacello Iliaco; and possibly room g in the Casa dei Vettii). Nevertheless, the more consistent pattern of relatively limited quantities of this material suggests that these items were either used or stored for personal use here.

Material that was more exclusively utilitarian/industrial was found in nine of these decorated rooms (23 percent of those with recorded contents). Cooking apparatus and storage were recorded in another three, possibly four, and an additional two contained a wealth of finds representing a mixture of domestic and utilitarian/industrial activities comparable to the front hall evidence. Building material was found in two, possibly three, others. Given the unlikelihood that these decorated rooms were intended for utilitarian purposes, some of the twenty-one rooms in this subgroup (table 5.4b) might have been undergoing change or might have been downgraded sometime after the commencement of their decoration. There was evidence in five of these rooms that the installation of shelving, or nails for suspension, would have defaced existing wall paintings. Few of the rooms in the former subgroup (table 5.4a), however, are included in this second subgroup. Of the four that are, two are only possible, and a third (room 43 in the Casa del Menandro) had a very mixed assemblage, possibly indicating an overlay of activities, including hoarding (see chapter 8). Some of the former group also had fragmentary pieces of statuary and furniture together with a domestic assemblage (for example, room D in the Casa degli Amorini Dorati, room c in the Casa del Principe di Napoli, and room c in the Casa di Giuseppe II). This combination may again represent an overlay of activities, conceivably a later deposition in deteriorated circumstances. Remains of more industrial material in rooms 3 and 6 in House I 10,8, together with more domestic material, suggest a similar phenomenon.

In summary, the prevailing pattern among the small closed and decorated rooms off the front hall suggests that the usual function of these rooms was related to private activities. Domestic activities that might be considered more communal (for example, cooking, eating, drinking, and storage) are not well represented. Actual evidence of bedding was rare, however, implying that decorated rooms of this type functioned as a type of "boudoir" rather than as a sleeping space. Some 25 percent had evidence of

Table 5.4a Small closed rooms off front hall, decorated: personal domestic material

House	Room	Recesses	Bedding	Built-in cupboards/ niches	Cupboards/ chests*	Small containers**
Casa di Julius Polybius	M	High			•	
	UU	Low/narrow	•			
Casa della Venere in Bikini	5	Low/narrow				
Casa del Menandro	43		•			
Casa del Fabbro	4	Low/narrow			• ?	
	5	Low/narrow				•
House I 10,8	3					•
	6		•			•
Casa dei Quadretti Teatrali	5					•
Casa del Sacerdos Amandus	c	Low/narrow		•		• ?
	f	Low/narrow				
Casa dell'Efebo	2	Low/narrow				• ?
	9	Low/narrow				
	11				•	
House I 7,19	a		•			•
	d	Low/narrow				• ?
Casa di Trebius Valens	e					•
Casa del Sacello Iliaco	d		•			
	h					• ?
	l		•			•
House VI 16,26	D	High				
	H					•
Casa degli Amorini Dorati	D					•
Casa di M. Lucretius Fronto	9	Low/narrow		•		
Casa del Principe di Napoli	c	Low/narrow				
House VI 15,5	f					• ?
Casa dei Vettii	g		• ?			•
House VIII 2,26	p					•
Casa di Giuseppe II	c					•
	f			•		
House VIII 2,29–30	1					•

* With domestic contents   ** With smaller amounts of domestic material

utilitarian activities, conceivably the result of downgrading after the inception of decoration.

Undecorated

Of the forty-four rooms of this type that appear to have been undecorated, or had only white plaster sometimes with a pink or yellow socle, fixtures and contents were recorded in thirty-one (tables 5.4c–d). Of these, twenty-three had fixtures, and fifteen of these had no loose finds. Six rooms had recesses; fourteen, including two with recesses, had evidence for shelving (figure

Table 5.4b Small closed rooms off front hall, decorated: utilitarian domestic/industrial material

House	Room	Industrial	Cooking apparatus/ storage vessels	Shelving/defaced decoration	Mixed assemblages	Building material
Casa di Julius Polybius	Y					•
	VV		•			
Casa del Menandro	43			•	•	
House I 10,8	3	•				
	6					• ?
	8	•		•		
Casa degli Amanti	4	•				
	7	•				
Casa di Stallius Eros	5					•
Casa dell'Efebo	11		• ?			
Casa di Trebius Valens	b	•				
Casa di Sacello Iliaco	1		•			
House VI 16,26	F	•		•		
Casa di M. Lucretius Fronto	6	•				
Casa del Principe di Napoli	c	•				
House VI 15,5	n				• ?	
	o				• ?	
Casa delle Nozze d'Argento	e	•				
	f		•			
Casa di Giuseppe II	m			•		
House VIII 2,29–30	f			•		

5.4). Other fixtures consisted of stairways, understair cupboards, an aedicula, and a vat. Thus, three of the rooms with recesses also had another fixture. With the exception of one in room l of House VIII 2,34, which was high and narrow, these recesses were of the low, narrow type conventionally assumed to have been a bed recess (see chapter 4). In four houses in Region VIII, the lack of finds in rooms with shelving, presumably intended for storage, could have resulted simply from poor recording. Such a lack is more noteworthy in the Casa degli Amanti, however, where decorated rooms 4 and 7 around the front hall contained finds. The latter example would seem to be an exception to the pattern of storage in undecorated rather than decorated rooms of this type.

Of rooms with recorded loose contents, only a skeleton was recorded in room q in House I 7,19, indicating eruption activity rather than room use, and only door fittings were recorded in room 1 in the Casa di Stallius Eros and possibly in room g in the Casa del Sacerdos Amandus. Such reported finds indicate that the excavators were unlikely to have overlooked other finds in these rooms and that, therefore, the rooms were probably devoid of further contents. This brings to fifteen (of a total of twenty-seven) the number of rooms in this group that were without contents in Regions I, V, and VI; thus, more than half of these rooms were substantially empty. Such an absence of finds is more significant here than in Region VIII.

While the fixtures indicate the intended use of these rooms at a certain stage in their life cycle, only sixteen of all the rooms in this group had contents that could have been related to their final occupation phase. Two of those with

Table 5.4c Small closed rooms off front hall, undecorated: fixtures

House	Room	Recesses	Shelving	Stairways	Understair cupboards	Aediculae/ painted niches	Vat
Casa della Venere in Bikini	3	•					
Casa del Menandro	2			•	•		
	5		•				
	6	•					
Casa del Fabbro	6		•				
Casa degli Amanti	5		•				
Casa di Stallius Eros	2	•			•		
Casa dell'Efebo	14		•				
House VI 16,26	C	•					
Casa della Ara Massima	C		•				
	E		•				
Casa di M. Lucretius Fronto	3		•				
Casa delle Nozze d'Argento	h	•	•				
	m		•				
House VIII 2,14–16	d					•	
	i'		•				
House VIII 2, 26	q		•				
Casa di Giuseppe II	e			•			
	k		•				
	1		•				
House VIII 2,34	1	•	•				
House VIII 2,29–30	a'						•
House VIII 5,9	3			•			

Table 5.4d Small closed rooms off front hall, undecorated: loose contents

House	Room	Utilitarian/ industrial	Mixed domestic	Mixed but more specialized	Specialized
Casa del Menandro	1				•
	2				•
	5	•			
	10				•
Casa del Fabbro	6		•		
Casa degli Amanti	2			•	
Casa dell'Efebo	14		•		
House VI 16,26	C		•		
Casa della Ara Massima	C	•			
	E		•		
	N				•
Casa del Principe di Napoli	a			•	
Casa delle Nozze d'Argento	m		•		
House VIII 2,14–16	e			•	
House VIII 2,28	r				•
House VIII 2,34	k			•	

pouring vessels, tableware, and material for weaving, writing, weighing, lighting, and ritual activities. They were perhaps too varied and too poorly represented to be diagnostic. For example, the contents of room k in House VIII 2,34 consisted of an iron rake and a small bronze-and-bone fibula. In five other rooms, three notably in the Casa del Menandro, the storage seems to have been even more specialized: objects related to personal and gaming activities in room 1 in the Casa del Menandro and room r in House VIII 2,28; objects for weaving in room 10 of the Casa del Menandro; serving and table dishes in room 2 in the Casa del Menandro; and kitchen utensils in room N of the Casa della Ara Massima. The latter had no garden or apparent service area; so, the use of rooms in the front-hall area might be expected to differ from that in other houses. The assemblage in room r in House VIII 2,28 included broken statuary. As in the decorated rooms, the deposition of this material may have occurred during disrupted conditions.

In summary, the most prominent fixture in undecorated rooms of this type was shelving, but recesses, niches, and understair cupboards were also significant. One of the rooms in this group (room a' in House VIII 2,29–30) appears to have been adapted for a specific purpose. Contents were recorded mainly in rooms with shelving, built-in cupboards, or recesses or where the room itself had actually been a cupboard (that is, room 10 in the Casa del Menandro). These contents consisted variously of general domestic storage, more utilitarian (possibly industrial) storage, or more specialized material.

As might be expected, the undecorated closed rooms around the front hall showed more evidence of bulk storage than did the decorated ones. While the contents of decorated rooms were less numerous and appear to represent more personal pursuits, the contents of both decorated and undecorated rooms showed a considerable range of household activities. This room type was the most numerous in the houses in this sample and therefore was likely, as a class, to have performed a variety of functions.

Figure 5.4 Evidence of shelving along walls, room Q, Casa di Julius Polybius. (Boxes against north wall, containing wall plaster fragments, are modern.)

shelving had utilitarian/industrial contents. Four others with shelving had copious, often mixed, domestic utensils. Therefore, rooms in this group with shelving in Regions I, V, and VI showed evidence of having been used for both domestic and industrial storage. A distinction between a use for domestic or for utilitarian/industrial storage that correlates with house size is not apparent. It is possible, however, that this use was related to overall living conditions before the eruption.

One room in this group without shelving (room C in House VI 16,26) had a recess and a mixed domestic assemblage, which seems more comparable to that found in decorated rooms of this type. Four other rooms without shelving had mixed domestic assemblages that seemed to be more specialized, consisting variously of

TYPE 5: OPEN-FRONTED AREAS OFF THE SIDES OF FRONT HALLS

These areas generally opened off the sides of the front hall, at the end towards the garden, although they sometimes were located in the middle of these sides. They were open-fronted in that they did not have a wall on the front-hall side. Nineteen houses in the sample had such spaces. Eight had two, often opposite each other, and two houses, with double front halls, had three. Thus, a total of thirty-one areas are categorized as this type.

Fixtures and contents were recorded in fifteen to seventeen of these spaces (table 5.5). In two, these contents consisted only of door fittings and isolated coins (room 4 in the Casa del Menandro and room 6 in the Casa delle Nozze d'Argento), implying that the lack of other recorded contents was not a result of bad reporting but probably an indication that these spaces were indeed empty. These two spaces are therefore not included in table 5.5. Fixtures consisting of shelving, built-in cupboards, and platforms were re-

corded in four to six of these areas. Room h in the Casa dei Vettii (figure 5.5) is frequently identified as a cupboard (for example, Strocka 1995:176). Parallels between the evidence of a closing wall on its north side and built-in cupboards in other houses in this sample (for example, room h in the Casa di Giuseppe II) suggest that it may have had a similar function (see also Casa dei Capitelli Figurati, Staub Gierow 1994: 56–57).

Only eleven spaces had loose contents. Storage containers, such as amphorae or chests filled with glass vessels, were found in five, including two of those with shelving. Many lamps were also recorded with mixed domestic storage in one of the latter spaces (room F in the Casa della Ara Massima), and fragmentary sculptural pieces in another (room cc in House VIII 2,14–16. Room m in the Casa di Trebius Valens seems to have had only a small bronze casket. Building or industrial material was recorded in four such areas, in two cases possibly with lamps. Only room r in House I 7,19 had a bed.

There is no clear pattern for these spaces, although evidence of shelving, built-in cupboards,

Table 5.5 Open-fronted areas off front hall with fixtures and contents

House	Room	Storage fixtures*	Storage containers**	Caskets/lamps	Bed	Building material
Casa di Julius Polybius	D	•	•			
	Q	•	•			
House I 10,8	2			•		• ?
House I 7,19	r				•	
Casa di Trebius Valens	m			•		
Casa del Sacello Iliaco	e		•			
Casa della Ara Massima	F		•	•		
House VI 15,5	g			• ?		•
Casa dei Vettii	h	• ?				
Casa delle Nozze d'Argento	7		•			•
House VIII 2,14–16	cc			•		
Casa di Giuseppe II	h	•				
House VIII 2,34	i					•
	h	• ?				
House VIII 2,29–30	h	•				

*Consists of shelving, built-in cupboards, platforms, and mezzanines   ** Includes storage vessels

Figure 5.5 View of room h from front hall, Casa dei Vettii

and storage containers implies they might have been used for the type of domestic storage recorded in the front halls and in the undecorated closed rooms. The presence of building material in three, possibly four, of them indicates that these areas, at least, were not used for their habitual functions at the time of the eruption. It is also conceivable that the bed had been placed in area r of House I 7,19 under makeshift conditions during repair work, which was evident throughout this house.

TYPE 6: MEDIUM/LARGE ROOMS OFF THE CORNERS OF FRONT HALLS

Rooms classified under this type were generally long, narrow, and closed, commonly with a narrow doorway in the end of the long wall, and usually located in the corner of the front hall. They did not exist in all houses. In many, rooms that may originally have been of this type appear to have been converted so that they opened onto the garden in their final structural phase. Such rooms are therefore classified as types 10 and 11.

A total of thirty-five rooms in twenty-three houses were classified as type 6 (table 5.6a–b).

Ten houses had two such rooms; only two had more than two: House VIII 2,14–16, which had two front halls, and the Casa della Ara Massima, which had no garden area. In eight, six of which were in Region VIII, fixtures with no loose finds were recorded. Loose finds were reported only in the more recently excavated houses in Regions I, V, and VI, in fourteen to sixteen of the twenty-four rooms of this type. Two-thirds (sixteen) of the rooms of this type from Regions I, V, and VI had wall decoration. Loose finds were reported in more than half of those (nine to ten). Six of the eight coarsely furbished rooms of this type contained loose finds.

In three rooms (all decorated), the fixtures consisted of long or short, low recesses. Room 4 of the Casa di M. Lucretius Fronto had two recesses. Unfortunately, no finds were recorded that could have provided evidence of how these recesses were used. Vessel fragments reported in room 10 in the Casa dell'Efebo may have come from the upper floor, and the fittings in room 4 in the Casa di M. Lucretius Fronto could have been from a chest. Other seemingly utilitarian fixtures occurred in nine, possibly ten, rooms of this type. These were predominantly shelving, understair cupboards, and possibly a mezzanine, but they also included niches, cistern

Table 5.6a Medium/large rooms off front hall: fixtures and building material

House	Room	Decorated	Recesses	Niches	Heating/ water*	Storage fixtures**	Stairway	Building materials***
Casa di Julius Polybius	P					•		
Casa del Menandro	3	•			•			•?
Casa dell'Efebo	10	•	•					
House I 7,19	b	•						•
	t					•		
Casa del Sacello Iliaco	c	•						•
Casa della Ara Massima	G	•				•?	•?	
Casa di M. Lucretius Fronto	4	•	•					
House VI 15,5	e	•	•					
Casa delle Nozze d'Argento	i					•		
House VIII 2,14–16	a			•		•		
	f					•		
	f	•		•				
	g'					•		
Casa di Giuseppe II	d	•			•			
House VIII 2,29–30	r				•	•?		

* Consists of hearths, ovens, cistern mouths, and drains   ** Consists of shelving, built-in cupboards, and mezzanines
*** Includes marble pieces

Table 5.6b Medium/large rooms off front hall: loose finds

House	Room	Decorated	Cupboards/ chests	Storage vessels	Utilitarian/ industrial	Utilitarian vessels*	Luxury**	Personal	Bed fittings
Casa di Julius Polybius	P			•					
	Z	•			•	•	•	•	
Casa del Menandro	3	•			•			•?	
House I 10,8	4		•	•		•			
Casa di Stallius Eros	4							•?	
Casa del Sacerdos Amandus	b	•	•		•				
Casa dell'Efebo	10	•		•?		•?			
Casa di Trebius Valens	d	•	•		•		•?		
Casa del Sacello Iliaco	c	•		•	•		•		•
House VI 16,26	E		•		•	•		•	
	G	•				•			•
Casa della Ara Massima	G	•	•		•	•	•	•	
	I						•		
Casa di M. Lucretius Fronto	4	•	•?						
Casa delle Nozze d'Argento	i		•	•					

* Includes cooking vessels   ** Includes vessels, furniture, and statuary

79

mouths, hearths, possibly a stairway, and a drain. While rooms with recesses were decorated, rooms with utilitarian contents could be either decorated or undecorated.

Building and reconstruction material was found in two, possibly three, rooms of this type, all decorated. Remains of cupboards and chests were recorded in six, possibly seven. In at least three rooms, all decorated, the containers held a variety of material ranging from utilitarian/industrial to utilitarian/domestic to personal. These assemblages suggest that some of the decorated rooms of this type were used for general household storage, at least at the time of the eruption. Storage vessels were found in three undecorated rooms, two of which had shelving. Evidence of dining furniture, or any luxury items conceivably related to dining, was rare. Only two rooms had evidence of what may have been dining furniture. Room c in the Casa del Sacello Iliaco had incomplete decoration and contained reconstruction material, storage vessels, and other utilitarian material, and room G in House VI 16,26 contained cooking and utilitarian vessels. Personal objects such as toilet items and jewelry were also relatively rare.

It is difficult to find a prevalent pattern for the use of this room type. The decorated rooms appear to have been used for utilitarian and mixed storage. Most of the undecorated rooms in Regions I, V, and VI also contained utilitarian material. Thus, while use of this room type, like that of room type 4, would have been as much dependent on its decoration as its structural form and location, a specific use was not particularly evident at the time of the eruption.

These rooms are said to have been used as winter dining rooms (Richardson 1983:63–64). With the possible exceptions of the recesses in three of them, however, their fixtures and fittings did not indicate this use (compare Foss 1994:108–109). If they had indeed once been used as such, they seem to have been subsequently used for a more utilitarian function. For some, this function must have occurred after they were decorated in the Fourth Style. Other rooms had utilitarian fixtures built against older wall decoration (for example, room 3 in the Casa del Menandro and possibly room d in the Casa

di Giuseppe II). If some, at least, were winter dining rooms, domestic material may have been stored in them temporarily during the summer.

Type 7: Open Rooms Leading to Gardens or Open-Sided Rooms opposite Main Entranceways

Rooms of this type were generally located on the opposite side of the front hall from the main entranceway (figure 5.6), although there were exceptions (for example, room d in the Casa del Sacerdos Amandus). They frequently formed a wide corridor to the garden but also often had large doors to shut them off or only a window-like opening on the garden side (for example, room f in the Casa del Sacello Iliaco). Twenty-four houses have rooms of this type, four with more than one (the Casa di Julius Polybius, the Casa dell'Efebo, House VI 16,26, and House VIII 2,29–30). Of the thirty-three rooms of this type, sixteen to seventeen had recorded contents (table 5.7). Ten of those with contents had painted wall decoration. Of all the rooms of this type, only one decorated room (room 7 in the Casa della Venere in Bikini) had any fixtures (a stairway with a cupboard underneath).

Freestanding cupboards and chests were recorded in nine to twelve rooms, more than half of which were decorated. Utilitarian domestic material (storage vessels, food-preparation vessels, and items for weighing, weaving, and needlework) was found in ten rooms, seven of which also contained storage furniture. Vessels for serving food and drink, lighting equipment such as lanterns and possibly lamps, statuary, and religious items were recorded in ten rooms. These included room f in House VIII 5,9 which seems to have had this type of material in commercial quantities or at least bulk domestic quantities. Of the other nine rooms with this material, four to five also had storage furniture and more utilitarian material. In three, possibly four, the assemblage included more personal material. For example, the assemblage in a cupboard in room L in House VI 16,26 included items seemingly concerned with toilet, gaming, needlework, and dress.

Figure 5.6 Front hall and room opposite main entranceway (type 7), Casa del Menandro

Table 5.7 Open rooms leading to garden or open-sided rooms opposite main entranceway

House	Room	Storage containers /chests	Utilitarian/ domestic	Serving luxury/ vessels/lamps/ religious items	Personal/ gaming	Beds/ furniture fittings	Building material/ tools
Casa di Julius Polybius	TT		•				
Casa della Venere in Bikini	7	•	•	•			
Casa del Menandro	8		•	•		•	•
Casa del Fabbro	7	• ?	•				
Casa dei Quadretti Teatrali	6	•	•				•
House I 6,8–9	d	•				•	•
Casa dell'Efebo	4	•				•	
	13	•	•	•	•		•
	15			•		•	
House I 7,19	c	• ?		•			
Casa dei Ceii	d	• ?		•			
Casa del Sacello Iliaco	f	•	•	•	•	•	
House VI 16,26	L	•	•	•	•		
Casa di M. Lucretius Fronto	7	•	•				
Casa del Principe di Napoli	e		•	•			
House VIII 2,29–30	q				• ?		
House VIII 5,9	f	•		•			• ?

Evidence for beds or couches was recorded in five rooms of this type, although in at least two rooms this furniture may have been in a fragmentary state at the time of the eruption. Room f in the Casa del Sacello Iliaco and room 15 in the Casa dell'Efebo had collections of bed legs that do not appear to have been from complete beds that belonged to these rooms. While the evidence for beds in this room type is not particularly significant, it is proportionately greater than in closed rooms off the front hall. Building material, marble fragments, and tools for construction, agriculture, and fishing were recorded in four, possibly five, of these rooms, all of which also contained furniture and domestic material, suggesting an overlay of activities and possibly downgrading.

The most prominent pattern for rooms of this type was that they had contained cupboards and chests with domestic material. Some might argue that such rooms, when decorated, might not normally have been used for domestic storage but had a more formal function. The frequent presence of storage furniture in rooms which were decorated, some in the Fourth Style, implies that storage was not necessarily a use for this room type under disrupted conditions only. The presence of beds or couches in some rooms of this type is noteworthy. While perhaps not significantly representative to indicate sleeping or dining use late in the life of the city, this pattern of activity was more prevalent in this room type than it was in type 4.

TYPE 8: INTERNAL CORRIDORS

These usually narrow corridors frequently led from the front hall to the garden, along one side of room type 7. They also led from the front hall and garden to rooms located away from the main axis of the house. In this sample, there were fifty-nine spaces of this type in twenty-three houses. They tended to be coarsely plastered or simply decorated. Fixtures were recorded in sixteen, the most common being stairways and understair cupboards, recorded in or leading off six of these corridors (table 5.8a). Corridor L of the Casa del Menandro had

two stairways, one with a trapdoor underneath leading to a cellar. At least two of the other stairways were built of masonry and had evidence of understair cupboards. Less frequent fixtures included latrines, cistern heads and downpipes, hearths, and niches. One of the hearths, or a small oven, was located in the understair cupboard of room D in the Casa delle Nozze d'Argento. In the other case, room 9 in House I 10,8, the corridor was more irregular in shape and included a cooking area. Recesses, all of the low and narrow type, were recorded in three corridors. As discussed in chapter 4, it is conceivable that the recess in corridor q of House VIII 2,34 had been a relic from an earlier structural arrangement. The same argument could not be made for the recesses in Houses I 10,8 and VI 16,26. Area q in House VIII 2,34 also appears to have had shelving or a mezzanine, implying that it had been used for storage as well as a passageway. The recesses might seem unusual fixtures for what was ostensibly a through-route, unless they were utility recesses rather than bed recesses (see chapter 4)

Loose finds were reported in twelve to fourteen of these internal corridors (table 5.8b). Many were door fittings or isolated finds that may have been dropped here during abandonment. For example, finds of tools, furniture fittings, pieces of sculpture, ceramic fragments, and coins from corridors 9, 16, and 53 in the Casa del Menandro and corridor k of the Casa dei Ceii, and a bronze basin in corridor a' of the Casa di Giuseppe II, might have been related to abandonment activity or post-eruption activity rather than habitual use of such corridors. They are therefore not included in table 5.8b. Collections of loose finds, which might have been significant to the functioning of these corridors during the final occupation phases, were recorded in seven. These collections included amphorae, tableware (in the cellar in corridor L of the Casa del Menandro), marble furniture (corridor 9 in House I 10,8), and a chest with luxury and personal items (corridor K in House VI 16,26: figure 4.3). While the latter might document normal storage in a recess, such contents, as well as building remains recorded in corridor

Table 5.8a Internal corridors: fixtures

House	Room	Recesses	Stairways*	Latrines/downpipes**	Shelving/mezzanines	Niches	Hearths
Casa del Menandro	51			•			
	53					•	
	L		•				
House I 10,8	14	•		•			
	9			•			•
House I 7,19	o		•				
Casa di Stallius Eros	f			•			
Casa del Sacello Iliaco	r					•	
House VI 16,26	K	•					
House VI 15,5	y		•				
Casa dei Vettii	3		•				
Casa delle Nozze d'Argento	D		•				•
House VIII 2,14–16	i				•		
House VIII 2,34	q	•			•		
House VIII 2,29–30	y			•			
	1		•				

* Includes understair cupboards   **Includes cistern heads

Table 5.8b Internal corridors: collections of loose finds

House	Corridor	Cupboards/chests	Amphorae	Food preparation and serving vessels	Tableware/luxury/personal items	Harness	Building material*
Casa di Julius Polybius	R		•	•			
	SS		•	•			
Casa del Menandro	L		•		•		•
House I 10,8	9			•			•
House VI 16,26	K	•			•		
Casa dei Vettii	3					•	
Casa delle Nozze d'Argento	A		•				

* Includes marble furniture fragments

L of the Casa del Menandro, could have blocked this access route at the time of the eruption.

As might be expected, these passageways between various parts of the house were generally devoid of fixtures and contents. Their precise functions seem to have been diverse. The proportions and location of each corridor had some bearing on its function. For example, corridor 3 in the Casa dei Vettii appears to have led to room 4, which was likely to have been a stable. It would therefore seem appropriate to have found an understair cupboard with horse harness in it in this area. Other fixtures indicate that a number of these corridors served other functions, as well as that of a passageway, related to access to upper floors, ablutions and access to water, food preparation, and storage. The number of storage vessels found in these corridors, particularly in service or industrial/commercial parts of the house, suggests they might have been practical and habitual locations for keeping such items.

Type 9: Main Gardens and Colonnaded Gardens, including Ambulatories, or Terraces

All the houses in the sample, except the Casa della Ara Massima, had gardens, generally behind the front-hall complex, although they could also be located to one side of it (figure 5.7). Most had only one such garden, but the Casa delle Nozze d'Argento, House VIII 2,14–16, the Casa di Giuseppe II, and House VIII 2,29–30 had two, making a total of thirty-three in the sample. These gardens usually had two distinctive areas—an open garden or terrace and colonnaded ambulatories. The ambulatories could run along one, two, three, or four sides of the open garden area.

The Open Garden

Almost invariably, open gardens had a cistern mouth, although it was sometimes located in the ambulatories or intercolumniations rather than in the actual garden.[5] Other fixtures were recorded in open areas of eighteen houses in this sample (table 5.9a). In twelve, there were varying combinations of pools, fountains, statue bases, and what seem to have been al fresco dining areas (consisting of either a masonry or a wooden structure under a wooden pergola; figure 5.8). While these fixtures might be classified as display and entertainment fixtures, at least one of the pools, that in House VIII 2,14–16, had reputedly been used for breeding fish. Religious shrines, in the form of aediculae, were found in two gardens, and smaller niches were located in five others. Some of the niches could conceivably have had religious or display functions. For example, a marble herm was found in the niche in the garden of the Casa del Fabbro. The niches in garden x of the Casa di Trebius Valens, however, were thought to have been used for serving food (Spano 1916:231; see figure 4.7). It is probable that such niches were used for one of several functions: religious, display, and utilitarian (see chapter 4).

Because cistern mouths tended to be concentrated in these areas, suggesting open rather than

Figure 5.7 View of garden m from southeast, Casa del Sacerdos Amandus

Table 5.9a Open garden area: fixtures

House	Garden	Pool/ fountains	Dining areas	Statue bases	Aediculae	Simple niches	Utilitarian fixtures
Casa della Venere in Bikini	8					•	
Casa del Menandro	c	•	•				
Casa del Fabbro	12		•			•	
House I 10,8	11					•	
House I 6,8–9	i						•
Casa di Stallius Eros	13					•	•
Casa del Sacerdos Amandus	m					•	
Casa dell'Efebo	23	•	•	•			•
Casa di Trebius Valens	x	•	•				
Casa degli Amorini Dorati	F	•		•			
Casa del Principe di Napoli	n				•		
House VI 15,5	u	•	•	•	•		
Casa dei Vettii	m	•		•			
Casa delle Nozze d'Argento	5	•	•				
House VIII 2,14–16	p	•					
House VIII 2,34	m'	•					•
House VIII 2,29–30	19a	•					
House VIII 5,9	h	•					

Figure 5.8 Garden 5 showing central pool, masonry *triclinium*, and poorly preserved decoration of west wall, Casa delle Nozze d'Argento. *Pompeii photo archive neg. D80833*

85

restricted access for household members needing to collect water, there was unlikely to have been a spatial separation between display and utilitarian or even personal activities here. This conclusion is reinforced by the presence of further utilitarian fixtures (stairways, water tanks, and hearths) in four of the garden areas. While hearths reported on terrace m' in House VIII 2,34 and possibly in garden i of House I 6,8–9 could have resulted from the downgrading of previously formal areas, downgrading is a less probable explanation for the presence of a water tank in garden 23 in the Casa dell'Efebo, a garden area that also contained a great range of display fixtures and fittings. If there was any separation of utilitarian and formal activities in these areas, it may have been temporal, during the course of the day.

Movable finds were reported from the open garden areas of all but one of the twenty-three most recently recorded houses with gardens (House I 6,8–9), while they were reported in the garden areas of only two of the houses in Region VIII, the latter again likely to be a result of poor recording methods during the earlier excavations rather than a lack of original furnishings (table 5.9b). Sculpture (marble, bronze, or glazed ceramic) and marble furniture, usually tables, were recorded in the garden areas of nine of these houses, many of which also had display fixtures. These types of furnishings further emphasize the significant role of this area for display.

Puteals were reported in the open gardens or intercolumniations in fourteen of these houses, as well as in the ambulatories of two others (the Casa dei Vettii and House VIII 2,14–16, also included in table 5.9b). Thus, they were more frequently found in garden areas than in the front hall. Ceramic basins were also recorded in the garden area and intercolumniations of two of these gardens, in the Casa degli Amanti and House VI 16,26, and may well have been associated with water provision and washing activities. Only one sundial, in garden F in the Casa degli Amorini Dorati, was definitely found in a garden context in this sample.

Amphorae were reported in eight of these open garden areas. In two gardens, these amphorae reputedly contained lime (garden m in the Casa del Sacerdos Amandus and garden h in House I 7,19). Large *dolia* were recorded in three garden areas (figure 5.9). With the exception of amphorae that may have contained building material, the location of both vessel types in these areas implies they had been used for either bulk domestic storage (for example, of such foodstuffs as wine, vinegar, or oil) or for other commercial/industrial purposes. In general, they were found in garden areas with little or no display furniture. Tortoises were found in garden h of the Casa dei Ceii and in garden CC of the Casa di Julius Polybius; the latter also contained a fruit-picking ladder.

Figure 5.9 View of garden area showing *dolia* in southeast corner, House VI 16,26. *Pompeii photo archive neg. D80709*

Table 5.9b Open garden area: loose contents

House	Garden	Sculpture and marble furniture	Puteals and basins	Amphorae	*Dolia*	Industrial and building material*	Scattered domestic material
Casa di Julius Polybius	CC		•				
Casa della Venere in Bikini	8		•				
Casa del Menandro	c		•				
Casa del Fabbro	12	•		•		•	
	10		•				
House I 10,8	11			•	•		
Casa degli Amanti	9		•				
Casa dei Quadretti Teatrali	16		•				•
Casa di Stallius Eros	13		•				•
Casa del Sacerdos Amandus	m	•	•	•			
Casa dell'Efebo	23	•		•		•	
House I 7,19	h			•	•		
Casa di Trebius Valens	x	•					
Casa del Sacello Iliaco	m			•		•	
House VI 16,26	M		•		•		
Casa degli Amorini Dorati	F	•	•				
Casa di M. Lucretius Fronto	10		•				
Casa del Principe di Napoli	n	•	•				•
House VI 15,5	u	•	•	•			
Casa dei Vettii	m	•	•				
Casa delle Nozze d'Argento	r	•					
	5						•
House VIII 2,14–16	ff		•				
	gg						•
House VIII 5,9	h		•	•			

* Includes fragmentary marble

Fragmentary marble and industrial building material, recorded in three of these garden areas, is likely to imply disrupted conditions, particularly in garden 23 of the Casa dell'Efebo which also had considerable display furnishings. Scattered domestic material (for example, bronze vessels, lighting and toilet items) found in six gardens may have been dislocated items, but it is difficult to ascertain whether as a result of conditions before, during, or after the eruption of AD 79.

The Ambulatories

Some of the gardens in this sample did not have ambulatories (for example, the Casa della Venere in Bikini, House I 10,8). For those that did, however, the types of fixtures and contents often recorded in the open gardens in other houses were also found in their ambulatories: *lararia* and aediculae, niches, stairways, and a hearth (table 5.9c). The Casa del Menandro had an aedicula in a small area opening onto the garden (room 25; figure 5.10), and the Casa

Table 5.9c Ambulatories: fixtures

House	Ambulatory	Aediculae	*Lararium* paintings	Niches	Stairways	Hearth
Casa di Julius Polybius	CC			•		
Casa del Fabbro	10				•	
Casa degli Amanti	9				•	
Casa dell'Efebo	19	•	•	•		
House I 7,19	g	•		•	•	
Casa di Trebius Valens	x					•
Casa del Sacello Iliaco	m				•	
House VI 16,26	M				•	
Casa degli Amorini Dorati	F	•				
Casa di M. Lucretius Fronto	10				•	

Figure 5.10 West ambulatory of garden c, from northwest corner looking towards room 25, Casa del Menandro

dell'Efebo had a stairway just off the ambulatory (in area 20). Thus, only four garden areas in the sample actually had any identifiable religious furnishings. Utilitarian fixtures seem to have been as common as religious or display ones.

Movable finds were reported in the ambulatories of sixteen to seventeen houses in this sample (table 5.9d). They included finds in common with those in the garden areas: marble tables and wooden or bronze seats, amphorae, and *dolia*. While amphorae were not generally found in open garden areas that had more formal furnishings, they could be found in the ambulatories of such gardens.

88

Table 5.9d Ambulatories: movable finds

House	Ambulatory	Tables/ seats	Amphorae/ *dolia*	Cupboards/ chests*	Food preparation material**	Fragmentary material***
Casa di Julius Polybius	CC	•		•	•	
Casa del Menandro	c	•	•	•	•	•
Casa del Fabbro	10			•	•	•
Casa degli Amanti	9		•	•	•	
Casa dei Quadretti Teatrali	12–13			• ?		
House I 6,8–9	i		•			•
Casa dell'Efebo	19			•		
House I 7,19	g			•		
Casa di Trebius Valens	x					•
Casa del Sacello Iliaco	m					•
Casa degli Amorini Dorati	F		•			•
Casa dei Vettii	M	•				
Casa del Principe di Napoli	l		•		•	
House VI 15,5	u		•			
Casa delle Nozze d'Argento	r		•	•		
House VIII 2,14–16	ff	•				
House VIII 5,9	h			• ?		

*With domestic/utilitarian contents   **Includes braziers   ***Includes building and industrial material

Chests and cupboards represent one of the most common classes of furnishings in these ambulatories. They usually contained domestic material, but sometimes had tools, weaving equipment, and other utilitarian/industrial material. These items were recorded in the ambulatories of seven to nine houses; those from areas 12 and 13 in the Casa dei Quadretti Teatrali were seemingly associated with more personal activities. This type of furnishing appears to have been normal for ambulatories, particularly as the houses in which they were found sometimes also had formal garden furniture in situ. As in the front hall, the ambulatories of the garden areas would have provided suitable, accessible locations for domestic storage. Evidence for cooking or food preparation, particularly in the form of braziers, was recorded in the ambulatories of at least six houses, and further braziers were found in a room off the ambulatories in three other houses:

room 18 in the Casa dell'Efebo; room 1 in the Casa dei Ceii; and room e in Casa del Principe di Napoli. Cooking and food preparation may have been a normal activity in ambulatories, particularly for meals taken in dining rooms opening off the garden or in open-air dining areas in the gardens themselves. The marble tables and seats recorded in the ambulatories could have been related to these dining activities, having been stored in these ambulatories, or they could have been associated with relaxing or with the pursuit of domestic/industrial activities (for example, needlework) in the ambulatories themselves.

Fragmentary furniture, sculpture, and industrial or building material were found in the ambulatories of six houses. There appears to be a general correspondence between gardens that had amphorae or *dolia* and such material. Some of these (for example, garden F in the Casa degli Amorini Dorati) also had luxury and display material, perhaps indicating the overlaying of different activities in the garden area.

Many studies have concentrated on the garden areas in Roman dwellings as the locations for sculptural display (for example, De Caro 1987; Neudecker 1988). According to Dwyer (1982:116–119, 123–128), colonnaded gardens were locations for water displays and viewing statues of Olympian deities, Dionysiac or rustic themes, and philosophers, poets, and prominent Romans. The notion of dining on masonry or wooden dining couches in open gardens has also continued to receive much attention (for example, Soprano 1950; Richardson 1988b; Dunbabin 1991). While many open garden areas had formal entertainment and dining fixtures and were furbished with luxury furniture and statuary, some of them were also used for bulk domestic storage or industrial/commercial activities. Some seem to have been used for both. The ambulatories also bore witness to bulk and domestic storage and possibly cooking. Perception of these gardens as formal areas, however, has so pervaded studies of domestic space in Pompeii that Andersson compared the *dolium* and tap in House I 7,19 to the cylindrical tufa fountain vases in the Casa del Torello, interpreting the former as an ornamental fountain arrangement although more domestic in character (1990:218). This interpretation seems to be a misunderstanding that arises from not considering the complete assemblage in this area and the state of the overall house. Jashemski has shown that these colonnaded gardens were not merely formal entertainment areas but often had large produce-bearing trees that could take up the entire open garden area (1979a:604).

Many of the smaller gardens, which were once decorated for entertaining, could conceivably have been converted for more utilitarian/industrial purposes during their final occupation. The analyses of the assemblages in a variety of houses in this sample, however, demonstrate that the gardens could have been used simultaneously for formal entertainment, religious activities, agricultural production, and storage, as well as utilitarian household activities. One important role of these areas would have been access to water, with inhabitants collecting it here on a regular basis. Given the presence of cistern heads and puteals, these areas were probably more important for water access than were the front halls. Cooking on braziers in these areas was not confined to poorer households and to the *"piccola borghesia"* (petite bourgeoisie) who had no true hearths in their houses (compare Salza Prina Ricotti 1978/1980:240, 278).

One should not imagine that Pompeian colonnaded gardens resembled sparsely furnished formal courts of eighteenth-century French and Italian villas. Such perspectives are based in part on impressions gained from the architectural remains of Roman villas that have been stripped of their contents. Rather, these areas were probably buzzing with daily household activities, possibly quietening down when the evening meal was taking place, but diners would have looked out on cupboards and amphorae, as well as statuary and pergolas. It is anachronistic to assume that utilitarian fixtures and furnishings would have been considered eye-sores to those entertaining or being entertained in Pompeian houses.

Type 10: Medium/Large Closed Rooms off Gardens/Terraces without Good Views

Type 10 rooms were usually long and relatively narrow and located in the corners of main garden areas. They tend to have a less open aspect than type 11. In particular, the wall onto the garden was usually less than half open. Nevertheless, there is no precise threshold in the openness of these two room types that distinguishes them; therefore, the patterns of their contents are considered together.

There were twenty-three rooms in fifteen houses classified as type 10. While some houses had more than one type 10 room (the Casa del Menandro, the Casa degli Amanti, House VIII 2,14-16, the Casa di Giuseppe II, and House VIII 2,34), others had none. This is not particularly significant, however, given their similarity to type 11. Fixtures were recorded in seven rooms and were thus relatively rare (table 5.10). In four, including all three rooms of this type in House VIII 2,34, these fixtures consisted of shelving: one high, narrow recess and one low, narrow recess; a built-in cupboard; and a stairway. In three others, they consisted of ovens or hearths.

Most of the rooms of this type either had no recorded contents, had only door fittings (for example, room 11 in the Casa degli Amanti), or had finds associated only with abandonment (for example, skeletons and their possessions in room 19 of the Casa del Menandro). The recording of such loose finds in these rooms suggests the rooms were otherwise devoid of contents. Building material recorded in two rooms of this type (room 7 in the Casa di Stallius Eros and room k in House I 7,19) is commensurate with the evidence from the rest of these houses, pointing to normal activities having been disrupted prior to the eruption. A plumb bob in room g of House VIII 5,9 seems out of keeping with the other finds in this room.

Only eight rooms of this type had recorded loose finds that seem to have been related to their final function prior to their use as a refuge during the eruption. Up to six seem to have contained a chest or possibly a cupboard. Some appear to have been empty. Contents, when present, consisted of utilitarian domestic items, possibly associated with food preparation and serving (for example, cooking pots, serving and storage vessels, and scales) or items associated with toilet and dress (for example, small glass

Table 5.10 Medium/large closed rooms off garden/terrace but without good view

House	Room	Food-preparation fixtures	Other utilitarian fixtures	Chests/ cupboards	Couches	Food-preparation contents*	Lighting equipment	Personal items	Building material
Casa della Venere in Bikini	10			•		•	•	•	
Casa del Menandro	17			• ?					
Casa degli Amanti	10				• ?		•		
Casa di Stallius Eros	7								•
House I 7,19	k								•
Casa di Trebius Valens	z			•					
House VI 16,26	T	•							
Casa degli Amorini Dorati	M			• ?					
House VI 15,5	1			•		•			
Casa di M. Lucretius Fronto	14			• ?	• ?	• ?	•		
Casa di Giuseppe II	p		•						
	th'	•							
House VIII 2,34	o		•						
	d'		•						
	z'		•						
House VIII 5,9	g	•				•	•		•

*Includes braziers

91

vessels, buckles, and jewelry). All these rooms, except room z in the Casa di Trebius Valens, were decorated in the Fourth Style. Of the fifteen rooms of this type, fixtures or loose finds were associated with storage in six to nine. Storage might therefore have been a relatively normal activity in rooms of this type, including the decorated ones.

Remains, possibly from couches, were recorded in two rooms. In addition to fixed hearths, equipment for food preparation was recorded in three. One of these also had a brazier, and a further three had utensils for food preparation, some of which were reported from cupboards. This pattern is reminiscent of the braziers and food-preparation material recorded in garden areas; they possibly indicate that cooking was carried out in this area, perhaps alongside dining. Lighting equipment was reported in four rooms that also had evidence of cooking activities and couches.

TYPE 11: MEDIUM/LARGE OPEN-FRONTED ROOMS OFF GARDENS/TERRACES, WITH WINDOW OR WIDE ENTRANCEWAY GIVING VIEW OF GARDEN OR LOWER FLOOR

This room type is similar to type 10 but with a more open aspect. It is located in almost any position in a garden area or off a terrace. It includes the spacious rooms on the lower floor of the houses of Region VIII that would have commanded a view over the Sarno River and the Bay of Naples (for example, room 6; House VIII 2,26; figure 4.2). Fifty-three rooms in twenty-three houses are categorized as type 11, some of the larger houses having four to five such rooms. Only eight were coarsely plastered, although the wall furnishings in another three were indeterminate. Finds were recorded in twenty-eight of these rooms, twenty-four of which had wall decoration (tables 5.11a–b). One room had only skeletal remains; five had only fixtures.

Fixtures included a fountain, two niches (one with a *lararium* painting), and six low recesses. They were therefore proportionally even less common here than in type 10, but with re-

cesses predominating. Tables and furniture fittings that are likely to have been from couches or beds were found in seven to ten rooms. Thus, there is more evidence of a relationship between recesses and the presence of couches or beds in rooms of this type than in the larger closed rooms around either the garden area (type 10) or the front hall (type 6), or indeed in type 4. Given the possibility that such furnishings went unrecorded, their occurrence in about a third of the rooms with recorded finds suggests dining, or at least reclining.

Bronze vessels, conceivably serving and table equipment, were recorded in nine or ten rooms. Glass and ceramic vessels, possibly associated with serving and dining activities, were recorded in eight rooms, at least half of which also had bronze vessels. Some of the bronze vessels may not have been used for serving or tableware. For example, the basin in room m in House VIII 5,9 was identified by the excavators as a type used for cooking. Also, in some cases, this material may have been stored rather than used in rooms of this type (for example, in undecorated room r of the Casa dei Vettii). Bronze or clay lamps and lampstands were recorded in six rooms, the more elaborate of which may have been associated with entertainment (for example, in room EE in the Casa di Julius Polybius). Some were more utilitarian (for example, a lantern in room w of Casa delle Nozze d'Argento and a lamp in room HH of the Casa di Julius Polybius) and could have been deposited during the eruption. There is a notable correspondence between the rooms that contained material associated with dining and lighting and evidence of beds or couches.

Chests and cupboards furnished six to ten rooms of this type, similar to the storage pattern observed in the large/medium closed rooms of the garden (type 10). Storage and other utilitarian vessels were recorded in nine rooms, and other utilitarian domestic and more industrial material were recorded in another seven. Thirteen of these also contained possible dining or entertainment equipment, suggesting that storage of such material in such an entertainment area may have been relatively habitual, both in this room type and in type 10. Some overlay of

Table 5.11a Medium/large open-fronted rooms off garden/terrace with window or wide entranceway giving view of garden or lower floor: fixtures and possible dining equipment

House	Room	Fountains/ *lararium* niches	Low, narrow recesses	Long, low recesses	Couches / tables	Bronze vessels	Ceramic and glass vessels*	Lamps
Casa di Julius Polybius	EE				•	•	•	•
	GG					•	•	
	HH				•	•	•	•
Casa del Menandro	12						•	
	15				•			
	18				•			
Casa del Fabbro	8				•			•
	9	• (*lararium* niche)	•		• ?	•		
House I 10,8	10						•	•
Casa dei Quadretti Teatrali	11				• ?			
	15				• ?	•		
Casa dell'Efebo	17			•	•			
House I 7,19	e						•	
Casa di Trebius Valens	p		•					
Casa degli Amorini Dorati	G					•		
Casa di M. Lucretius Fronto	13				•	•	•	
Casa del Principe di Napoli	k					•		•
House VI 15,5	k		•					
Casa dei Vettii	r					• ?	•	
Casa delle Nozze d'Argento	w							•
House VIII 2,26	6		•					
House VIII 2,28	x	•(fountain)						
House VIII 2,29–30	p	•(niche)						
House VIII 5,9	m		•			•		

* Includes tableware and serving vessels

depositional activity, however, might have occurred during later disruption, including during the final eruption.

Personal and toilet items were recorded in six rooms of this type, but in two (room HH in the Casa di Julius Polybius and room 9 in the Casa del Fabbro) this material was associated with skeletons and therefore with the abandonment processes. Room 10 in House I 10,8 also had building material, and room n in the Casa delle Nozze d'Argento appears to have been in-completely decorated and therefore in a disrupted state.

Statuary, complete and fragmentary, and other pieces of marble were reported in four rooms. Building material was also recorded in one of these. The presence of building material in four rooms of this type suggests that the normal activities of these particular rooms had been disrupted. The presence of statuary might suggest salvaging during the final eruption. Its association with building material, however,

Table 5.11b Medium/large open-fronted rooms off garden/terrace with window or wide entranceway giving view of garden or lower floor: utilitarian and personal contents

House	Room	Chest/ cupboards	Utilitarian vessels*	Utilitarian/ industrial	Personal	Sculpture**	Building material
Casa di Julius Polybius	EE	•	•			•	
	GG		•	•			
Casa del Menandro	11	•	•				
	15	• ?					
	18		•				
Casa del Fabbro	8	•	•	•			
	9			•			
House I 10,8	10	•	•		•		•
Casa dei Quadretti Teatrali	15			•			
Casa dell'Efebo	17					•	
House I 7,19	e	•		•			•
Casa degli Amorini Dorati	G	• ?	•		•		
Casa di M. Lucretius Fronto	12	•					
	13					•	•
Casa del Principe di Napoli	k	• ?		•			
House VI 15,5	h						•
Casa dei Vettii	r	• ?				•	
Casa delle Nozze d'Argento	n		•		•		
House VIII 5,9	m		•	•	•		

*Includes storage vessels   **Includes marble fragments

suggests that it may instead have been related to pre-eruption salvaging (see the Casa dei Vettii).

Contents seem to have been more common in room type 11 than type 10, although there are more than twice as many of the former rooms in the sample. As in room type 10, chests and cupboards were a common furnishing. In room type 10 they were more frequently recorded than beds, couches, or tables, whereas in room type 11 they were as frequent. While food-preparation contents and fixtures were frequently recorded in room type 10, other material identifiable as serving or tableware was not. The pattern is the reverse in room type 11. Thus, although one might conclude that these large open rooms around the garden were more likely to have been used for dining and entertainment than were the closed ones, storage of domestic utensils seems to have been common in both types.

TYPE 12: SMALL CLOSED ROOMS OFF GARDENS/TERRACES OR LOWER FLOORS

Type 12 rooms were similar in form to room type 4 but were located in the main garden area. Seventy rooms in twenty-seven houses in this sample are categorized as this type. The houses lacking type 12 rooms are the Casa della Venere in Bikini, the Casa del Fabbro, and the Casa della Ara Massima. Again, the distinction between these rooms and larger closed rooms (type 10) is proportionate to house size rather than absolute (for example, rooms J and I in the Casa degli Amorini Dorati). As with room type 4, they are divided into those that had painted decoration and those that did not. There are eleven examples for which no documentation of the decoration is available. It is most probable that these rooms were undecorated (for example, rooms e, f, g, and h in House I 6,8–9). They are therefore categorized as such.

Decorated

Thirty-three rooms of type 12 had documented painted decoration. Sixteen of these had no recorded finds or fixtures, and another six had

fixtures only (tables 5.12a–b). Only eleven such rooms had recorded loose finds.

Fixtures included recesses, niches, and built-in cupboards. Furniture fittings, conceivably from beds, were found in one, possibly, two rooms of this type. More common were finds associated with personal activities, ablutions, and luxury/religious activities (for example, a

Table 5.12a Small closed rooms off garden/terrace or lower floor, decorated: luxury/personal fixtures and contents

House	Room	Recesses	Niches*	Furniture/ beds	Personal**	Cloth working/ lighting
Casa di Julius Polybius	AA		•		•	•
	II	•		•		
House I 7,19	f	•				
Casa dei Ceii	f				•	•
Casa di Trebius Valens	s		•			
	u				•	•
Casa degli Amorini Dorati	I					•
Casa di M. Lucretius Fronto	20				•	•
Casa di Giuseppe II	i'			• ?	•	•
House VIII 2,34	a'	•				
House VII 5,9	n		•			

* Includes built in cupboards   ** Includes ablution, luxury, and religious material

Table 5.12b Small closed rooms off garden/terrace or lower floor, decorated: storage, utilitarian fixtures, and contents

House	Room	Shelving	Cupboards/ containers	Storage vessels	Other vessels*	Utilitarian/ industrial	Building material**
Casa di Julius Polybius	AA		•		•		
Casa dei Quadretti Teatrali	14			•	•	•	•
Casa dell'Efebo	22		• ?		•		
Casa dei Trebius Valens	u				•		
Casa dei Ceii	f		•				
	g	•	•		•	•	
Casa degli Amorini Dorati	I		•			•	
	R		•				
Casa di M. Lucretius Fronto	20				•	•	•
Casa di Giuseppe II	i'		• ?		• ?		•
House VIII 2,34	a'	•					
	g'	• ?					

* Includes food-preparation, serving, and table vessels   ** Includes sculpture fragments marble table, bronze statuettes, shells, and a small altar), clothworking (weaving, spinning, and needlework), and lighting. Thus, the predominant pattern of use for rooms of this type was for personal activities, but with little evidence for sleeping. Generally, there was a more pronounced pattern for contents associated with ablutions and a wide range of clothworking equipment here compared with the small closed rooms around the front hall.

Two to three of these decorated rooms had shelving. Storage furniture was recorded in up to seven rooms, with storage vessels in another. Six to seven rooms had recorded contents related to food preparation or dining, and four had more utilitarian/industrial material (that is, a travertine basin, tools, and scales). Thus, all the decorated rooms of this type with recorded finds contained some storage or utilitarian material or were fitted with shelving. Shelving, in particu-

lar, might seem unusual for decorated rooms and suggests that they had been downgraded. The prominent pattern of storage furniture suggests, however, that at least some sort of storage might have been habitual in rooms of this type, particularly for material associated with food preparation and dining. Material related to ablutions and toilet must either have been stored or used in these rooms. The presence of building material and fragmentary statuary in three rooms suggests that any storage in these rooms may have been makeshift and associated with disrupted circumstances.

Undecorated

Coarse furbishing was recorded in twenty-seven rooms of this type; another eleven have no record of any painted decoration. Of all these, eight had no recorded finds, and six had fixtures but no significant loose finds (tables 5.12c–d).

Table 5.12c Small closed rooms off garden/terrace or lower floor, undecorated: fixtures

House	Room	Stairways	Water systems*	Shelving	High recesses/ niches**	Recesses	*Lararium* painting
Casa di Julius Polybius	BB				•		
Casa del Menandro	21			•			
House I 10,8	12			•			
Casa dei Quadretti Teatrali	10				•		
House I 6,8–9	h		• ?				
Casa di Stallius Eros	8		•				
	12	•	•				
Casa del Sacerdos Amandus	g'			•			
	p	•					
Casa dell'Efebo	18			•			
House VI 16,26	O				•		
	R	•					
Casa degli Amorini Dorati	J			•			
	K		•				
	L		•	•			
Casa di M. Lucretius Fronto	17					•	
Casa dei Vettii	o			•			
Casa delle Nozze d'Argento	k				•		•
House VIII 5,9	l			•			

*Includes latrines, cistern heads, and downpipes   **Includes built-in cupboards

96

Table 5.12d Small closed rooms off garden/terrace or lower floor, undecorated: loose contents

House	Room	Storage furniture	Storage vessels	Utilitarian/ domestic*	Utilitarian/ industrial	Tableware/ personal**	Building material***
Casa di Julius Polybius	BB	•	•		•	•	
Casa del Menandro	14		•				
	21			•	•?		
House I 10,8	12		•	•	•	•	
Casa degli Amanti	17			•		•	
	18	•					
	19			•		•	
Casa dei Quadretti Teatrali	10	•				•	
Casa di Stallius Eros	8			•			
Casa del Sacerdos Amandus	p		•	•			
Casa dell'Efebo	18		•	•			
House I 7,19	i		•	•			•?
Casa dei Ceii	m			•		•	
Casa del Sacello Iliaco	o						•
Casa degli Amorini Dorati	J				•	•	
	K				•?		
	L					•	
Casa di M. Lucretius Fronto	15				•		•
	17			•			
Casa del Principe di Napoli	i			•			
Casa dei Vettii	o		•				
Casa delle Nozze d'Argento	k				•		
House VIII 2,14–16	l"					•	•
House VIII 2,34	i'			•			•

*Includes lighting **Includes serving vessels ***Includes marble fragments

Twenty-four rooms in this group had loose finds conceivably related to habitual use.

Fixtures included stairways, latrines, cistern mouths and water pipes, shelving, and built-in storage areas (that is, understair cupboards, high and narrow recesses, and niches). One room had a short, low recess, conceivably also used for storage (see chapter 4), and another had a lararium painting. Room 17 in the Casa di M. Lucretius Fronto also had an unidentifiable masonry structure. Thus, fixtures related to storage were the most frequent type in these undecorated rooms.

The loose contents included storage furniture (for example, cupboards and chests) in three rooms and storage vessels (for example, amphorae) in seven. The amphorae in room i of House I 7,19 were filled with lime and conceivably associated with evident restoration work in this house. Utilitarian/domestic contents (for example, clothworking, cooking, and weighing equipment) and lighting equipment were recorded in twelve rooms. Five to seven had more utilitarian/industrial material (for example, harness, tools, or fishing equipment), and nine had finer-quality material (for example, serving vessels, tableware, toilet items, and gaming implements). Some rooms contained a mixture of utilitarian and finer material, suggesting mixed storage. There was a significant pattern for the storage of relatively utilitarian material in these rooms around the garden area, both domestic and more industrial. Building material and fragments of architectural or display sculpture recorded in four to five rooms suggest disrupted conditions.

As might be expected, the undecorated examples of this type had more fixtures related to utilitarian functions than the decorated examples. While the undecorated rooms showed ample evidence of storage activities, shelving was also present in some of the decorated rooms, and storage furniture was more evident in decorated than in undecorated rooms. While it should be noted that there was mixed storage in both decorated and undecorated rooms, there seems a slight tendency for such storage to have been more utilitarian and industrial in undecorated rooms. The storage in decorated rooms was more likely to be related to toilet and entertainment, including food preparation. The assemblages in these rooms, particularly the decorated ones, seem to document less specialized and more communal activities (for example, dining and food preparation) than those in the comparable small rooms around the front hall, which usually had only small quantities of material not consistent with storage activities.

The number and uses of rooms of this type, and others around the garden area, undoubt-edly varied according to the size and status of the house. Consequently, they may have been more sensitive to changing living conditions than were room types around the front hall. This was probably even more true, but less obvious, for these smaller rooms. The predominant pattern was that undecorated rooms stored a variety of materials, not excluding utilitarian and bulk storage. Decorated rooms could have been similarly used, although with less evidence of permanent storage and of less utilitarian material. Ablution and toilet activities may have been carried out in these rooms, but there was a marked lack of evidence for sleeping.

TYPE 13: SMALL OPEN-FRONTED AREAS OFF GARDENS/TERRACES OR LOWER FLOORS

Rooms of this type were similar in form to room type 5, although less uniform in size, proportion, and location. There could also be a number of them around a single garden. Twenty-two spaces are categorized as type 13 but in only twelve houses. Five were in the Casa del Menandro and six in House VIII 2,14–16. Some were very small; room 3 in the Casa degli Amorini Dorati was little more than a large built-in cupboard with no recorded finds. Only seven had any significant contents, with five in the Casa del Menandro (table 5.13). The contents, all in small quantities, consisted variously of statuary in a *lararium* aedicula, furniture (including a chest), braziers, lamps, ceramic vessels, toilet equip-

Table 5.13 Small open-fronted areas off garden/terrace or lower floor

House	Room	*Lararia*/ statuary	Chests/ furniture	Braziers	Ceramics/ lamps	Toilet/ spinning	Building material
Casa del Menandro	13		•				•
	22				•		
	23						•
	24			•			
	25	•					
Casa dei Ceii	1		•	•			
Casa del Principe di Napoli	m					•	

98

ment, and a spinning implement. Two areas had evidence of building material.

The small number of spaces of this type, the lack of pattern, and the quantities of material found prohibit any specific conclusions. The complete lack of material in most of them, the limited amount of material in a few, and the recording of only a single bronze coin in room t of the Casa di Trebius Valens imply that, under normal conditions, they were probably relatively empty spaces. Any material recorded in these spaces was similar to that found either in the ambulatories of the colonnaded gardens (for example, braziers and chests) or in the small closed rooms in this area (personal items, for example).

TYPE 14: ROOMS WITH COOKING HEARTHS OR ASSOCIATED ROOMS (KITCHEN AREAS)

By definition, rooms categorized as type 14 had a built-in bench identified as a cooking hearth (Salza Prina Ricotti 1978/80:241–243; Foss 1994: 79–80; figure 5.11), or they were dependent on a room so furbished, that is, accessible only through it. Dependent rooms that appear to have functioned entirely as latrines are categorized separately (see type 15). In this sample, benches or hearths ranged in size from approximately 0.6 to 1 m high, 0.5 to 1.35 m deep, and 0.75 to 3.25 m long. Rooms of this type were not restricted to a particular location in the house plan. At least one such room was documented in each house in the sample, although those in the Casa di Stallius Eros and House I 10,8 are categorized differently. The Casa di Stallius Eros had a circular hearth in the front hall (room type 3); in House I 10,8 there was a cooking hearth in corridor 9 (room type 8). No hearth was actually reported in the Casa della Ara Massima, but Stemmer believed room K had once had one (1992:35).

A total of forty-four rooms are categorized as type 14.[6] In six houses, more than one room is categorized as such because two rooms were dependent. In four houses, two or even three separate rooms with built-in hearths were identified. These houses tend to be the larger ones, particularly those that had more than one front hall or had lower levels as in Insula VIII 2. Neither was the case for House VIII 5,9, however, which had two separate areas of this type. Only four rooms of this type had no finds or fixtures other than a hearth.

Besides the defining hearth, the other most frequent fixtures were latrines (table 5.14a–b). As mentioned, other houses often had separate latrines that opened immediately off this room type. Gemma Jansen has argued (1997:128) that the latrine itself could often have been used for disposing of waste material from cooking and

Figure 5.11 Bench and cooking pots in kitchen w, Casa dei Vettii (Sogliano 1898a: Fig. 13)

food preparation. Cistern mouths, downpipes, and other drains besides latrines were recorded in five to six houses; sinks and fixed basins for water storage (Jansen 1997:130) were recorded in eight. Water was presumably also collected from other locations in other houses (for example, open garden areas).

Lararium paintings were recorded in six rooms and niches, and built-in cupboards in nine. None of the recorded niches was located in

Table 5.14a Rooms with cooking hearth or associated rooms (kitchen areas): fixtures

House	Room	Latrines	Water systems*	Water storage**	*Lararia*	Niches***	Stairways
Casa di Julius Polybius	Nk		•				
Casa della Venere in Bikini	9	•					
Casa del Menandro	45	• ?			•	•	
	52			•	•	•	
Casa del Fabbro	11				•		
Casa degli Amanti	16				•		
Casa dei Quadretti Teatrali	8			•			•
Casa del Sacerdos Amandus	h	•					
	i			•			
Casa dell'Efebo	8	•					
	21	•					
House I 7,19	m			•			
Casa di Trebius Valens	i	•				•	
Casa dei Ceii	i	•					
Casa del Sacello Iliaco	n	•					
House VI 16,26	Z	•					
Casa degli Amorini Dorati	X	•	•				
	V			•			•
Casa della Ara Massima	K		• ?				
Casa di M. Lucretius Fronto	18				•		
	21	•				•	
Casa del Principe di Napoli	g	•	•			•	•
Casa dei Vettii	w		•	•			
Casa delle Nozze d'Argento	s				•		
	H	•					
House VIII 2,26	f	• ?		•			
	2	•				•	
House VIII 2,28	e					•	•
Casa di Giuseppe II	d'	•	•				
House VIII 2,34	r					•	
House VIII 2,29–30	10	•				•	
	13	•					
House VIII 5,9	o			•		•	•

*Consists of cistern mouths, downpipes, and drains   **Consists of sinks and fixed basins   ***Includes understair cupboards direct association with the *lararium* paintings, suggesting that these fixtures did not necessarily have a religious function (compare Dwyer 1982: 114; Orr 1988:294–295) but may have served utilitarian purposes (see chapter 4). Stairways were located in five rooms of this type. Less common fixtures were long, low recesses in the walls of room 7 of the Casa dell'Efebo, ovens in room i of the Casa di Trebius Valens and room a of House VIII 2,29-30, an unidentifiable podium in room s of the Casa delle Nozze d'Argento, and possibly a table in room m' of House VIII 2,14–16.

At least twenty-four of these rooms had some recorded loose contents. These included movable cooking apparatus (for example, tripods, marble vessel supports, bronze cooking pots, and ceramic vessels with evidence of fire blackening) and truncated amphorae and amphora bases, reputedly used to rest cooking pots on. Other food-preparation equipment, which does not appear to have been specifically for cooking (for example, certain bronze, ceramic, and glass vessels; handmills; mortars; and weights), was recorded in fourteen to fifteen

Table 5.14b Rooms with cooking hearth or associated rooms (kitchen areas): loose contents

House	Room	Cooking apparatus	Amphora bases	Food preparation/ serving	Amphorae*	Serving/ tableware*	Misc.
Casa di Julius Polybius	Nk		•	•			
Casa della Venere in Bikini	9	• ?				• ?	
Casa del Menandro	45			•			•
	52			• ?			
Casa del Fabbro	11	•		•			
Casa degli Amanti	16			•	•		•
Casa degli Quadretti Teatrali	8			•			•
Casa del Sacerdos Amandus	h				•		
	i	•		•		•	
Casa dell'Efebo	7			•			
	8	•				•	•
House I 7,19	m'		•				
Casa di Trebius Valens	r			• ?			•
Casa dei Ceii	i			•	•		•
Casa del Sacello Iliaco	n	•	•	•			
House VI 16,26	Z						•
Casa di M. Lucretius Fronto	18/21	•		•	•		•
Casa del Principe di Napoli	g				•	• ?	•
	h			•	•	•	•
Casa dei Vettii	w	•		•			•
Casa delle Nozze d'Argento	s	•				•	•
	H			•		• ?	
Casa di Giuseppe II	d'					•	•
House VIII 5,9	d	•		•		•	
	o				•		

*Includes other storage vessels **Includes lamps

rooms, representing some 60 to 70 percent of the rooms with reported finds; storage vessels, particularly amphorae, were recorded in seven.

Finer-quality vessels, vessels identified as tableware (for example, *terra sigillata* pottery, small glass vessels, bronze *casseruole*, and decorated bronze vessels), and lamps were reported in up to nine rooms of this type. Such material was conceivably out of place in this area, but its relatively frequent occurrence may be the result of its having been brought here either to fill with food and drink or for washing. Lamps could have been commonly used in what would often have been quite a dark room. Given traditional assumptions that small glass bottles were personal items, however, it is difficult to explain their frequent presence in this room type. Perhaps their functions were more diverse than generally believed.

Other miscellaneous contents that might seem out of place in this context (for example, surgical implements, statuary, a puteal, remains of storage furniture, and tools) were recorded in thirteen rooms. It is conceivable that tools and storage furniture belonged in such a context, but some of the other items suggest that the activities in many of these rooms had been disrupted or that the rooms had gone out of use prior to the eruption. This was probably true for room i in the Casa dei Ceii (figure 5.12) and room w of the Casa dei Vettii where broken, large-scale statuary was found. However, it is conceivable that an Egyptian statue in room Z of House VI 16,26 belonged in this context under normal conditions.

Salza Prina Ricotti (1978/1980:239–240) noted that hearths were found in 93 percent of rich houses, 66 percent of medium houses, and 40 percent of poor houses in Pompeii. She concluded that braziers were used in houses without them. However, this study shows that braziers were used in houses that also had such hearths, sometimes more than one hearth and more than one brazier. Braziers seem to have been used for a different type of cooking (it is tempting to see an analogy with such modern cooking practices as barbecuing or fondue cooking). Dell'Orto was of the opinion that food was reheated on portable stoves because the kitchen

Figure 5.12 Kitchen i, viewed from north, Casa dei Ceii

was usually some distance from the dining room (1990:187). This explanation is unsubstantiated at least in the Casa del Fabbro, the Casa degli Amanti, the Casa dell'Efebo, and House VIII 5,9, four of the six houses in this sample in which braziers were recorded in the garden area.

Lararia are believed to have been a characteristic of kitchens (Dwyer 1982:114; Salza Prina Ricotti 1978/1980; Orr 1988:295). Taking into account the limited chance of preservation of such paintings, they were not as frequent a part of kitchen furnishings as is generally believed. It would seem inappropriate to assume that all niches in kitchens had a religious function. Also, the statuary found in the kitchen areas in this sample was usually both fragmentary and of a size and subject matter seemingly unsuitable for household shrines (compare Dwyer 1982:121–

122). The presence of statuary here may have been the result of disrupted domestic conditions.

The more prominent pattern of food-preparation equipment unrelated to cooking may have resulted from post-eruption looting of bronze vessels. Alternatively, it could suggest that while initial food preparation and storage may have been carried out in rooms of this type, a certain amount of cooking could have been done on movable braziers in closer proximity to the diners, as shown in the garden areas. In houses with more than one room with a hearth, the second or third hearth was sometimes nearer to the main dining/entertainment areas (for example, Houses VIII 2,26 and VIII 2,29-30), revealing a need for the food to be prepared near the diners. Neither observation supports Foss's notion that cooking sights and smells needed to be kept away from the diners (1994:165–168). Using analogies with nineteenth- or early twentieth-century kitchens can mislead us into applying to the past recent, culturally specific attitudes about cooking and food-preparation activities, with their labor divisions and by-products of noises, smells, and seemingly unsightly apparatus. It is perhaps more appropriate to take the massive changes in western cooking practices in the last hundred years as a measure of how much these practices might have changed over the last two thousand. Anecdotal textual references to unsavory smells in the Roman period must be properly contextualized (for example, Seneca *Ep.* 104.6; compare Foss 1994:42).

TYPE 15: LATRINES AS ENTIRE ROOMS

As noted above, latrines were frequently located in kitchens. They could also occur as separate rooms in a variety of locations in the house plan. Of eleven recorded cases in ten houses in the sample where the latrine seems to have been a separate room, six were next to the kitchen (figure 5.13), one was in the garden area, and four were near entranceways to the house. While the location of latrines was probably also related to available drainage systems (see Jansen 1991:158; 1997:128), different attitudes to hygiene and privacy from those of

modern western societies are apparent. Jansen argued (1997:125–126) that Pompeians did not want to be seen while in the latrine. But this would have been impossible because many latrines were located in kitchens, and Jansen seemed to be aware of this.

Apart from the obvious fixture (see Jansen 1991:155–158), for many of which only the sloping platform remained (Jansen 1997:124, Figs. 10.1–2, 127), the only other recorded contents were a basin and tap in room s1 in the Casa delle Nozze d'Argento, tools and spinning and needlework implements in room 9 of the Casa dei Quadretti Teatrali, and a puteal in room e' of House I 6,8–9 (table 5.15). The latter assemblage seems out of place and suggests either that this room has been wrongly identified or had been out of use at the time of the eruption, or that the assemblage had fallen from the floor above.

Figure 5.13 Painted walls and ceiling, latrine s1, Casa delle Nozze d'Argento

Table 5.15   Latrines as entire rooms: other fittings and contents

House	Room	Basins/puteals	Furniture fittings	Clothing working	Tools
Casa dei Quadretti Teatrali	9		•	•	•
House I 6, 8–9	e'	•			
Casa delle Nozze d'Argento	s1	•			

TYPE 16: OTHER ROOMS OUTSIDE FRONT HALL/GARDEN COMPLEXES

Seventy-nine rooms are classified as type 16. They include a number of forms but are generally small and relatively closed. They do not include room types 14 and 15, also often located away from the main axis. These rooms occur in nineteen houses in the sample and tend to be concentrated in the larger houses that had suites of rooms outside the front-hall/garden complex. For example, eighteen rooms of this type were in the Casa del Menandro, twelve in the Casa di Giuseppe II, and nine in House VIII 2,29–30. They usually lacked any evidence of wall or pavement decoration. Loose contents were recorded in twenty-eight to twenty-nine of these rooms (table 5.16b). Another fifteen had fixtures only (table 5.16a). Loose finds in rooms C and D in the Casa del Menandro were part of the fill brought in when the rooms went out of use.

Latrines and a sink (in room T of the Casa degli Amorini Dorati) occurred in these rooms, located near the front hall, near back entrances, or on lower ground floors. Room v in House VIII 2,34 had a cistern mouth, as did room v of House VIII 2,28. Evidence for shelving, mezzanines, ledges, or suspension nails were recorded in six to seven rooms of this type. Room 8 in the Casa dei Vettii had both shelving and a built-in cupboard. While shelving was the most frequently occurring fixture in rooms of this type, it was notably less frequent here, both proportionately and in total, than in the small, closed undecorated rooms either around the front hall (room type 4) or around the garden area (room type 12). Low, narrow recesses were located in three rooms of this type and a high recess, or built-in cupboard, in one (room x' of the Casa dei Vettii, one of the rare decorated rooms in this

category). Two of the low recesses were in unventilated underground rooms, and one was under a stairway. Although these rooms could conceivably have been used for sleeping, it seems improbable. It is more likely that these recesses served purposes other than for beds (see chapter 4). As in room type 14, niches recorded in five of these rooms had no evident religious significance, particularly a large rectangular niche in room H of the Casa di Julius Polybius.

Domed ovens and *fornelli* were located in four of these rooms. The ovens, which appear to have been heating systems for bath complexes, were also found in association with rooms containing what appear to have been supports for a table (rooms C and D in the Casa del Menandro and room 3 in the Casa di Giuseppe II). Mau identified these as bread-making tables (1887: 133). The ovens might therefore have served the dual purpose of heating the bath and baking bread. This interpretation draws attention to the variety of cooking types and cooking areas within a domestic context. The exact purpose of the *fornelli*, however, is by no means established. Some appear to have been used for heating, but as Foss concluded (1994:79), it is doubtful they were used for cooking. Two rooms of this type had stairways leading to the upper floor. One (room u, in the Casa di Giuseppe II) appears to have also provided a through-route from the front-hall area to the lower levels, and the other (room 29 in the Casa del Menandro; figure 5.14) contains what has been identified as a manger and was therefore probably a stable, perhaps with accommodation for feed and/or harness storage above.

In eight rooms, loose finds included furniture remains. The finds were mostly from storage containers (including a casket), but the remains of what had possibly been folding tables or stools and a puteal (in room u of the Casa

Table 5.16a Other service areas outside front-hall/garden complex: fixtures

House	Room	Water system*	Shelving**	Recesses	Niches	Fornelli/ ovens	Platforms***	Stairways
Casa di Julius Polybius	H				•			
Casa del Menandro	54					•		
	A			•				
	B						•	
	C	•					• ?	
	D					•		
	20					•		
	29						•	•
	31						• ?	
	35		•					
	37		•					
	38		• ?					
	40	•	•					
House I 10,8	13			•				
Casa di Stallius Eros	10	•						
House VI 16,26	Y				•			
Casa della Ara Massima	L	•						
Casa degli Amorini Dorati	T	•						
Casa dei Vettii	8		•					
	x'			•				
	z				•			
House VIII 2,14–16	l'						•	
	o'				•			
House VIII 2,28	v				•			
Casa di Giuseppe II	u						•	•
	f		•					
	f'		•					
	2			•				
	3					•		•
	4				•			•
House VIII 2,34	v	•						

*Consists of latrines, sink, and cistern mouths   ** Includes nails, ledges, and mezzanines   *** Includes hearths, tables, and tubs

di Giuseppe II) were also reported. Storage vessels, particularly amphorae, were recorded in thirteen of these rooms, implying they were frequently used for bulk storage. Only three rooms (rooms 35, 37, and 38 in the Casa del Menandro) contained both shelving and amphorae, although three others had recesses or niches and amphorae. Fourteen to fifteen rooms contained varieties of other utilitarian domestic material (material related to cooking and food preparation, lighting, cloth production, and possible ceramic serving and tableware), eight or nine of which also had storage amphorae. Thus, rooms of this type seem normally to have contained a

Table 5.16b Other service areas outside front-hall/garden complex: loose contents

House	Room	Furniture/ containers	Storage vessels	Utilitarian domestic	Tools	Luxury/ personal	Building material
Casa di Julius Polybius	H	•	•	•		•?	
Casa del Menandro	54			•		•?	
	A		•	•	•	•	
	B	•	•	•		•	•
	20		•				
	29		•				
	32						•
	35	•				•	
	36	•	•	•			
	37		•	•		•	•
	38	•	•	•		•	
	40			•	•	•	
House I 10,8	13		•	•			
Casa di Stallius Eros	9			•			•
Casa dei Ceii	n		•	•		•?	
House VI 16,26	U					•	
	X			•		•?	
Casa della Ara Massima	L					•	
Casa degli Amorini Dorati	Y	•				•	
House VI 15,5	4				•		
	5		•				
Casa dei Vettii	4	•				•	
	8			•		•?	
Casa delle Nozze d'Argento	E		•	•		•	
	F					•?	
House VIII 2,28	v					•?	
Casa di Giuseppe II	u	•					•
	3		•	•?			
House VIII 5,9	b		•			•	

variety of domestic material, possibly for storage. Interestingly, tools were reported in only three rooms of this type.

In twelve and possibly up to nineteen rooms of this type, some luxury material (decorative lampstands, statuary, and silver and bronze tableware) or personal material (jewelry, writing and gaming equipment, or other material related to apparel, ablutions, or toilet activities) was reported. In three, this material consisted

only of glass bottles, which conceivably had uses other than those just listed. Notably latrines and ablution material could occur in these areas, together in the case of room L in the Casa della Ara Massima. However, it is not certain whether the latter material was habitually stored or utilized in all such areas (for example, in rooms A, B, 35, and 40 in the Casa del Menandro).

Animal bones in room n of the Casa dei Ceii may have been the remains of meals or cooking

Figure 5.14 Platform along west wall of room 29, Casa del Menandro

activities, particularly as charcoal was also recorded here. The presence of a horse skeleton in room 4 in the Casa dei Vettii implies that this room, like room 29 in the Casa del Menandro, was a stable. For the Casa dei Vettii, this interpretation is given further weight by the presence of a horse harness in the cupboard under the stairs in corridor 3. The other loose finds in room 4 were largely personal. It is equally conceivable that they, or the horse, or both, were moved here during disruption. Possible building material (particularly roof tiles, architectural decoration, and marble fragments), recorded in five rooms, may have been used in repairs.

The combination of the locations and fixtures in these rooms indicates they were not essentially a coherent group. For example, some were located off the front-hall area, others off the garden area or secondary entranceways, and still others in lower ground-floor areas. Most of the contents, however, indicate that rooms of this type were used for utilitarian activities (for example, heating water, baking bread, storage, and animal quarters). It has traditionally been assumed that they were used as service areas or for servant and animal quarters (for example, Maiuri 1933:186–224). There was certainly less

evidence of decorated rooms in these areas than in the main front-hall/garden access. Nonetheless, evidence of shelving indicates that storage was as likely to have occurred in the main part of the house as in these assumed service areas. There seems little reason to believe that slaves had their own quarters (see George 1997b:22). These observations and the frequent occurrence of luxury and personal items in these areas away from the main axes of the house should put into question assumptions about the separation of the areas of Pompeian houses into service and non-service facilities.

TYPE 17: STAIRWAYS

The areas classified as room type 17 are those that were completely taken up with stairways. Their obvious function—to provide access to upper or lower floors—needs no further discussion. There were twenty-four such areas in eighteen houses in the sample, houses in Region VIII with lower ground floors often having two. Many of them had built-in cupboards or storage areas underneath, which have been included in the contents for the room off which it opens. As might be expected, little was found on these stairways (table 5.17) or, indeed, on

Table 5.17 Stairways

House	Room	Amphorae/other vessels	Jewelry	Cistern mouth	Building material*
Casa di Julius Polybius	B				•
Casa degli Amanti	3	•			
Casa del Sacerdos Amandus	ST	•			
Casa dell'Efebo	20		•	•	
Casa delle Nozze d'Argento	I	•			
House VIII 2,28	k		•		•

* Includes sculptural fragments

any other stairways in the sample. The only other fixture recorded in association with them was a cistern mouth under stairway 20 in the Casa dell'Efebo. Bronze rings found there and on stairway k in House VIII 2,28 may have been deposited during the abandonment process. Presumably, the partial remains of statuary found on the latter also indicate disrupted conditions, as would building material under the stairway in room B in the Casa di Julius Polybius. The main pattern was for amphorae and other vessels, often utilitarian, to be left on the landing, as was the case on three type 17 stairways, on the stairway that was part of corridor SS in the Casa di Julius Polybius (see room type 8), and on the stairway in room o of House VIII 5,9 (see room type 14). The assemblage in the Casa di Julius Polybius included two bronze jugs and a brazier. Vessels and other apparatus may have been left habitually on the landing while in transit to and from the upper floor. Although none of these rooms have explicit evidence, such material may have been used for eating in the upper-floor rooms.

TYPE 18: SECONDARY INTERNAL GARDENS AND COURTYARDS, USUALLY NOT COLONNADED

By definition, these open areas were generally not part of the main axis of the house. They were often accessible through an internal corridor or another room that opened off the front hall or main garden. Rooms of types 14, 15, and 16 often open off type 18 areas. Thirteen such areas in ten houses in the sample are categorized as this type. With the possible exception of area 50 in the Casa del Menandro, none provided direct access to the street. Fixtures only were recorded in five of them, and loose finds were reported in seven (tables 5.18a–b).

The fixtures included pools or water-catchment areas. In garden 2 of the Casa delle Nozze d'Argento, there was a swimming pool and fountain with sculptural decoration (figure 5.15). The remains of pools or tubs built into the south wall of garden 50 in the Casa del Menandro may once have served as areas for water storage. Cistern mouths were also recorded in two courtyards, one with a puteal in situ. An oven or a furnace in area 6 of the Casa dell'Efebo was reputedly used for heating water in room 5, and the one in area s of the Casa del Sacello Iliaco for industrial activity (figure 5.16). Stairways were located in three of these areas. Other, less frequent fixtures included a lararium aedicula, a high recess, and an understair cupboard. The latter two in area 5 of House I 10,8 seem curious in this open-air area.

The most frequently occurring loose contents were storage vessels (amphorae and dolia). Smaller domestic vessels (for example, smaller ceramic vessels and bronze buckets) were reported in two rooms, but more common was utilitarian material (for example, mortars, grinding stones, weights, tools) that might be categorized as industrial or domestic/industrial. Two of these areas also had building material.

The general impression is that utilitarian activities were carried out in these areas. The

Table 5.18a Secondary internal gardens and courtyards: fixtures

House	Room	Pools/water catchment	Cistern mouths	Ovens/ furnaces	Stairways	Recesses*	*Lararium* aediculae
Casa del Menandro	44		•				
	50	• ?			•		
House I 10,8	5				•	•	
Casa dell'Efebo	6	•		•			
House I 7,19	n	•					
Casa del Sacello Iliaco	s			•			
Casa dei Vettii	v	•			•		•
Casa delle Nozze d'Argento	2	•					
House VIII 2,14–16	i"		•				

*Includes understair cupboards

Table 5.18b Secondary internal gardens and courtyards: loose contents

House	Room	Storage vessels	Domestic vessels	Utilitarian/industrial equipment	Building material
Casa del Menandro	44	•	•	•	•
Casa del Sacello Iliaco	s			•	•
Casa degli Amorini Dorati	P	•			
Casa dei Vettii	s	•		•	
	v		•		
Casa delle Nozze d'Argento	2	•		•	
	G	•			

Figure 5.15 Garden 2, Casa delle Nozze d'Argento. ICCD - *Ministero per i beni e le attività culturali, Roma, gabinetto fotografico neg. N49639*

Figure 5.16 Structure in southeast corner of area s, Casa del Sacello Iliaco

exceptions, perhaps, are the painted area n in House I 7,19 and area P in the Casa degli Amorini Dorati, which seemed to have served as light-wells and possibly provided water. Even garden 2 in the Casa delle Nozze d'Argento, with its swimming pool and ornamental fountain, contained utilitarian/industrial material. Maiuri reported evidence of planting in area 50 in the Casa del Menandro and suggested the area had been a productive garden (1933:216). This evidence might reflect, to a certain extent, the activities recorded in the main garden areas where utilitarian fixtures, amphorae, and *dolia* were reported and whose productive role has been noted (Jashemski 1979a:604). There is a general sense, nevertheless, that garden areas not in the main axis of the house were more utilitarian.

TYPE 19: SECONDARY ENTRANCES AND ENTRANCE COURTYARDS

There are twelve entranceways in ten houses in this sample categorized as type 19. They usually provided access to the house but not directly from the street to a front hall. This category includes areas at the front of the house, such as areas A and C in the Casa di Julius Polybius (figure 5.17) that do not conform architecturally to type 3, as well as corridors and courtyards that provided entranceways to other parts of houses. Five entranceways had fixtures, and loose finds were reported in seven (table 5.19). As might be expected, loose finds were invariably reported in the entranceways that formed courtyards rather than in those that were corridors.

The fixtures consisted predominantly of cistern mouths, one with a puteal. A stairway, a *fornello*, and two troughs were also recorded in these areas. As in room type 18, the commonest loose contents consisted of storage vessels, mainly amphorae but also *dolia*. Thirty-four amphorae were found in the entrance from area B to adjoining room E of the Casa delle Nozze d'Argento. In many other areas, considerable quantities of amphorae were also reported. All these areas had direct access to the street and seem to have been used for distributing bulk materials. The quantities of amphorae in many of these areas suggest some specific commercial/industrial activity or indicate the quantities of amphorae necessary for running a household. It might also be significant that both the *fornelli* in courtyard 34 of the Casa del Menandro (figure 5.18) and in room 20 of the same house (room type 16) were associated with a number of amphorae.

Again, as in room type 18, other utilitarian ceramic and bronze vessels, as well as utilitarian/industrial material, were reported in these entranceways. One also had what might be clas-

Figure 5.17 Northwest corner of area A showing earlier decoration, building material, and amphorae, Casa di Julius Polybius

Table 5.19 Secondary entrances and entrance courtyards

House	Room	Fixtures	Storage vessels	Utilitarian domestic vessels	Utilitarian/ industrial equipment	Luxury material	Building material
Casa di Julius Polybius	A	• (cistern mouth)	•	•			•
	C		•				•
Casa del Menandro	34	• (*fornello*/ troughs)	•		•		
Casa degli Amorini Dorati	S	• (stairway)					
House VI 15,5	2		•				
Casa delle Nozze d'Argento	B	• (cistern mouth)	• ?				
House VIII 2, 26	VIII 2, 27	• (cistern mouth)	• ?	• ?	• ?	• ?	

sified as luxury items (bronze lampstand, small glass and bronze vessels, jewelry, and a coin hoard).[7] This latter material might have been collected together during disruption. Building material was recorded in both front areas of the Casa di Julius Polybius.

As might be expected, these entranceways seem to have been used for utilitarian activities and possibly for commercial and industrial activities. However, it should be noted that the door of entranceway 2 to House VI 15,5 had probably been decorated with bronze bosses and other ornaments, as well as a bell. The combination of such ornamentation and the types of goods that might have passed through these entranceways emphasizes the multiple character of such residential establishments in a pre-industrialized society.

Figure 5.18 Amphorae stacked against south wall and around *fornello*, courtyard 34, Casa del Menandro (Maiuri 1933: Fig. 90)

TYPE 20: ROOMS OPEN TO THE STREET

These spaces were usually at the front of the house, had a wide opening to the street, and often a narrower access to the front hall. In only eight houses in the sample was this type of room directly attached to the main dwelling. Three rooms in House VIII 5,9 are classified as type 20, although room 1a should probably not be included in this analysis as it did not have direct access to the house. (On the other hand, the rooms to either side of it did.) Of the eleven rooms of this type, six had fixtures and five to six had contents, all in small quantities (tables 5.20a–b).

Fixtures included niches, *podia* of indeterminate use, and downpipes, possibly indicating a connection with the upper-floor water systems. Only room b of House I 6,8–9 appears to have had a wooden bench and shelving, with two *dolia* set in the ground, suggesting that this area had been used for dispensing merchandise. Unfortunately, there is no evidence as to what that merchandise might have been. The loose finds were not very informative here.

Most type 20 rooms thus had no fixtures to provide obvious evidence that they had been used for commercial or industrial activity. Apart from the bench in House I 6,8–9, the other fixtures found here, but not commonly found in other parts of the house, were *podia* (figure 5.19). Such a fixture was found in room s (room type 14) in the Casa delle Nozze d'Argento, which could indicate that it had been related to food preparation, although this does not seem very probable.

Loose contents included utilitarian material (that is, scales, a lantern, cloth-making equipment, and a small travertine base), amphorae, and other vessels possibly related to food preparation and serving. Three rooms also had material that might seem to have been more personal (that is, a buckle, *fritilli*, and small vessels). Two had possible evidence of building material. In general, these contents and their assemblages were not distinctively different from those found in areas inside the house. It is notable that no especially large quantities of material were found in rooms of this type. While the evidence is not substantial, it indicates either that activities carried out in these areas attached to the main dwelling were not very different from those carried out inside the house or that possibly the contents had been packed up and removed prior to abandonment.

Table 5.20a Rooms at front of house open to street (shop): fixtures

House	Room	Shelving	Niches	Counters/fixed *dolia*	Podia	Downpipes
Casa della Venere in Bikini	I 11, 7		•		•	
House I 6, 8-9.	b	•		•		
Casa di Stallius Eros	3		•			
House VIII 5,9	1a				•	•
	1b					•

Table 5.20b Rooms at front of house open to street (shop): loose contents

House	Room	Utilitarian domestic	Amphorae	Food preparation and serving vessels	Personal/ gaming	Building material
Casa di Julius Polybius	V	•		•		
Casa della Venere in Bikini	I 11, 7					• ?
Casa del Menandro	42		•	•		
Casa degli Amanti	I 10, 10	•	•		•	
House I 6,8–9.	b				• ?	
Casa di Stallius Eros	3	•			• ?	•

Figure 5.19 Podium in shop I 11,7, Casa della Venere in Bikini. *ICCD - Ministero per i beni e le attività culturali, Roma, gabinetto fotografico neg. N55651*

113

TYPE 21: BATH AREAS

Areas have been identified as bathing facilities in six of the houses in the sample (table 5.21). In the Casa dell'Efebo such a facility consisted of one small room with a bronze basin (figure 5.20). The other houses had suites of up to five rooms with hypocaust flooring or lead piping to carry water. The Casa di Giuseppe II also had a separate pool, area z', whose painted decoration suggests that it had a formal function as a pool for bathing. A total of eighteen rooms have been classified as this type.

Because there was little in the way of fixtures and contents to indicate the functions of these spaces, the architectural form has been used for type assignment. Room 46 in the Casa del Menandro had a shallow central pool and appears to have been a type of room not found in the other bath complexes in Pompeian houses (figure 5.21). As with room z' in the Casa di Giuseppe II, room 6 in House VIII 2,29–30 was completely taken up by a tub, and there was an outdoor swimming pool in garden 2 in the Casa delle Nozze d'Argento (figure 5.15). In each of four complexes (in the Casa del Menandro, the Casa di Trebius Valens, the Casa delle Nozze d'Argento, and the Casa dei Giuseppe II), one room had an apse and was located closest to the heating device; hence, it was undoubtedly used

for a hot bath. Two of the rooms with apses also had recesses that had reputedly been used for a bath (figure 5.22), but only one actually had a metal tub. Another (room 8 in the Casa di Giuseppe II) had four small recesses reputedly for wooden seating. This latter room has been identified as a cold area, but it was of an architectural form similar to room 49 in the Casa del Menandro, which has been assumed, conversely, to have been a sweat room. The latter room contained truncated amphorae filled with building material and appears to have been out of use at the time of the eruption. Another amphora, recorded in room y in the Casa di Trebius Valens, was possibly used for carrying water. The only other such area with loose finds was area z' in the Casa di Giuseppe II; some of these finds could conceivably have been associated with ablutions (that is, a metal *patera* and a small glass bottle). The lack of baths and bathing equipment, despite the fact that the latter was reported in other areas of the houses in this sample, could imply that some of these complexes were not operative at the time of the eruption. On the other hand, bathers were likely to have carried their own bathing equipment with them and would not have left it in the bath area.

It should also be noted that bath complexes were located close to service areas. To enter the

Table 5.21 Bath areas

House	Room	Pools	Apses	Recesses	Basins/tubs	Amphorae	Personal items
Casa del Menandro	46	•					
	48		•	•			
	49					•	
Casa dell'Efebo	5				•		
Casa di Trebius Valens	q		•				
	y					•	
Casa delle Nozze d'Argento	t		•		•		
Casa di Giuseppe II	z'	•					•
	7		•	•			
	8		•				
House VIII 2,29–30	6	•					

Figure 5.20 Basin in room 5, Casa dell'Efebo. *ICCD - Ministero per i beni e le attività culturali, Roma, gabinetto fotografico neg. N57459*

Figure 5.21 View from southeast corner showing central pool (with modern cover), room 46, Casa del Menandro

baths in the Casa di Giuseppe II, for example, one would have had to pass through room 3, which contained an oven that seems also to have been used for bread making. In the Casa delle Nozze d'Argento, the pool was in an open area that seems to have acted as a service garden. This draws our attention to the much more public acts of ablutions and toilet in the Roman world than is traditional in most modern Western societies, even within these private baths.

Figure 5.22 Recess in north wall, room 48, Casa del Menandro

TYPE 22: UPPER FLOORS

Much of the material recorded as being from upper levels in the Pompeian excavations may well have been found above ground level because the deposit was disturbed. There are only a few houses in this sample where individual upper-floor rooms are actually identified (that is, in the Casa di Julius Polybius and the houses in Insula I 10). Even in these houses, however, some of the material is likely to have been from disturbed contexts. At the same time, some of the assemblages recorded in the other houses can be fairly securely attributed to upper-floor areas and possibly even to specific rooms (for example, the Casa dell'Efebo). In the following discussion, material attributable to individual rooms is first described and then compared with assemblages from less certain contexts.

Given the lack of evidence for actual rooms in the upper stories, fixtures were rarely recorded. Vertical ceramic drainpipes, recorded in the walls of ground-floor rooms, might be presumed to provide evidence of fixtures in the upper floor (figure 5.23). These were noted in fourteen locations in the sample. This number should by no means be taken, however, as the total of such fixtures in this sample, as many may not be visible, hidden behind plaster and wall masonry. These downpipes, therefore, are not included in table 5.22a. The Casa dell'Efebo appears to have had at least three downpipes (in rooms 2, 6, and 9), as did House VIII 5,9 (in rooms 1, 1a, and 1b). The room directly above room Z in the Casa di Julius Polybius had a cupboard under the stairs and a niche, reputedly a latrine (see Jansen 1997:125, Figs. 10.3–4). Evidence of a latrine was also recorded above room 2 of the Casa dell'Efebo. This evidence might contradict Sutherland's belief (1990:149–164, Figs. 60–61) that above rooms 2 and 3 there was a large room possibly used for dining. If downpipes provided evidence of upper-story niche latrines (see Jansen 1997:127), there would have been at least three latrines in the upper floor of the Casa dell'Efebo and in the front of House VIII 5,9. It seems more probable that downpipes found in ground-floor areas served a variety of

drainage functions, one of which may have been to carry away excess roof water (see Jansen 1991:158). A bathtub and bed were also recorded in upper-story rooms in the Casa dell'Efebo (table 5.22a).

Of the thirty upper-floor areas identified, sixteen to seventeen had evidence of amphorae and storage vessels. Such material was witnessed in all but one (that is, above stairway B) of the eleven upper-story rooms in the Casa di Julius Polybius. The less frequent recording of this material in the other houses may be related to less careful reporting of fragmentary material in earlier excavations. Nevertheless, the occurrence of such material in upper rooms suggests that storage was common in these areas, possibly of vessels containing foodstuffs but also conceivably of vessels for transportation of water. The transportation of amphorae to the upper floor has already been noted by their presence on stairways (room type 17).

More than two-thirds of these identifiable upper-floor rooms seem to have had cupboards

Figure 5.23 View of room 9 from south end showing cooking hearth and downpipe of amphora bodies, House I 10,8. *Pompeii photo archive neg. D103387*

Table 5.22a Upper-story rooms: fixtures and utilitarian material

House	Above area	Fixtures	Beds/tubs	Cupboards/chests	Amphorae/dolia	Utilitarian domestic	Clothworking*	Tools
Casa di Julius Polybius	A			•	•	•		
	B					•		
	D				•	•		
	E				•	•		
	M				•			
	Q			•	•			
	S,U,Y					•		
	Z	• (niche/cupboard)			•?	•		
	BB				•			
	CC			•	•	•		
	SS				•	•		
Casa del Fabbro	7			•		•?		•
	8				•			
	9			•				
	10			•	•	•		•
House I 10,8	7–10						•	
Casa degli Amanti	18				•	•		
Casa dei Quadretti Teatrali	a			•			•	
House I 6,8–9	b				•	•		
Casa di Stallius Eros	I 6, 14				•		•	
Casa del Sacerdos Amandus	a			•				
	g			•?				
Casa dell'Efebo	2	• (latrine)						
	4		•	•		•		
	9–10		•	•		•		
Casa dei Ceii	d				•			
Casa della Ara Massima	B			•				
	G			•				
Casa di M. Lucretius Fronto	7				•	•		
Casa dei Vettii	d and k			•	•	•		

* Includes spinning, weaving, and needlework

and chests and/or utilitarian domestic material. The latter consisted predominantly of unspecified bronze, glass, and ceramic vessels, some of which could have included tableware. It also included equipment for food preparation, weighing, and possibly painting. Clothworking implements were recorded in three areas. Thus, the upper-story rooms seem to have contained a range of utilitarian domestic material not dissimilar to that found in the lower rooms. Two picks were reported in the Casa del Fabbro but, in general, more utilitarian/industrial material was less evident here than in the lower parts of the house.

A certain amount of less utilitarian material was also reported in fifteen of these areas (table 5.22b). It consisted of a seemingly high proportion of lighting material (clay and bronze lamps, lanterns, and bronze lampstands) but also included tableware, statuary, and religious material (small altars and possibly shells). Seemingly personal, toilet, and pharmaceutical material was apparent, especially small glass bottles but also other small ceramic and glass vessels, mirrors, washing equipment, writing equipment, apparel, ornaments, jewelry, and surgical and personal hygiene implements. Ornaments included items identified as coming from a harness but which could also have been for human apparel (see chapter 4). Remains of luxury furniture (that is, marble tables and fittings from couches, chairs, and stools) were recorded in two of these areas. It should not be discounted, however, that the excavators were often looking for complete objects, and such small, light mate-

rial was more likely to have survived floor collapse than heavier items such as amphorae. With the possible exception of lighting material, these types of contents were recorded in smaller proportions in the Casa di Julius Polybius than in other houses. This situation, and the significant evidence for amphorae in this house, suggests that the use of upper floors varied among houses. For example, the area above room 7 in the Casa del Fabbro contained a collection of surgical and pharmaceutical material unparalleled elsewhere, but the assemblage also included considerable quantities of bronze tableware and material related to personal hygiene.

Similar patterns were observed for material found in upper levels that was less securely attributable to the upper floor (tables 5.22c–d). Such material was reported in twenty-two houses in the sample. While the presence of amphorae was again notable in the Casa di Julius Polybius, it was less evident in the other houses. Most evident were utilitarian domestic material, lighting equipment, and personal and toilet items. Fragments of luxury furniture and

Table 5.22b Upper-story rooms: luxury and personal material

House	Above area	Luxury furniture	Lighting	Tableware	Statuary/ religious	Personal*
Casa di Julius Polybius	D		•			
	E		•			
	CC		•			
	SS			•	•	
Casa del Fabbro	7			•		•
	9	•	•			•
	10			• ?		•
House I 10,8	7–10		•	•	•	
Casa dei Quadretti Teatrali	a		•			•
House I 6,8–9	b	•				
Casa di Stallius Eros	I 6,14		•			
Casa dell'Efebo	4			•	•	
Casa della Ara Massima	B		•	• ?		•
Casa dei Vettii	d and k		•			•
Casa delle Nozze d'Argento	7		•		•	•

* Includes toilet and pharmaceutical

Table 5.22c Upper levels: utilitarian material not safely attributable to upper-floor rooms

House and area	Above area	Cupboards/ chests	Storage vessels*	Utilitarian domestic	Clothworking**	Misc.
Casa di Julius Polybius	G		•			•
	I			•		
	L			•		
	O		•	•		
	FF		•	•		
	GG		•	•		
	HH		•	•		•
	N		•			
Casa della Venere in Bikini				•		
Casa del Menandro			•		•	•
Casa del Fabbro			•	•	•	•
Casa dei Quadretti Teatrali				•		
Casa di Stallius Eros					•	
Casa dell'Efebo		•		•		
House I 7,19		•			•	
Casa del Sacello Iliaco			• ?	• ?		
House VI 16,26				•		
Casa di M. Lucretius Fronto		•				•
Casa del Principe di Napoli- north			•			•
Casa del Principe di Napoli- south		•				
House VI 15,5–east		•				
House VI 15,5–north of front hall		•				
House VI 15,5–west			•			
Casa delle Nozze d'Argento			•	•		
House VIII 2,14–16				•		•
House VIII 2,34				•		

* Includes amphorae   ** Includes spinning, weaving, and needlework

miscellaneous material (for example, a tufa column, a hypocaust, a sundial, tools, weapons, and marble fragments) found in the upper levels were likely to have been disturbed from lower levels.

In general, therefore, upper-floor areas seem to have been used for similar activities as lower-floor areas, with perhaps less evidence of industrial and entertainment activities, and, at the other end of the scale, less display activities, but with notable evidence of personal activities. This observation may draw our attention to the prominence of separate, rented living quarters in such areas. At the same time, in the Casa di Julius Polybius, which had the most precise recording, storage activities were predominant in the upper rooms in the front area.

SUMMARY

Since the amount of information in the foregoing discussion may not be readily digestible, it

Table 5.22d Upper levels: luxury and personal material not safely attributable to upper-floor rooms

House and area	Above area	Luxury furniture	Lighting	Tableware	Statuary*	Personal / toilet
Casa di Julius Polybius	F					•
	FF			•		
	II					•
Casa della Venere in Bikini			•			
Casa del Menandro		•		•	•	• ?
Casa di Stallius Eros			•			
Casa dell'Efebo				•		•
Casa del Sacello Iliaco			•	• ?		•
House VI 16,26					•	•
Casa della Ara Massima		•				•
Casa degli Amorini Dorati		•			•	•
Casa di M. Lucretius Fronto			•			
Casa del Principe di Napoli - south				•		•
House VI 15,5–east						• ?
House VI 15,5–north of front hall			•	• ?		•
House VI 15,5–west			•	• ?		
Casa dei Vettii–north		•	•			•
Casa delle Nozze d'Argento			•			
House VIII 2,14–16		•				•
House VIII 2,28			•		•	• ?
Casa di Giuseppe II				•	•	
House VIII 2,34			•			•
House VIII 5,9			•			

* Includes religious items

seems appropriate to summarize the activities that appear to have been represented by the assemblages in each of these main areas of the house: front-hall area, main-garden area, other ground-floor areas, and upper floors.

Front-Hall Area

The distribution patterns suggest that front halls, while forming the stage for display and religious activities, were the centers around which many of the household activities revolved, with similar activities being carried out in the open rooms (type 5) to either side. The contents of the small, closed, and decorated rooms off these areas imply that these rooms were used for more private or personal domes-

tic activities, although the lack of definitive sleeping evidence suggests that they did not serve as bedrooms in the modern sense. The rooms to either side of the main entranceways (type 2) had fairly utilitarian/domestic functions, as did the small undecorated rooms off the front halls. The frequent occurrence of shelving in these small undecorated rooms off the front halls implies that they were used for storage, which could be utilitarian/domestic, both for bulk commodities and more specialized storage. With the possible exception of domestic storage, no clear pattern of activity was discernible in the larger closed rooms (type 6), suggesting that they lacked a distinctive function, at least at the time of the eruption. The prevalent pattern for rooms leading from the front hall to the garden (type 7) was of storage furniture for domestic materials, similar to the front halls themselves. Thus, there is ample evidence that the front areas of these houses were used for general domestic activities, both seemingly utilitarian and personal, as well as for the reception of visitors and a certain amount of more commercial activities. Notable domestic activities for which evidence was generally lacking in this area include food preparation and dining.

Main-Garden Area

The main-garden area, in general, must have been the most ostentatious part of a house. The opulence of the display presumably depended on the occupants' wealth and, perhaps, social status. Many of the smaller dwellings seem to have given over such display areas for more utilitarian purposes during the final occupation of the town, often after these areas had been decorated in the Third Style. Even in the houses with a wealth of display in the garden areas and with spacious and richly decorated banqueting rooms, utilitarian and everyday domestic activities were not excluded. Open gardens often seem to have been used as kitchen gardens rather than as purely formal display areas, as reconstructed in the Casa dei Vettii or the Casa degli Amorini Dorati (see, for example, Sogliano 1898a: Pl. 8; Jashemski 1979a: Figs. 56–57, 60). It seems that it was not improper to have latrines in these areas or to carry out ablutions and collect water here. Domestic storage and other household activities were undoubtedly carried out in the ambulatories and the surrounding rooms. Bulk storage could be found side by side with banqueting halls, and food preparation could be carried out in these areas, very possibly in front of the diners.

Other Ground-Floor Areas

The assemblages in the kitchen areas (room type 14) indicate food preparation but, as noted above, it is very probable that some cooking was carried out closer to the formal dining areas. It is therefore perhaps not quite accurate

to assume that these kitchen areas functioned as their counterparts in large nineteenth- and early twentieth-century European domestic establishments.

Other areas outside the main front-hall/garden complex seem to have been predominantly utilitarian. In some, however, personal and more luxury assemblages were also recorded. The activities witnessed in these areas, therefore, varied considerably. Where many of these areas included back entranceways and secondary courtyards, the activities in them and the goods that passed through them seem to have been associated with the domestic activities of the household, as well as any commercial/industrial activities of the establishment, and with repair work. Such activities emphasize the multiple character of these residential establishments in a pre-industrialized society. This particular sample showed a marked lack of evidence of commercial activity in the rooms opening on to the street (type 20).

Upper Floors

Evidence from upper-floor assemblages indicated activities similar to those in the lower floors, but with perhaps less sign of industrial activities and less entertainment or display. They suggest that the occupants used these spaces for routine domestic activities such as sleeping, eating, and possibly small, unpretentious gatherings. This pattern may indicate separate living quarters in such areas, even if a separate entranceway was not evident (compare Pirson 1997:175–178). The occupants of these quarters may have had more limited needs, or opportunities, than those in the larger house below and thus few ostentatious furnishings. They may also have carried out more industrial or commercial type activities elsewhere. Some upper-floor areas showed little evidence of habitation and seem to have been used for bulk storage.

CONCLUSIONS

Room contents have been employed as an indication of how the spaces in Pompeian houses functioned during the last years of the life of the town and also how they were likely to have functioned for much of their history. Patterns of fixtures and, less easily, movable fittings or of considerable collections of material, in particular, have been assessed for the information they provide on these conditions. As noted by Dell'Orto, movable furniture was not extensively used in Pompeian houses because many of the furnishings consisted of fixtures (1990: 171). The resulting patterns also give the impression that although there were areas of Pompeian houses that had formal and entertainment functions and were furbished to impress visitors, the Pompeians did not necessarily share the modern European obsession with hiding from these visitors the evidence of the day-to-day workings of a domestic and industrial establishment. Thus, there is no simple linear graph to represent the relationship among the public, private, and service areas of a house (see Wallace-Hadrill 1994, I: 11), as one might produce for a Georgian house or a nineteenth-century Italian villa (for example, Ames 1982:212–213).

NOTES

1. See Jameson (1990) on the use of space in Greek houses and anthropological studies such as David (1971: esp. 111).

2. Given the problems associated with the use of contemporary analogy, it is difficult to provide an English term for this space as it has no precise modern equivalent. In his translation of Vitruvius, Granger referred to these as "courtyards" (Vitruvius, transl. Granger:24). Lord Lytton (1834: chapter IIIA) referred to this part of the Pompeian house as the "hall." For the purposes of this study, I have chosen to label it the "front hall."

3. Berry (1997: esp. 185, 193) and Laurence (1997:11) seem to have misrepresented my analysis and interpretations (compare Allison 1994a:42–46). Berry's findings appear rather to corroborate my own, as noted by Wallace-Hadrill (1997:238).

4. Room i in the Casa dei Ceii conforms architecturally to this type but is defined here as room type 14. Room c could potentially have been included in this group, but it was considerably larger than most other rooms of this type and is therefore classified as type 6.

5. As outlined in chapter 3, these are not included in the database.

6. Room 45 in the Casa del Menandro is included in this group although, strictly speaking, it may have been altered and used for other purposes prior to the eruption.

7. The material reported in entranceway VIII 2,27 (Fiorelli 1860–64, III:69–71) is very similar to that reported from room v in House VIII 2,28 (Fiorelli 1860–64, II:160–164) and may well have been the same assemblage. If so, it has not been possible to verify the correct find spot for this collection.

Figure 6.1 Objects from chest against west wall in hall 41 (inv. nos 4960–65), Casa del Menandro.
(Bone container and lid are not part of this assemblage.)

6.

Distribution of Household Activities

THE DISCUSSION IN CHAPTER 5 showed that household activities, as documented by the contents of particular room types, were not always strictly segregated according to these structural and locational types and that many overlapped. It therefore seems appropriate to reassess these data, commencing from the standpoint of the activities themselves and examining their distribution across the sample and across room type. Thus, this chapter first presents the activities and discusses their spatial distribution throughout the house. Then, drawing on textual information about the performers of these household activities, the spatial patterning is investigated for insights into the interrelationships of the various groups of people using these spaces, particularly any evidence of segregation within Pompeian houses according to status, age, and gender.

Some of the activities likely to have taken place in Pompeian houses and to have left identifiable remains are introduced here along with their distribution. Certain artifacts and assemblages, however, could potentially document a number of activities. Also, the study deals largely with inorganic material, and therefore it is difficult to determine the actual function of, for example, empty vessels. This is particularly relevant to assessing storage patterns. It is often not possible to ascertain whether containers and utensils had been stored as commodities themselves, were used to store organic material, or were found in the location where their contents would have been used. Because the precise function of each artifact, if there indeed was one, could not always be determined, the results of this exploration may need to be modified after more detailed analysis has been carried out on the actual artifacts (Allison, n.d.).

FOOD PREPARATION

Evidence of food-preparation activities comes in three main forms: cooking and washing fixtures; movable cooking apparatus (for example, braziers and truncated amphorae); and various vessels likely to have been involved in food preparation. Large utilitarian bronze and ceramic vessels are the most likely cooking vessels (see figure 5.11). Smaller bowls, jugs, and jars were likely to have been used in food serving or food storage. Pestles and mortars are not discussed here unless they were associated with other food-preparation utensils, because such implements could have had a variety of functions.

Cooking hearths, which have been used to define rooms of type 14, are also not included in this discussion, as their spatial distribution has been dealt with in chapter 5. Table 6.1a lists other locations where artifact distribution appears to document food preparation. Of the twenty-eight possibilities, only five are in areas at the front of the house (that is, room types 1–7). Hall 41 in the Casa del Menandro was not actually in the front area. In the Casa delle Nozze d'Argento, the rooms off the main entranceway may have provided food for outside the house rather than inside. It is by no means certain that the fixtures in the south ambulatory of garden x in the Casa di Trebius Valens, in room b of the Casa delle Nozze d'Argento, or in room d of the Casa di Giuseppe II were used in food preparation. Large ovens that served bath complexes (in room D in the Casa del Menandro and in room 3 in the Casa di Giuseppe II) reputedly were also used for bread making and conceivably the preparation of other foodstuffs. Corridor 9 in House I 10,8 had been enlarged to accommodate

Table 6.1a Distribution of food-preparation activities, by room type

House	Room	2	3	6	7	8	9	10	11	12	13	16
Casa di Julius Polybius	SS					•						
	CC						•					
Casa del Menandro	c						•					
	18								•			
	24										•	
	41		•									
	C											•
	D											•
Casa del Fabbro	10						•					
House I 10,8	9					•						
Casa degli Amanti	9						•					
House I 7, 19	i									•		
Casa di Trebius Valens	x						• ?					
Casa dei Ceii	g									•		
	1										•	
House VI 16,26	G			•								
Casa di M. Lucretius Fronto	17									•		
	20									•		
Casa del Principe di Napoli	e				•							
	1						•					
Casa delle Nozze d'Argento	b	• ?										
	c	•										
	D					• ?						
Casa di Giuseppe II	d			•								
	3											•
	4											•
House VIII 5,9	g							•				
	h						•					

a cooking hearth (see figure 5.23), and food-preparation material found on the stairway in corridor SS of the Casa di Julius Polybius was likely to have been stored there, possibly in transit rather than for use in this location, although the latter is not impossible.

Aside from room type 14, then, the main evidence for activities related to food preparation was found in the garden itself (room type 9) and in small rooms off the garden (type 12). It is probable that the material found in rooms of type 12 had been stored there, handy to its place of use. Small, movable braziers were particu-larly evident in such rooms. Many rooms of type 14 were also near the garden area or the rear part of the house. Thus, most food preparation appears to have taken place in the garden area, including in the garden itself.

Table 6.1b includes those rooms that contained food-preparation utensils, most likely as stored items, particularly because many were found in cupboards. A cooking pot found in the entranceway of the Casa dei Quadretti Teatrali may have been stored in a cupboard that conceivably had fallen from the upper floor. Only one of the many vessels found in the cupboards

Table 6.1b Probable storage of food-preparation utensils, by room type

House	Room	1	3	4	10	12	16
Casa della Venere in Bikini	2		•				
	10				•		
Casa del Menandro	2			•			
	A						•
Casa del Fabbro	3		•				
House I 10,8	12					•	
Casa dei Quadretti Teatrali	a	•	• ?				
Casa dell'Efebo	18					•	
Casa dei Sacello Iliaco	b		• ?				
House VI 15,5	1				•		
Casa di M. Lucretius Fronto	14				• ?		
Casa delle Nozze d'Argento	m			•			

in the front hall of the Casa del Sacello Iliaco may have been used for cooking. Vessels stored in room 2 of the Casa del Menandro seem to have been tableware or serving vessels (figure 6.2). Some were burnt on the base, indicating that they had also been used in food preparation or food heating (figure 6.3). Although the evidence is limited, apparently there was not a pronounced preference for storing food-preparation material towards the rear of the house as there was for food-preparation activities. Such material, as part of the household wealth, may have been stored in the front area even if it was not used in this part of the house.

FOOD STORAGE

Given that organic remains were not generally recorded, food storage usually could not be verified, with limited exceptions (for example, in the Casa del Sacello Iliaco, hazelnuts under the stairway off room 1 and fish bones in a vessel from a cupboard in the front hall). While some of the amphorae recorded in this sample could have been used for water or commercial/industrial purposes, including distribution of foodstuffs outside the house, it is also probable that many of them, as well as other ceramic and glass storage jars, may have served as containers for

Figure 6.2 Four sizes of Pompeian Red Ware dishes (inv. nos 4268A, C, E, and O), found in room 2, Casa del Menandro

Figure 6.3 Pompeian Red Ware dishes showing burning on base (inv. nos 4268A and O), found in room 2, Casa del Menandro

foodstuffs (liquid and solid) for use within the household.

Up to seventy-eight ground-floor rooms in the sample had possible evidence of such food storage, both in the front (table 6.2a) and in the rear (table 6.2b) of the house. Eight houses had possible evidence of food storage in the upper floors, and three stairways supported evidence of what had conceivably been temporary food storage. Approximately two-thirds of the storage in the front part of the house was in the front hall itself and in the small closed and open rooms to either side. Many of the latter were undecorated rooms, although not exclusively.

Table 6.2a Front area of house: distribution of food storage activities, by room type

House	Room	1	2	3	4	5	6	7	14	16	19
Casa di Julius Polybius	H									• ?	
	O			•							
	D				•						
	P						•				
	Q				•						
	C										•
	N			•							
Casa della Venere in Bikini	7							•			
Casa del Fabbro	3			• ?							
	6				•						
Casa dei Quadretti Teatrali	a	•									
	b			• ?							
House I 6,8–9	c			•							
Casa dell'Efebo	A'			•							
	10						•				
	14				•						
Casa dei Ceii	i								•		
Casa del Sacello Iliaco	b			•							
	l				•						
	e					•					
	f							•			
House VI 16,26	B			• ?							
Casa della Ara Massima	F					•					
	G						•				
Casa del Principe di Napoli	a				•						
	b			•							
	g								•		
	h								•		
House VI 15,5	b			•							
	o or n				•						
Casa delle Nozze d'Argento	i						•				
	m				• ?						
	7					•					
House VIII 2,29–30	v		• ?								

Table 6.2b Rear and upper areas of house: distribution of food storage activities, by room type

House	Room	3	8	9	11	12	14	16	17	18	19	20	22
Casa di Julius Polybius	BB					•							
	EE				•?								
	GG				•								
	A'												•
	D'												•
	E'												•
	M'												•
	Q'												•
	BB'												•
	SS'												•?
Casa del Menandro	c			•									
	11				•								
	14					•							
	A							•?					
	L		•										
	34										•		
	38							•?					
	41	•						•?					
	42											•	
	44									•			
Casa del Fabbro	12			•									
	UF*												•
House I 10,8	11			•									
	12					•							
	13							•?					
Casa degli Amanti	3								•				
	9			•									
	16						•						
	UF												•
House I 6, 8–9	i			•									
	UF												•
Casa di Stallius Eros	UF												•
Casa del Sacerdos Amandus	ST								•				
	P					•							
Casa dell'Efebo	18					•							
	23			•									
Casa dei Ceii	n							•					
	UF												•
Casa del Sacello Iliaco	UF												•?
House VI 16, 26	M			•									
Casa degli Amorini Dorati	P									•			

Continued on next page

Table 6.2b Rear and upper areas of house: distribution of food storage activities, by room type (continued)

House	Room	3	8	9	11	12	14	16	17	18	19	20	22
Casa di M. Lucretius Fronto	18/21						•						
House VI 15, 5	2										•		
	5							•					
Casa dei Vettii	o					•							
	s									• ?			
	UF												•
Casa delle Nozze d'Argento	r			•									
	2									•			
	A		•										
	B										• ?		
	E							•					
	G									•			
	I								•				
House VIII 2, 26	VIII,2 27										• ?		
House VIII 5,9	o						•						
	b							•					

* UF = upper levels

While this evidence in the front-hall areas generally consisted of vessels stored away in cupboards, that in House VI 16,26 may have been associated with a *lararium*. In the rear of the house, the ambulatories of the garden seem to have been one of the main areas for food storage, as was the case also with the small, undecorated closed rooms off them (type 12) and possibly other presumed service rooms away from the garden area (type 16). Amphorae recorded in rooms of type 16, however, may often have been associated with building activity or bulk storage unrelated to normal household consumption.

Vessels with food contents found in a *cisternola* in corridor L of the Casa del Menandro may have been stored for household consumption or placed as ritual offerings. Some of the large storage vessels found in garden and secondary courtyard areas (for example, garden M of House VI 16,26; see figure 5.9) were possibly for the processing of agricultural produce (for example, wine and oil). Others (for example, in courtyard B of the Casa delle Nozze d'Argento or courtyard 34 of the Casa del Menandro; see figure 5.18) may have been for produce in the process either of transportation into the house or

of distribution outside. Some such vessels, however, may have been for building or fertilization processes (for example, those filled with lime).

It is not possible to ascertain whether certain bulk storage, as evidenced by the presence of amphorae and other large storage vessels, was for foodstuffs. Nor was it possible to ascertain whether it was for household use or use outside the house (for example, in the area of hall O of the Casa di Julius Polybius, in the front halls of House I 6,8–9, the Casa dei Vettii, House VIII 2,28, the Casa di Giuseppe II, in room E of the Casa delle Nozze d'Argento, and room m of House VIII 5,9). In addition, some of these collections of vessels may represent evidence of food storage associated with disrupted conditions leading up to or during the final eruption (for example, in room EE in the Casa di Julius Polybius and in room 11 in the Casa del Menandro). What is perhaps significant is that there was more evidence in the front area of the house for food storage than for food preparation. Food storage in the main courtyard areas of the house might conceivably be related to the role of certain foodstuffs as part of the household wealth.

FOOD CONSUMPTION

Dining furniture and tableware are the most likely evidence for food consumption. Fixed couches, or possible evidence of remains of movable ones, may indicate areas that had been used for the serving and consumption of food and drink. This furniture was predominant in room type 7, leading through to the garden; in the open garden area itself; and in room type 11, off the garden area (table 6.3). A relatively high

Table 6.3 Distribution of serving and consumption of food and drink, by room type

House	Room	6	7	9	10	11	14
Casa di Julius Polybius	Nk						•
	EE					•	
	HH					•	
Casa della Venere in Bikini	9						•?
Casa del Menandro	8		•				
	c			•			
	15					•?	
	18					•?	
Casa dell Fabbro	9					•	
	11						•
	12			•			
Casa degli Amanti	10				•?		
Casa dei Quadretti Teatrali	15					•?	
House I 6, 8–9	d		•				
Casa del Sacerdos Amandus	i						•
Casa dell'Efebo	4		•				
	8						•
	10	•					
	15		•?				
	23			•?			
	17					•	
Casa di Trebius Valens	x			•			
Casa dei Ceii	i						•?
Casa del Sacello Iliaco	c	•					
	f		•				
House VI 16, 26	G	•					
Casa degli Amorini Dorati	G					•?	
Casa di M. Lucretius Fronto	13					•	
	14				•?		
Casa del Principe di Napoli	g						•?
House VI 15, 5	u			•			
Casa dei Vettii	w						•?
Casa delle Nozze d'Argento	s						•?
	5			•			
	H						•?
House VIII 5, 9	d						•?

proportion of examples was recorded in room type 7. Only two type 6 rooms, assumed to have been dining rooms, contained any possible evidence for couches, one of which had been undergoing repair (in room c in the Casa del Sacello Iliaco). Only one of this type (room 10 in the Casa dell'Efebo) had possible evidence of tableware.

If the presence of couches indeed indicated the location of eating and drinking activities, in this sample open areas towards the back of the houses (for example, figure 6.4) were preferred for serving and consumption, at least at the time of year when Pompeii was buried, generally accepted to have been summer. A number of beds or couches were found in rooms of type 4 and one in a room of type 5 (room r in House I 7,19), which are dealt with below under "Sleeping," but it is not impossible that the consumption of food and drink had taken place on them. Otherwise, there was no evidence of food consumption in the front part of the house.

Vessels likely to indicate the serving and consumption of food take the form of bronze, ceramic (particularly *terra sigillata*), and possibly glass tableware, and serving containers such as jugs. These items include vessels used for hand washing before eating (see Nuber 1972:83–90, 117–118, Pls. 20.2, 29). It is by no means established that all these vessel types were necessarily associated with food consumption (see Allison 1999b:66–67). None of the couches in garden areas were directly associated with any of these types of vessels, but this may not be surprising. Of the nine possible examples of type 10 and 11 rooms with evidence of couches, four had possible evidence of associated serving vessels and tableware. Some of the vessels found in room type 14, the kitchen area, appear to have been serving vessels or tableware. It is not possible to ascertain whether they were used or stored in this location.

STORAGE OF MATERIAL FOR FOOD CONSUMPTION

Many of the examples of tableware and serving vessels were indeed probably recorded in their place of storage rather than in their place of use (for example, in cupboards). Apparent storage of this material occurred predominantly in the front hall, in undecorated examples of room type 4, in room type 12, and some examples in room type 16 (table 6.4). Food-consumption

Figure 6.4 Reconstructed couches along west and north walls, room 17, Casa dell'Efebo

Table 6.4 Storage of tableware and serving vessels, by room type

House	Room	1	3	4	6	7	8	9	11	12	14	16	18	20	22
Casa di Julius Polybius	A												•?		
	H											•			
	SS						•?								
	Z				•										
	CC							•							
	AA									•?					
	EE								•?						
	A'														•?
	S',U'–Y'														•?
	SS'														•?
	FF'														•
Casa della Venere in Bikini	2		•												
Casa del Menandro	2			•											
	B											•			
	40											•			
	41		•												
	42													•	
	43			•											
	UF														•
Casa del Fabbro	3		•?												
	UF*(7)														•
	UF(10)														•?
House I 10, 8	12									•					
	UF(7–10)														•
Casa degli Amanti	17									•					
Casa dei Quadretti Teatrali	b		•												
	10									•					
Casa dell'Efebo	1'	•?													
	13					•									
	14			•											
	UF(4)														•
	UF(9/10)														•?
	UF														•
Casa di Trebius Valens	a		•?												
	u									•					
Casa dei Ceii	g									•					
	n											•			
Casa del Sacello Iliaco	b		•												
	UF														•
House VI 16,26	C			•											
Casa della Ara Massima	E			•?											
	UF(B)														•?
Casa di M. Lucretius Fronto	2		•?												

Continued on next page

Table 6.4 Storage of tableware and serving vessels, by room type (continued)

House	Room	1	3	4	6	7	8	9	11	12	14	16	18	20	22
Casa del Principe di Napoli	b		• ?												
	h										•				
	UF														•
House VI 15, 5	b		• ?												
	UF														• ?
Casa delle Nozze d'Argento	m			•											
	E											•			
Casa di Giuseppe II	i'									•					
	UF														•
House VIII 2, 34	c		•												
House VIII 5, 9	f				•										

UF = upper levels

material found in room 43 in the Casa del Menandro was part of a very mixed assemblage that hints at hoarding during disrupted conditions. Otherwise, this material was not found in decorated examples of room type 4. Likewise, in room EE in the Casa di Julius Polybius (figure 1.3), it is unclear whether the vessels were in their place of use or storage, or whether this would have been relatively permanent storage or temporary storage during disruption. Such vessels were often reported also in upper-floor contexts, but it is uncertain if this material had been used or stored in these locations. Generally, it was not found in contexts that could be easily assigned to an upper-floor room. Only in the area above room 4 of the Casa dell'Efebo were such vessels associated with a bed or couch. Considerable quantities of *terra sigillata* cups and lamps were reported in room f of House VIII 5,9, but this storage seems to have been related to commercial activity rather than to domestic storage.

Again, despite the lack of evidence of actual food consumption in the front part of the house, utensils for such consumption seem to have been stored in this area. Interestingly, this material does not seem to have been very prominent in the ambulatories of the garden areas. As for the storage of foodstuffs and food-preparation materials in the front area, this storage pattern may be related to the role of this material as a household asset and may also demonstrate a need to maintain its visibility so that it could be accounted for.

SLEEPING

The principal finds correlated with sleeping are, again, any evidence for bedding or couches. As discussed in chapter 4, recesses have not been considered as evidence of sleeping as they were likely to have had more widespread uses. Table 6.5 includes all possible examples of bedding, mainly in the form of the remains of beds and couches, including those already discussed as possible indications of food consumption (table 6.3). There were thirty-three rooms with sleeping evidence. The greatest numbers of these furnishings were in room types 10 and 11, but there was also a notable presence in room types 4 and 7 and conceivably in some of the upper floors. Given the large number of rooms of type 4, however, evidence of bedding was recorded in only a relatively small proportion. Examples of possible bed fittings were found in other contexts (for example, in room c of the Casa del Sacello Iliaco and room 15 of the Casa dell'Efebo), but these were likely to have been hoarded during disruption. Generally speaking, aside from the pattern in rooms of type 11,

Table 6.5 Distribution of possible evidence for sleeping, by room type

House	Room	4	5	6	7	10	11	12	22
Casa di Julius Polybius	UU	•							
	EE						•		
	HH						•		
	II							•?	
Casa del Menandro	8				•				
	15						•		
	18						•		
	43	•							
	UF								•
Casa del Fabbro	8						•		
	9						•?		
	UF*(9)								•?
House I 10, 8	6	•							
	10						•?		
Casa degli Amanti	10					•?			
Casa dei Quadretti Teatrali	15						•?		
House I 6, 8–9	d				•				
	UF(b)								•
Casa dell'Efebo	4				•				
	15				•				
	17						•		
	UF(4)								•
House I 7, 19	a	•							
	r		•						
Casa del Sacello Iliaco	c			•?					
	d	•							
	1	•							
	f				•				
House VI 16, 26	G			•					
Casa di M. Lucretius Fronto	13						•		
	14					•?			
Casa dei Vettii	g	•?							
Casa di Giuseppe II	i'							•?	

UF = upper levels

which is assumed to have been evidence of dining, there does not appear to have been one particularly dominant pattern for the choice of sleeping area. It is conceivable that sleeping may have taken place in various parts of the house, distributed between front and back areas, and possibly related to gender, age, status, and season.

Ablutions and Personal Hygiene

Much of the evidence for ablutions in Pompeian houses is in the form of fixtures such as latrines, basins and pools, and bath complexes, as well as ceramic downpipes that may have been connected to latrines or ablution areas on the upper floor. Some thirty-three latrines were recorded on the ground and lower floors in this sample (table 6.6a). Of these, twelve to thirteen were near the front of the house, predominantly in kitchens but also in corridors or as separate rooms off kitchens. It does not seem uncommon to have had latrines in kitchens that opened directly off a front hall (for example, room 8 in the Casa dell'Efebo, room g in the Casa del Principe di Napoli, room i in the Casa dei Ceii [see figure 5.12], and room s1 in the Casa delle Nozze d'Argento [see figure 5.13]). Other latrines were found in kitchens and small closed rooms off the garden area, as well as in areas away from the main front-hall/garden axis and in the upper floors. It would seem that such facilities were evenly spread throughout the house. Other areas undoubtedly for personal ablutions were pools and bath complexes

Table 6.6a Distribution of latrines and downpipes, by room type and areas*

House	Room	8	14F	15F	12G	14G	15G	14O	15O	16O	22
Casa di Julius Polybius	Z'										•
Casa della Venere in Bikini	9							•			
Casa del Menandro	45							• ?			
	51	•									
	C									•	
House I 10,8	14	•									
	UF(9)										•
	UF(14)										•
Casa degli Amanti	14						•				
Casa dei Quadretti Teatrali	9			•							
House I 6, 8–9	h				• ?						
	e'						•				
Casa di Stallius Eros	UF(f)										•
	10									•	
	12				•						
Casa del Sacerdos Amandus	h		•								
Casa dell'Efebo	8		•								
	21					•					
	UF(2)										•
Casa dei Trebius Valens	i		•								
Casa dei Ceii	i		•								
Casa del Sacello Iliaco	n					•					
House VI 16, 26	Z							•			
Casa degli Amorini Dorati	K				•						
	Y	•									
Casa della Ara Massima	L									•	

Continued on next page

Table 6.6a Distribution of latrines and downpipes, by room type and areas* (continued)

House	Room	8	14F	15F	12G	14G	15G	14O	15O	16O	22
Casa di M. Lucretius Fronto	21					•					
Casa del Principe di Napoli	g		•								
House VI 15, 5	q								•		
Casa dei Vettii	1						•				
Casa delle Nozze d'Argento	s1						•				
	H							•			
House VIII 2, 26	f		•?								
	2							•			
House VIII 2, 28	f			•							
Casa di Giuseppe II	d'		•								
House VIII 2, 34	t			•							
	v									•	
House VII 2, 29–30	10							•			
	13							•			
House VIII 5, 9	k						•				
	UF(1a)										•
	UF(1b)										•

* F = front, G = garden, O = other, UF = upper levels

(room type 21). As discussed in chapter 5 (see table 5.21), there was no direct connection between these and latrines, the latter being most often associated with kitchen areas. This association might have been made because of drainage systems, but it would have had considerable impact on social practice. The vat in room a' of House VIII 2,29–30 could conceivably have been used for personal ablutions, although the excavator believed it had an industrial purpose.

Loose finds that were likely to have been related to personal ablutions consisted of possible toiletries and washing equipment (for example, mirrors, combs, tweezer, strigils, basins and *forme di pasticceria*, and small glass bottles; see figure 6.5). Many examples of small bottles and *forme di pasticceria* are not included in table 6.6b because it was not possible to assess their likely functions unless they were recorded in association with other personal hygiene material (Allison 1999b:66–67).

Figure 6.5 Personal items found in room 37 (inv. nos 4918–19, 4921, 4923–24), Casa del Menandro

Table 6.6b Distribution of loose items possibly associated with personal hygiene, by room type

House	Room	3	4	7	9	11	12	13	16	22
Casa di Julius Polybius	EE					•?				
Casa della Venere in Bikini	2	•								
Casa del Menandro	B								•?	
	37								•	
	38								•	
	41	•								
Casa del Fabbro	3	•								
	5		•							
	UF*(7)									•
	UF(9)									•?
	UF(10)									•?
House I 10, 8	3		•?							
	12						•?			
Casa degli Amanti	9				•?					
	19						•?			
Casa dei Quadretti Teatrali	14						•			
	UF(a)									•?
Casa dell'Efebo	11		•							
Casa del Sacello Iliaco	1		•?							
Casa dei Ceii	b	•?								
	f						•			
Casa di Trebius Valens	u						•			
House VI 16, 26	U								•	
	X								•	
Casa degli Amorini Dorati	J						•			
	L						•			
Casa della Ara Massima	L								•?	
	UF									•?
Casa del Principe di Napoli	m							•?		
	UF									•?
House VI 15, 5	b	•								
	o		•							
Casa dei Vettii	UF									•?
Casa delle Nozze d'Argento	m		•							
	E or F								•	
House VIII 2, 34	UF(m')									•?
House VIII 2, 29–30	q			•						

* UF = upper levels

Items of these types found in room type 3 had generally been stored in cupboards. Strigils from hall 41 of the Casa del Menandro were possibly on a shelf, but the assemblage in this room was very mixed. There were prominent patterns of ablutions and personal hygiene material in both decorated and undecorated small closed rooms off both the front hall and the garden area and in small rooms away from the main front-hall/garden axis. In general, such material was not found in open areas. It is notable also that this material was not found near areas with fixtures for ablutions or for the collection of water, such as in the garden area. This suggests that water for personal hygiene was brought into the rooms in which this material was found or that the material was stored away in those areas and taken out to appropriate areas for performing ablutions. This type of material appears to have been frequent in the upper levels. Thus, as with the distribution of latrines, there was no apparent restriction of personal ablutions to a particular part of the house. While it has always been assumed that basins found in the front area were for display purposes, they may also have held water for ablutions. After all, many wellheads that would have been used to supply household water were located in the front hall.

LUXURY AND LEISURE

Without preconceptions about what constitutes luxury, prestige, and leisure activities in a Pompeian house (see Wallace-Hadrill 1994:141–147), it is difficult to assess what material would have been associated with these activities. In many ways it may be inappropriate to separate out any such material in this context. For example, many pieces of luxury furniture and vessels were associated with eating and drinking and cannot be easily separated from that category. Therefore, this discussion concerns material that might be classified as having served primarily for display purposes rather than more seemingly functional prestige material, such as that used for lighting or dining.

Table 6.7a therefore includes predominantly large-scale sculpture and furniture, particularly that made of sculpted marble (for example, tables, large-scale statuary, and fountain fittings), and fixtures (for example, marble bases and stands) that had no apparent utilitarian function or whose display qualities seem to surpass any such function. It also includes collections of smaller-scale sculpture that seem to have had a similar display function as larger pieces (for example, in garden r of the Casa delle Nozze d'Argento and garden u of House VI 15,5). It also includes some larger bronze vessels (for example, large decorated bronze basins or *labra*). However, it does not include other luxury, but essentially serviceable, items such as folding bronze tables, beds or couches with bronze and silvered fittings, elaborate lampstands, decorated silver and bronze vessels, or silver trays supported by bronze statuettes (as found in room 13 of the Casa dell'Efebo). The separation of this material, particularly the sculpture, from material classed as religious may also be inappropriate. For example, did the placement of a herm in a semicircular niche in garden 12 of the Casa del Fabbro constitute religious behavior when, as demonstrated in chapter 4, one should not assume that all niches in Pompeian houses had a religious purpose? Bartmann argued that, while sculptural display in the domestic setting can be seen as "an allusion to paradisiacal afterlife" (1991:74), it embodied the Roman concept of decor, which she believed had a more secular function, namely, to demonstrate the owners' cultural and political status.

Most display material was recorded in open areas: the front halls and the gardens. Because much of the material found in the other room types was in a fragmentary condition, it may have been stored there, possibly salvaged during disrupted circumstances. Possible exceptions were a table found in room G of the Casa della Ara Massima and a statue in room EE in the Casa di Julius Polybius (figure 1.3), but even this more complete material may have been salvaged from elsewhere in these houses. None of the material of this kind in upper levels was found in identifiable rooms, and it is likely that it had been disturbed after the eruption. Thus, display of luxury and prestige goods undoubtedly took place in

Table 6.7a Distribution of large scale display material, by room type

House	Room	3	4	6	7	9	11	14	16	17
Casa di Julius Polybius	EE						•			
Casa della Venere in Bikini	2	•								
	7				•					
Casa del Menandro	b	•								
	8				•					
	41	•								
Casa del Fabbro	3	•								
	12					•?				
Casa del Sacerdos Amandus	m					•				
Casa dell'Efebo	A"	•								
	15				•					
	17						•			
	23					•				
House I 7, 19	p	•								
Casa di Trebius Valens	a	•?								
	d			•						
	x					•				
Casa dei Ceii	b	•								
	i							•		
House VI 16, 26	B	•								
Casa della Ara Massima	G			•						
	I			•						
Casa degli Amorini Dorati	F					•				
	Y								•	
Casa di M. Lucretius Fronto	2	•								
House VI 15, 5	u					•				
Casa dei Vettii	m					•				
	r						•			
	w							•		
Casa delle Nozze d'Argento	d	•								
	r					•				
House VIII 2, 28	r		•							
	k									•
Casa di Giuseppe II	b	•								

open areas. At the same time, the assemblages in many houses in the sample did not include such prestige material.

Table 6.7b includes smaller-scale material that was likely to have been for luxury and prestige of a more personal kind. This applies partic-ularly to jewelry, stamp seals, and toiletry items whose description suggests that they were prestigious. Many of the reports of jewelry consisted of isolated glass beads. It is quite possible that these, and individual pieces of bronze jewelry (for example, bracelets), could have been lost

Table 6.7b Distribution of personal luxury and prestige material, by room type

House	Room	2	3	4	5	6	7	9	10	11	12	16	17	19	22
Casa di Julius Polybius	Z					• ?									
	CC							•							
Casa della Venere in Bikini	2		•												
	10								•						
Casa del Menandro	1			•											
	B											•			
	35											•			
Casa del Fabbro	3		•												
	10							•							
	UF(7)														•
House I 10, 8	10									• ?					
Casa dei Quadretti Teatrali	b		•												
	12–13							• ?							
Casa dell'Efebo	14			•											
	20												•		
House I 7, 19	a			•											
Casa di Trebius Valens	e			•											
Casa dei Ceii	f										• ?				
Casa del Sacello Iliaco	f						•								
House VI 16, 26	E					•									
Casa della Ara Massima	F				•										
Casa degli Amorini Dorati	G								•						
House VI 15, 5	p	•													
	n or o			•											
Casa dei Vettii	c		•												
	4										•				
	UF(d/k)														•
Casa delle Nozze d'Argento	n								•						
	D or F										• ?				
House VIII 2, 26	VIII 2,27													• ?	
House VIII 2,28	r			•											
	v										• ?				
	k												•		
Casa di Giuseppe II	c			•											

items and their distribution haphazard. Such items are included in the table only if more than one was recorded, or if they were in assemblages that suggested they had not been individually lost. Pieces of jewelry or prestige goods evidently associated with victims of the eruption are also not included. Similarly, isolated finds in upper levels that could be provenanced to a particular room have not been included. Given observations (for example, Mouritsen 1988:14) that a large proportion of stamp seals bore the names of freedmen or servants, these seals might not seem to have been luxury or prestige items. However, they are classified as such here as they were items that would have been carefully guarded as valuable and may have signified status of a predominantly commercial nature.

Despite the material excluded, small-scale luxury material seems to have been distributed quite widely throughout the house. In the front part of the house, such material appeared predominantly in cupboards in the front hall and in rooms of type 4. In the other parts of the house, it was scattered through a range of room types. Many of the finds in the latter seem to have been in assemblages that could be considered hoards (for example, in room B in the Casa del Menandro). Other examples may have been in assemblages that were dropped during abandonment of the house. Nevertheless, as this material consists mainly of jewelry and luxury toilet objects that are traditionally associated with élite women, its wide distribution might support a lack of segregation along gender lines, particularly among the free members of these households. If anything, it occurs more frequently in closed rooms around the front hall (type 4) or away from the main house axis (type 16; see figure 4.18) than in those around the garden area (type 12).

Table 6.7c includes material that might be associated with leisure, such as gaming and musical equipment. Items associated with gaming include dice, knucklebones, and small buttons or counters. So-called *fritilli* are not included, as their link with such a specific activity is somewhat spurious (see chapter 4). Musical instruments appear to have consisted of parts of wind instruments and cymbals. The distribution of leisure material suggests that it was concentrated around the front area of the house, particularly in cupboards in the front hall and in room types 4 and 7. It also occurred in cupboards and chests, in what appear to have been storerooms, and in other parts of the house. As might be expected, such material was usually found in its place of storage, sometimes in collections seemingly hoarded during disruption (for example,

Table 6.7c Distribution of leisure material, by room type

House	Room	3	4	7	9	10	12	16	22
Casa di Julius Polybius	M		•						
	CC				•				
Casa della Venere in Bikini	2	•							
	10					•			
Casa del Menandro	1		•						
Casa del Fabbro	3	•							
	10				• ?				
House I 10, 8	12						•		
Casa dei Quadretti Teatrali	b	•							
	12–13				• ?				
Casa dell'Efebo	13			•					
Casa del Sacello Iliaco	b	• ?							
	h		• ?						
House VI 16, 26	C		•						
	L			•					
Casa della Ara Massima	UF(A)								•
House VI 15, 5	o or n		•						
Casa dei Vettii	4							•	
House VIII 5, 9	b							• ?	

in room 4 in the Casa dei Vettii). Thus, the distribution pattern for this material does not reveal much about where leisure activities took place. However, gaming material was notably found in small containers in association with toiletry or jewelry items (for example, in room 10 in the Casa del Fabbro and in area 12–13 in the Casa dei Quadretti Teatrali) and found to be concentrated around the front-hall area.

RELIGIOUS ACTIVITIES

Identifying material culture associated with religious activities is a complex issue. Some material of religious or symbolic significance, or used in religious activities, can be indistinguishable from items in other categories. Tables 6.8a and 6.8b therefore include material identified as primarily of religious significance or function rather than as part of a prestigious display or another, more utilitarian, function. Material that might have been associated with religious activities consists of both fixtures and loose finds.

Fixtures include aediculae (household shrines), *lararium* paintings, and semicircular niches painted with scenes related to the Lares (see Boyce 1937; Fröhlich 1991; for further references: Orr 1988). Niches lacking such paintings or association with seemingly religious paraphernalia are not included here (see chapter 4). Aediculae were invariably located in courtyard areas and the open areas off courtyards, conforming to the

Table 6.8a Distribution of fixtures associated with religious activities, by room type

House	Room	3	4	9	11	12	13	14	18	20
Casa di Julius Polybius	N	•								
Casa del Menandro	b	•								
	25						•			
	42									•
	45							•		
	52							•		
Casa del Fabbro	9				•					
	11							•		
Casa degli Amanti	16							•		
Casa dell'Efebo	A'	•								
	19			•						
House I 7, 19	g			•						
House VI 16, 26	B	•								
Casa degli Amorini Dorati	F			•						
Casa di M. Lucretius Fronto	18							•		
Casa del Principe di Napoli	n			•						
House VI 15, 5	b	•								
	u			•						
Casa dei Vettii	v								•	
Casa delle Nozze d'Argento	k					•				
	s							•		
House VIII 2, 14–16	d		•							
House VIII 2, 28	d	•								
Casa di Giuseppe II	c		• ?							
House VIII 2, 29–30	k'	•								

Table 6.8b Distribution of loose finds potentially associated with religious activities, by room type

House	Room	3	4	5	6	8	9	12	14	16	22
Casa di Julius Polybius	CC						• ?				
	SS'										•
Casa della Venere in Bikini	2	• ?									
Casa del Menandro	1		• ?								
	35									•	
	41	•									
House I 10,8	3		• ?								
	UF(7–10)										• ?
Casa degli Amanti	2		•								
Casa dei Quadretti Teatrali	b	•									
Casa dell'Efebo	2		• ?								
	23						• ?				
	UF(4)										•
House I 7, 19	g						•				
Casa di Trebius Valens	u							•			
Casa dei Ceii	b	•									
	n								•		
Casa del Sacello Iliaco	c				•						
House VI 16, 26	B	•									
	K					•					
	Z								•		
Casa di M. Lucretius Fronto	20							•			
House VI 15, 5	b	• ?									
Casa delle Nozze d'Argento	r						•				
House VIII 2, 14–16	cc			•							
Casa di Giuseppe II	c		•								

perceived need for *lararia* to be open to the air (Orr 1988:294–295) and to their association with communal or household ritual. One aedicula was located in a closed room (room d in House VIII 2,14–16). Otherwise, any presumed religious fixtures located away from open areas consisted of *lararium* niches and *lararium* paintings. The latter tended to be located in kitchens or immediately outside kitchen areas (for example, in hall N in the Casa di Julius Polybius and front hall A' in the Casa dell'Efebo). The exception is the one in the front hall B in House VI 16,26. The locations of these paintings has been taken to emphasize a relationship between food and religion (see Foss 1994:43–45). They were re-

corded in only six kitchens across the sample (see chapter 5). It has also been assumed (for example, Foss 1994:45; George 1997a:316–317) that these *lararia* served a different purpose from the aediculae and addressed the religious needs of a different group of householders (that is, slaves and servants). With the exception of the relatively large Casa del Menandro and Casa dell'Efebo, however, the paintings tended to be reported in houses without aediculae.

Portable material that could conceivably be associated with religious activities includes movable altars, as well as seashells and statuettes. It might also include animal parts, such as boars' teeth[1] and deer antlers, as found in a cup-

Figure 6.6 East ambulatory of garden F with shrine area at south end, Casa degli Amorini Dorati

Figure 6.7 Shrine against west wall with plaster casts of three busts and a head, room 25, Casa del Menandro

board in the front hall of the Casa della Venere in Bikini, room 1 in the Casa del Menandro, and in corridor K of House VI 16,26. Material from upper levels, but not from an identifiable context, is not included in the table.

Large-scale sculpture appears to have been used primarily for prestige display. It seems less probable that much of the small-scale sculpture found in these houses would have played a similar role in the decor of the house. Indeed, in addition to Lares, and heads and busts assumed to have been ancestral portraits, one of the shrines in the garden of the Casa degli Amorini Dorati contained statuettes of Jupiter, Juno, Minerva, and Mercury and the other contained an Egyptian statuette and a statuette of Fortuna (figure

6.6). The shrine in room 25 of the Casa del Menandro contained a wooden statuette of a young seated male, believed by Maiuri to have been a deity or to have represented a *genius* (Maiuri 1933:102; figure 6.7). Statuettes included in table 6.8b tend to be those identified as a particular deity or found in association with other seemingly religious paraphernalia. The general distinction between the function of large-scale statuary as display and small-scale statuary as religious is obviously rather imprecise (see George 1998:87). A statuette seemingly associated with a fountain in the garden of the Casa dell'Efebo, for example, undoubtedly formed part of the garden display but might also have had symbolic significance.

Skeates has argued (1991) that the conch shell (*Charonia nodifera* or *Charonia sequenzae*) has a long history in southern Italy as a trumpet for religious use. Not all the shells included in table 6.8b are of this type. However, as other types of shells were found in association with this particular type (for example, in hall 41 in the Casa del Menandro; see figure 4.17), it seems possible that the collection of this material may have had some symbolic significance. The association of boars' teeth (or tusks) and deer antlers with religious activities also seems tenuous. Although it is conceivable that this material may have been collected for bone working, the assemblages in which it was found suggest that it was more probably some type of keepsake. There is evidence, in Spain and possibly in Italy, that such tusks and antlers had been given as dedications to Diana.[2]

Other objects with possible religious significance have not been included in table 6.8b (for example, lamps and vessels containing food, such as were found in room 22 and in the *cisternola* under corridor L of the Casa del Menandro) because it was not always possible to separate such material from the same types of objects that had more utilitarian functions. Such material was included only when it was found with an altar in the proximity of the *lararium* painting in the front hall of House VI 16,26 and in an aedicula in the front hall of House VI 15,5 (see figure 4.6).

In general, the distribution of this portable material follows a vaguely similar pattern to that of the religious fixtures, occurring most frequently in open areas. This material may sometimes have been stored in such locations, however. The statue of Apollo, for example, found in the front hall of the Casa dei Quadretti Teatrali had been placed in a cupboard. There is also a notable pattern for such material being located in small closed rooms, especially room type 4, and in the upper floor, but not in kitchen areas.

HOUSEHOLD PRODUCTION

Household production includes evidence of production activities or of bulk storage of this production, either for household use or for dis-tribution outside the dwelling (for example, preserving of horticultural produce). Evidence for food preparation associated with immediate consumption within the household is not included here because it has already been discussed earlier in this chapter.

An industry that seems to have been important to the household is cloth production. Evidence occurred in the form of material used in weaving (for example, loomweights), spinning, needlework, and dyeing. It is not always clear whether particular weights were in fact loomweights or used for weighing generally. Numbered weights (for example, in room m of the Casa dei Ceii) could have been used either for weaving or for weighing. According to John Paul Wild (1970:63 n. 1), loomweights were inscribed with their value because knowledge of their weight was important for balancing the loom. Uses of these weights may also have been interchangeable. Amphorae, reputedly for collecting urine for processing wool (for example, in room 1 of the Casa del Fabbro), are not included here as there was no substantiating evidence.

Table 6.9a includes fifty-five possible locations for cloth production. The majority were in the front-hall area (figure 6.8) and notably in small closed rooms off it (room type 4). The evidence in the front hall consisted mainly of material for weaving, probably indicating that it had taken place in this area, although sometimes loomweights had been stored here (for example, in a cupboard in the front hall of the Casa del Sacello Iliaco).[3] Equipment for cloth production, mainly for spinning and needlework, found in both decorated and undecorated rooms of type 4, was likely to have been stored in these rooms for use in other, better-lit areas, possibly the front hall. While such material was notably absent from main-garden areas, there was a significant pattern for clothworking material to be found in the small, closed rooms off the garden (room type 12). Such material also occurred, although infrequently, in the upper levels and in the areas of the ground floor away from the main front-hall/garden axis. Thus, the most likely location for cloth production was the front

Table 6.9a Distribution of cloth-production equipment, by room type

House	Room	2	3	4	6	7	9	11	12	13	14	16	18	20	22
Casa di Julius Polybius	CC						•								
	A'														•
	AA'														•
	FF'														•
Casa del Menandro	1			•											
	8					•									
	10			•											
	54											•			
Casa del Fabbro	2		•												
	3		•												
	5			•											
	6			•											
	7					•									
	10						•								
House I 10, 8	1		•												
	12								•						
	UF														•
Casa degli Amanti	4			•											
	7			•											
	9						•								
	I 10, 10													•	
Casa dei Quadretti Teatrali	b		•												
	UF(a)														•?
Casa di Stallius Eros	b		•?												
	3													•	
	8								•						
	9											•			
Casa del Sacerdos Amandus	1		•												
	c			•											
Casa dell'Efebo	11			•											
	13					•									
Casa dei Ceii	b		•												
	f								•						
	m								•						
Casa di Trebius Valens	x						•								
Casa del Sacello Iliaco	b		•												
	f					•									
House VI 16, 26	H			•											
	E				•										
	L					•									

Continued on next page

Table 6.9a Distribution of cloth-production equipment, by room type (continued)

House	Room	2	3	4	6	7	9	11	12	13	14	16	18	20	22
Casa della Ara Massima	E			•											
	G				•										
Casa del Principe di Napoli	a			•											
	c			•											
	k							•							
	i								•						
	m									•					
House VI 15, 5	p	•													
	n or o			•											
Casa delle Nozze d'Argento	r						•								
Casa di Giuseppe II	d'										•				
	i'								•						
House VIII 2, 29–30	k'		•												
	m'		•												
House VIII 2,34	c		•												

Figure 6.8 Lead weights found on west side of front hall, House I 10,8

hall, perhaps with some occurring in the garden, but less on upper floors or in the alleged service areas of the house. This suggests that cloth production was a highly visible activity and therefore an important part of the "public" activities in the household.[4] What is not discernible from this study, however, is any distinction between cloth production destined for household use and that for distribution outside.

Other household industries for which there was apparent evidence in the contents of these houses are horticulture or agriculture. This evidence consists predominantly of iron tools, such as pruning knives, axes, picks, hoes, and shears (figure 6.9). These tools seem to have been spread throughout the house (table 6.9b), although usually in limited numbers. It is possible that some of this distribution resulted from the use of such tools during the final escape (for example, a hoe in room 1 of the Casa del Fabbro, an axe in room b of the Casa delle Nozze d'Argento, a hoe in the front hall of the Casa dei Quadretti Teatrali, and an iron hammer with remains of a cartwheel in the front hall of House VIII 2,34). Alternatively, they may indicate abnormal or disrupted conditions (for example, in room 43 in the Casa del Menandro). Such tools were rarely located in the garden proper or in second-

Table 6.9b Distribution of horticultural/agricultural equipment, by room type

House	Room	2	3	4	7	9	11	12	14	16	22
Casa del Menandro	41		•								
	43			•							
	54									•	
	A									• ?	
Casa del Fabbro	1	•									
	10					• ?					
House I 10,8	8			•							
	12							•?			
Casa degli Amanti	7			•							
Casa dei Quadretti Teatrali	b		• ?								
	15						• ?				
	UF(a)										• ?
Casa dell'Efebo	13				•						
House I 7, 19	e						•				
Casa di Trebius Valens	r							•			
Casa dei Ceii	g							• ?			
Casa delle Nozze d'Argento	b	•									
House VIII 2, 34	c		•								
	k			•							
House VIII 5, 9	m						•				

ary courtyards. Without more detailed study of the types of tools and their possible uses, it is difficult to interpret this pattern, except to note that these tools may not have been for use in the garden of the house in which they were found but rather for cultivation outside the dwelling.

Figure 6.9 Some of the tools found in the center of room 43, Casa del Menandro

There is significant evidence that weighing was carried out in these houses (table 6.9c). This evidence consists of scales and weights, particularly those that cannot have been loomweights. Some of this equipment may have been used in food preparation for household consumption. It was largely absent, however, from the kitchens (room type 14). More probably, this equipment may have been related to the control of commodities coming into or leaving the house. It is also possible that some of it could have been part of the equipment for building repairs (for example, in garden m of the Casa del Sacello Iliaco; see figure 8.10). This type of material was found throughout the main front-hall/garden axis of the house but notably not in areas away from it, which may highlight the importance of weighing commodities in the more "public" areas of the house. Again, without more specific study of the ranges and sizes of this material (for example, types of weights and sizes of scales), it is not possible to identify their various functions

Table 6.9c Distribution of weighing equipment, by room type

House	Room	3	4	6	7	9	10	11	12	14	20	22
Casa di Julius Polybius	V										•	
	BB								•			
	GG						•					
Casa della Venere in Bikini	10						•					
Casa del Menandro	45									•		
Casa del Fabbro	3	•										
	7				•							
	9							• ?				
House I 10, 8	8		•									
Casa degli Amanti	7		•									
	19								•			
	UF(18)											•
Casa dei Quadretti Teatrali	6				•							
	UF(a)											• ?
Casa del Sacerdos Amandus	b			• ?								
Casa dell'Efebo	UF(4)											•
	UF(1')											•
House I 7, 19	e							•				
Casa del Sacello Iliaco	f				•							
	m					•						
Casa della Ara Massima	G			•								
Casa degli Amorini Dorati	I								•			
Casa di M. Lucretius Fronto	2	•										
Casa del Principe di Napoli	d	•										
Casa dei Vettii	UF (d and k)											•

and the types of commodities that were likely to have been weighed.

Amphorae, *dolia*, and large glass jars were evidently used for the transportation and storage of commodities in bulk. Residue analyses were not usually carried out on these Pompeian vessels to determine what they contained at the time of the eruption, although as noted above, the contents were sometimes quite evident to the excavators (for example, hazelnuts were stored in an amphora under the stairway in room 1 of the Casa del Sacello Iliaco, and amphorae in courtyard 44 of the Casa del Menandro contained building repair materials). Inscriptional evidence throughout the Roman world indicates that amphorae were principally containers for olive oil, wine, and fish products (Peacock and Williams 1986:31; compare Callender 1965:36–39; Panella 1977:147–148). This evidence is not necessarily reliable, however, for identifying end use. From evidence provided by the examples just mentioned, they could also have held other contents, both edible and inedible.

Table 6.9d includes the locations of vessels whose quantities suggest they were found outside their place of immediate use. This table, therefore, includes some of the same data as in tables 6.2a–b. The amphorae in room type 14 (kitchen), where usually only one or two were located for immediate use, do not feature in this

Table 6.9d Distribution of bulk storage, by room type

House	Room	3	4	5	6	7	8	9	11	12	16	18	19	22
Casa di Julius Polybius	H										•			
	O	•												
	D			•										
	Q			•										
	P				•									
	C												•	
	N	•												
	A'													•
	D'													•
	M'													•
	Q'													•
	Z'													•?
	BB'													•
Casa della Venere in Bikini	7					•								
Casa del Menandro	c							•						
	11								•					
	14									•?				
	L						•							
	20										•			
	34												•	
Casa del Fabbro	12							•						
House I 10, 8	10								•					
	11							•						
Casa degli Amanti	9							•						
House I 6, 8–9	c	•												
	i							•						
Casa dei Stallius Eros	UF													•
Casa del Sacerdos Amandus	p									•				
Casa dell'Efebo	10				•?									
	23							•?						
Casa del Sacello Iliaco	b	•												
	e			•										
	m							•						
House VI 16, 26	B	•												
	F		•											
	M							•						
Casa della Ara Massima	G				•									
Casa degli Amorini Dorati	P											•		
Casa del Principe di Napoli	d	•												
House VI 15, 5	u							•						
	2												•?	

Continued on next page

Table 6.9d Distribution of bulk storage, by room type (continued)

House	Room	3	4	5	6	7	8	9	11	12	16	18	19	22
Casa dei Vettii	c	•												
	o									•				
Casa delle Nozze d'Argento	7			•										
	i				•									
	r							•						
	2											• ?		
	A						•							
	B												• ?	
	E										• ?			
	G											•		
Casa di Giuseppe II	b	•												
House VIII 5, 9	m							•						

table. Likewise, reports of single amphorae in other room types without associated industrial material (for example, in room 2 in the Casa dell'Efebo) are not included. Locations where amphorae appear to have contained building material (for example, area A in the Casa di Julius Polybius [see figure 5.17], room 14 in the Casa dei Quadretti Teatrali, and in the garden of the Casa dell'Efebo) are also omitted.

This type of storage occurred in many room types but was most evident in the front hall and main garden. There was also a pronounced pattern for such storage in the upper floor of the Casa di Julius Polybius, which was better preserved and recorded than the upper floors of other houses in the sample. It might seem improbable that the front hall was used for permanent storage of bulk commodities, and so this pattern may indicate that such material was often brought into the house through the front entrance and deposited here for distribution within the house. Alternatively, this pattern may signify that produce from inside the house was deposited here for distribution outside the house. As noted above, material found in the main garden, particularly in the open garden area (for example, in garden M of House VI 16,26; see figure 5.9), implies that commodities such as garden produce (for example, wine, oil, or fruit) that had been produced or processed here was being stored either for household use

or for distribution outside. The occasional presence of storage vessels in other room types, particularly decorated rooms (for example, room 11 in the Casa del Menandro and room G in the Casa della Ara Massima), suggests haphazard storage in disrupted circumstances.

Besides these main groups of evidence for household production, the material remains also indicate isolated examples of commercial or industrial activities that apparently took place in certain houses but were not necessarily widespread practices throughout the sample. In room f of House VIII 5,9, for example, the unique find of seemingly commercial quantities of ceramic cups and lamps from different sources, including South Gaul, suggests that the occupants of this house were engaged in some sort of trade in pottery. The associated discovery of what appears to have been raw clay implies that this business may also have involved pottery production. Whether or not it did, there seems to have been little definitive spatial separation between domestic and commercial activities in this house.

Other examples of unique and seemingly discrete assemblages of industrial activities were found in the Casa del Fabbro, consisting of what appears to have been furniture production or furniture repair in room 8; more general carpentry and perhaps metalworking in the ambulatory of the garden; and, in the upper floor, surgical, pharmaceutical, or toilet activities that seem more extensive than the needs of the house occupants would have required. For the Casa del Sacello Iliaco, it has generally been assumed that the quantities of gypsum and other seemingly industrial material in the rear of the house were associated with its repair (for example, Strocka 1984b:131; see figure 8.10). The apparent scale of the enterprise, including the installation of a large oven in area s (see figure 5.16), however, suggests that the production of building material may also have been for distribution outside the house. A less evident example of seemingly more small-scale industrial activity was found in room 21 in the Casa del Menandro. The assemblage in this room seems quite different from others in the sample.[5]

Fixtures do not feature prominently in the discussion of household production. In general, most fixtures in these houses were associated with more domestic activities. Some that might have been associated with industrial activities are the so-called *fornelli*, such as in room 3 of the Casa del Menandro (figure 6.10) and the vat in room a' in House VIII 2,29–30. The *fornelli* had been used for heating but seem inappropriately shaped and located for food preparation. They could have been used in a variety of activities (for example, room heating, metalworking, lime production, or glassworking).

COMMENTS

The foregoing analysis has explored some of the activities likely to have been associated with the house contents in this sample. It does not include all the material in the sample because, for some of it, the function is still indeterminate. At the same time, much of the material probably had more than one function. Loomweights, for example, may have also been used to weigh other commodities, and jugs were likely to have been used in food preparation, food serving, and food storage. This study highlights that the difficulties inherent in ascribing specific functions to artifacts, or groups of artifacts, are often as much a result of the nature of scholarship in this area of archaeology (Allison 1997a, 1999b) as of the nature of the actual archaeological evidence.

Figure 6.10 So-called *fornello* against decorated south wall in room 3, Casa del Menandro

While more detailed study of these artifacts and their assemblages can provide more secure information concerning their functions (Allison, n.d.), without recourse to textual analogy such a study is unlikely to prove very rewarding, particularly in developing a fuller understanding of the symbolic meaning with which some of this material was likely to have been imbued (see Miller 1995:643–665).

Despite these limitations, certain distribution patterns have emerged in this analysis. It is also evident that a specific spatial-functional relationship, according to the categories identified above, cannot automatically be established. This emphasizes the role that nineteenth-century ideologies of "separate spheres" play (see for example, Rosaldo 1980; Vickery 1993), not only in current perceptions of the separation between public and private space, but also in perceptions of the significance of spatial divisions within the household. While some of the houses in Pompeii were very large and had a diverse range of spaces, many of the activities that took place in them seem to have been divided along different lines from those of more recent societies, even pre-industrial ones (compare Carandini 1984 I: 187–206; Wallace-Hadrill 1994:12–14).

The next important question is, how can these assemblages and the activities with which they appear to have been associated inform us about the inhabitants of these houses? Can they be used to differentiate between the parts of houses used by household members and those used by outsiders, or to differentiate between areas used by different household members? Can we assign particular assemblages to particular individuals or groups of individuals? Can we isolate activity areas that were status, age, or gender specific?

VISITORS

Assuming that invited guests and high-status visitors to Pompeian houses entered into places that had prestigious display furnishings, then both the front hall and the formal gardens of these houses would have been open to them

(see table 6.7a). Only the fact that the colonnaded gardens were usually further inside the house implies that they might have been more secluded (compare George 1997a:300). However, the more ostentatious furnishings appear to have been more prevalent in gardens than in front halls (figure 6.11). Given that the location of the front hall probably made it a more public area, the householders probably reserved their most luxurious vistas for their most intimate guests. Bath-suites were often located in the main areas, generally off the garden, but again it is not possible to ascertain whether visitors from outside the household were invited to use them (see Pliny *Ep.* 2, 7 and 5, 6; Foss 1997:216). As already noted, however, these courtyard areas did not appear to be reserved solely for formal activities and entertainment. Rather, they appear to have also been centers around which routine household activities revolved. There appears to have been little concern among Pompeian householders for hiding their domestic activity from such outsiders. Perhaps only the smaller rooms to the sides of these main circulation areas were more private and less accessible to visitors.

Figure 6.11 Garden m from northeast corner, Casa dei Vettii. *Pompeii photo archive neg. D80831*

Contact with outsiders involved with the commercial or industrial enterprises of the establishment, particularly the distribution of household production and bulk items for household consumption, may have been through secondary entrances, but there was evidence that such activities could also be conducted through the front-hall areas, even in houses that also had back entranceways. It would seem inaccurate, then, to apply a modern analogy to Pompeian houses, which distinguishes between the "aristocratic elegance" of the front-hall area and "the vulgarity of the trades and businesses" carried out in separate areas or through separate entrances (Raper 1977:193).

Prestigious but functional material that was likely to be used for the entertainment of guests (for example, silver vessels or decorated bronze vessels) was found in a variety of locations around the house, including assumed service areas. While some of the luxury material, particularly large scale, was discovered in its place of use, many of the smaller artifacts were found in their storage locations (see table 6.7b). Nevertheless, it is possible that they were also close to their place of use.

ENSLAVED AND FREE

If the members of Pompeian households were nuclear families with slaves, other dependent children, freedmen, and freedwomen (see for example, Gardner and Wiedemann 1991:3; Parkin 1994; George 1997a:301 n.5), then we might hope to find spatial differentiations of the activities of these groups.

Differentiations between enslaved and free individuals, however, are problematical for much of archaeology. These are concepts known through written evidence, both from ancient authors and epigraphy. They are essentially indistinguishable in the material record without accompanying epigraphic evidence (for example, inscribed stamp seals) or recourse to textual or modern analogy, which is not necessarily always appropriate (for example, Carandini 1984 I:187–206; George 1997a:316–317). Assumptions that there were indeed service areas with slave

quarters in Pompeian houses (for example, Maiuri 1933:199–212) are based on analogies with more recent European practice, without any specific justification for such analogy. As Michele George (1997b:22–24) has argued, separate slave quarters were not a necessity for a Roman house.

It is probably justifiable to assume that many of the service activities were usually carried out by slaves and therefore that the utilitarian assemblages, including those related to food preparation and household industries, might be used to identify the spaces that they frequented. It cannot be assumed, however, that this was exclusively so. If it had been, the occurrence of such assemblages in various parts of the house, with the possible exception of the small decorated rooms off the front hall (room type 4) and the large rooms off the garden (room types 10, 11), suggests that slaves were not restricted to specific areas of the house, except perhaps on a temporal basis (for example, at particular times of the day: see Laurence 1997:11).

From this pattern, one might wish to argue that slaves did not generally frequent the small decorated rooms off the front hall or the upper floors. The kinds of personal assemblages found in these areas were also found in the assumed service areas of the house. Artifact assemblages cannot be used to isolate slave activity without bringing in external assumptions about what slaves did in a Pompeian household and what artifacts they would have used. Anyone making such assumptions should be critically aware of the degree to which these rely on modern analogical inference, as opposed to explicit and contextualized textual analogy.[6]

AGE

Identifying age differentiation, particularly of the very old and the very young, through a distribution of household activities based on analysis of the material culture, is also difficult. As no recorded artifacts in this sample could be attributed to children, these assemblages cannot be used to trace their activities. Wallace-Hadrill has noted a lack of evidence for the spatial segregation of children in the extant structural remains of Roman houses (1994:9). His argument (1994:9–10), however, is not based on anything intrinsically readable in the archaeological remains. Rather, it is based on an analogy with such separate spaces in "the modern Western house," two literary references, and Philippe Aries' thesis that childhood was not a social phenomenon prior to the seventeenth century. In contrast, Beryl Rawson and others (for example, Rawson 1997) have shown that children in fact played an important and distinguishable role in Roman social life. Failure to distinguish their footprints in Pompeian households through artifact assemblages is not likely to be due to their lack of social definition. It is more likely to be because of a lack of specific material culture pertaining to children or, perhaps more pertinent, our lack of study and therefore knowledge of what constituted that material culture. Similar issues may affect the identification of material culture pertaining to the elderly, although it seems less probable that further research will help to distinguish traces of their activities (see Parkin 1997).

GENDER

It is also difficult to find any gender distinctions in these assemblages without making assumptions about gender roles. Substantial feminist anthropological and archaeological literature has demonstrated the amount of bias brought to bear on the engendering of activities in the past (for example, Rosaldo and Lamphere 1974; Conkey and Spencer 1984; Wylie 1991). Recent studies of women in the Roman world (for example, Bernstein 1988; J. K. Evans 1991:101–165; Gardner 1991; Crook 1992) have shown the wide range of roles that free, freed, and slave women could have taken. In the same vein, the extent of the range of male activities within the household needs closer scrutiny. The following examples are therefore in the nature of an exploration of the possibilities of the relationships between gender and space in Pompeian households.

Laurence argued for a temporal distribution of occupancy of Pompeian houses that was based on a binary male/female separation (1994: 122–132). He argued that the front hall would have been a male space in the early morning and left very much a female space for the remainder of the day. Certain members of the household undoubtedly vacated it during parts of the day, particularly the *paterfamilias* in his civic and public roles, and servants involved in industrial and commercial activities outside the household. The engendering of these activities, however, needs more critical assessment. Equally, it seems reasonable to envisage that the overlap of activities documented in the material remains reflects the considerable overlap between the various activities that took place here as well as the simultaneous presence of various household members and outsiders of diverse ages, gender, and status who performed these activities.

Also, only if one assumes that cloth production was carried out by women—whether free, freed, or slave—could one possibly identify areas frequented by women. Evidence for spinning and weaving was predominantly found in the front hall and in small, mainly undecorated rooms off the hall (room type 4), with some equipment in small, closed rooms off the garden (room type 12). It is by no means certain that women carried out all such production. The term *textor* indicates that males also engaged in weaving (for example, Martial *Ep.* 12, 59.6; Juvenal *Sat.* 9,30). From the current state of our knowledge, there seems little reason to assume that males' involvement in this industry did not include the production that took place within the household.

Toiletry items have frequently been considered women's objects. Mirrors, particularly, have been "symbolically associated with women" in the Classical world (Kampen 1996:22). In Pompeian houses, such material was found predominantly in the small, closed rooms off the front hall (room type 4) and garden area (room type 12), as well as in small rooms away from the main axis. If this material can be shown to have been associated with women's activities, it would suggest that they had a prominent use of these more private rooms. On the other hand, ablutions, for which toiletry items were used, were undoubtedly carried out by male household members as well, including the use of mirrors for shaving (see Wyke 1994:135–138). This distribution pattern rather highlights the private nature of these activities. Attempts to separate female from male toilet activities by ascribing certain types of toiletries to the former are somewhat subjective, without more critical analyses of the evidence for the performance of these activities in Roman society.

Textual evidence also indicates that it is difficult to segregate food preparation and food consumption according to gender. This was highlighted by Foss (1994:47–50) who emphasized the depiction of professional male cooks in literary sources, such as the writings of Cato, Columella, Varro, and particularly M. Gavius Apicius, but also demonstrated that food could be prepared by either male or female cooks, whether free or enslaved. Dining was also not segregated, according to the textual evidence, although the roles of men and women may have differed during this activity. More rigorous analyses of the lines of segregation of these activities, as evidenced in the texts, is needed before the material cultural evidence can be interpreted (see Dixon 2001).

SUMMARY

This analysis provides little specific evidence that status, age, gender, or any other supposed "hierarchies of power" were defining elements in the organization of the living patterns that can be identified through the distribution of household activities within Pompeian houses. Again, this is partly owing to the lack of detailed investigation of such issues through Roman material culture. Wallace-Hadrill argued that status could be ascertained by the architecture and decoration (Wallace-Hadrill 1994:143–174). In other words, the "hierarchies of power," as a product of the prescribed intentions of the

builders of Pompeian houses, would be expressed in the daily workings of these houses. However, the evidence of Pompeian daily life either does not reflect that intention or reflects it in a way that is much more foreign to our current ideals than we are prepared to believe of a Roman town on Italian soil. Much more rigorous research that takes account of cultural biases is needed before house contents can throw more light on these issues.[7]

CONCLUSIONS

While this analysis demonstrates certain patterns of the spatial division of household activities that might seem unexpected given assumptions made about universalities in domestic behavior, it also demonstrates the difficulty of separating out household activities through artifact assemblages. This is partly owing to the lack of detailed study of the consumption patterns in Roman material culture or indeed any other past material culture (Miller 1995). It may also be a symptom of our reliance on categories that equate with our own perspective of how domestic behavior is organized.

While the written sources provide information concerning Roman households (see Gardner and Wiedemann 1991), it is apparent that these are not suited for the inquiry into the spatial distribution of household activities. Because of the particular agenda of ancient authors, the textual evidence provides little or only anecdotal information on the daily functioning of a Roman house, let alone on that of a Pompeian one for which such evidence is practically nonexistent. The seemingly limited results attained through analysis of artifact assemblages, however, should not be dismissed as uninformative. Rather, they should provide a basis from which we both question our assumptions about domestic universals and material culture consumption and critically assess our interpretations of textual information, its explicit relevance, and its universality within a very diverse Roman world.

NOTES

1. The word used in the excavation reports is "*dente.*" While it therefore appears to refer to teeth rather than tusks, the recorders may have used this term for the generic concept of dentition.

2. See Dessau 1962: ILS 3259, a dedication in Spain made by Q. Tullus Maximus in which he dedicated boars' tusks, *dentes aprorum*, and deer antlers, *cervom altifrontum cornua*, to Diana. An inscription was also found at Cosa in 1997, referring to the use of *cornua* to open the way for Diana to her sanctuary. These could conceivably have been antlers, although such a conclusion would make the current argument rather circular. I am grateful to Rabun Taylor (University of Minnesota) for these references.

3. In general, loomweights have been recorded singly or in groups of four to five. There were only three possible instances in this study where significantly larger quantities were recorded (House I 10,8, the Casa del Principe di Napoli, and House VI 16,26). It is not possible to ascertain whether this reflected the lack of interest of the excavators in such finds, post-eruption disturbance, or if indeed these weights had often occurred in small groups prior to the eruption.

4. Michael Jameson's assumption that in Greek houses "looms possibly set up in an odd corner (compare with an ironing board or sewing machine today)" would seem an inappropriate analogy for either Greek or Roman domestic practice (1990:102–103). Even in the segregated domestic worlds of the nineteenth and early twentieth centuries, looms, spinning wheels, and sewing machines could be found in relatively public and formal rooms (for example, a spinning wheel in an ante-drawing room in late nineteenth-century South Australia: Lane and Serle 1990: Fig. 149).

5. A closer examination and analysis of the finds is needed before further comment can be made (Allison, n.d.).

6. In this regard, George (1997b:19–22) has not been adequately critical of the generalized use of analogical inference in previous studies that purport to have isolated slave quarters.

7. The author's current research is concerned with gender and Roman spaces.

Figure 7.1 Masonry seats to either side of main entrance, House I 10,8

7.

Textual Nomenclature for Spaces

TRADITIONALLY, SCHOLARS concerned with spatial function in Pompeian houses have not analyzed relationships between the structural room types and their contents, and the distribution of household activities. Rather, spatial functions have been deduced through labeling the structural types with textual nomenclature according to their apparent concordance with the nomenclature prescribed, particularly by Vitruvius (see table 5.a; figure 2.2). Further textual references to the household activities carried out within so-named spaces are then employed to provide information concerning the uses of so-labeled structural types in Pompeian houses (for example, Mau 1899:240–273; Becker 1876; McKay 1977:32–59, Figs. 8–10; Shelton 1988:59–62). While this approach might seem outmoded and has recently been criticized (for example, Wallace-Hadrill 1994:6; Leach 1997:50; Nevett 1997), it is still prevalent among publications on Pompeian houses and, in particular, more general publications on Roman housing (for example, Clarke 1991:2–19; George 1997a, 1997b, 1998; Descœudres et al. 1994; Ellis 2000).

The works of three specific Roman authors—Varro, Vitruvius, and Pliny the Younger—have been instrumental in providing the nomenclature with which scholars have labeled spaces in Pompeian houses. They have also been the principal sources for information concerning the locations and functions of the various spaces in Roman houses. This labeling process, however, has seldom paid attention to the purposes for which these authors were writing. None of their works was actually intended as a presentation of Roman, let alone Pompeian, domestic behavior. The following paragraphs briefly summarize these works, highlighting the writers' concerns and their uses of the nomenclature that has subsequently been applied to spaces in Pompeian houses.

Briefly, Varro, a linguist and antiquarian of Roman culture, was concerned with the derivations of Latin words. He was interested in how rooms in Roman houses acquired their names. He described (*De ling. lat.* 5, 161–162) how the central court of a house came to be called the *cavum aedium* and the *atrium*, and how the rooms around this court had a number of different purposes and gained their names from these original uses: they were called *cellae* or *penaria* for storage, *cubicula* for lying down, or *cenacula* for eating. He also described how *cenacula* were later moved upstairs and observed that the Romans had several rooms for dining. He gave little insight into how so-labeled rooms might have been used in his day. For example, even if it could be shown that, despite the acknowledged unreliability of his etymologies (for example, Mau 1899:267–268), rooms around an *atrium* had continued to be called *cubicula*, *cellae*, *penaria*, or *cenacula* in Varro's day, those labels may have had little bearing on their function at that time.

Vitruvius was an academic architect with a prescriptive approach to the prerequisites for designing various types of Roman buildings (see Leach 1997:50; Millette 1999). In his architectural treatise on the ideal Roman house (6, 3), he described the recommended dimensions and locations of its components. He commenced with the *cavum aedium*, which he later referred to as the *atrium*. He then described the *alae*, on either side, and the proportions of the *tablinum* in relation to the width of the *atrium*. He stipulated that the *fauces* be proportional to the *tablinum* and that the *peristyla* lie crossways. His recommended proportions for a *triclinium*, which can also be an *exedra* or *oecus*, were that its length be twice its width. Thus we learn that the *fauces*, *atrium*, *alae*, *tablinum*, and *peristyla* should be spatially related to one another. While Vitruvius proceeded (6, 4) to discuss the preferred aspects of seasonal *triclinia*, *balnearia*, *cubicula*, *bybliothecae*, *pinacotheca*, and *plumariorum textrina*, he told us nothing about the location of these other room types, either relative to one another or within the house plan. We learn only (6, 5) that *cubicula*, *triclinia*, and *balneae* are private rooms, whereas *vestibula*, *tabulina*, and *atria* are areas that people can enter uninvited. Vitruvius suggested that the latter group might therefore be grander in the houses of people of rank. He also emphasized (7, 4.4; 7, 5.2) that room type and room function played an important part in the choice of decoration. In general, however, he showed little concern for these houses as lived spaces. It is only through analogy with Pompeian houses that a visual realization of his house plans has been created (compare Becker 1876: Plans A and B; see Allison 1993).

Pliny the Younger, famed for his writing skills rather than architectural interest, discussed in flowing prose the places where he lived (see de la Ruffinière du Prey 1994:8–9). He described his luxurious villas at Laurentium (*Ep.* 2, 17) and in Tuscany (*Ep.* 5, 6) using terminology and phraseology that he hoped would entice his friends to visit him, as well as to reinforce his self-representation as an intellectual. For example, through one letter (*Ep.* 2, 17) he took Clusinius (?) Gallus on a guided tour of his *Laurentium*.[1] The tour commenced from the *atrium* that led onto a *porticus*, in turn leading to a *cavaedium* and a *triclinium* that opened onto the seafront. To the left was a large *cubiculum* and then a smaller one. Round the corner was located another *cubiculum*, built around an apse and fitted with shelves like a library. Next came the heated *dormitorium*. Pliny described another room that could be used as either a large *cubiculum* or a moderate *cenatio*. Behind it was another *cubiculum* with a *procoeton*, from which was divided yet another *cubiculum* and *procoeton*. Then came the *frigidarium*, the *unctorium*, the *hypocauston*, and other rooms connected with the *balineum*. Close by was a *sphaeristerium*. The upper story had four *diaetae*, as well as a *cenatio*, an

apotheca, and a *horreum*, below which was a *triclinium*. In another part of the complex, Pliny described a *cryptoporticus* with a *xystus* in front. At the far end of the latter was Pliny's favorite *diaeta*, containing a *heliocaminus* and a *cubiculum*. Opposite the intervening wall was a *zotheca*, large enough to hold a *lectus* and two *cathedrae*. Next to it was a *cubiculum noctis et somni*. A *cubiculum hypocauston* had been added here, and there was also a *procoeton* and a *cubiculum* that faced the sun. Pliny was describing a spacious aristocratic villa, emphasizing those rooms that he considered of social and intellectual importance. His style of writing and the lack of any identifiable remains related to these villas have rendered any attempts to reconstruct their plans fruitless (see Drummer 1994). For example, reconstructions of Pliny's Laurentine villa (see Pinon et al. 1982:104-142; de la Ruffinière du Prey 1994) have resulted in villas bearing close resemblances to those of the investigator's own past (for example, French eighteenth-century villas).

There are only a few examples of written evidence in Pompeii for the names of spaces in Pompeian houses. That is, limited epigraphical evidence has survived in Pompeii that can enlighten us as to the names Pompeians would have used for the spaces in their houses, but it does not tell us which spaces were actually referred to (compare Della Corte 1965: No. 821; Pirson 1997: 168). Hence, there is no direct literary evidence for a study of room use in Pompeian houses (compare Foss 1994:57; Laurence 1995:313, 1997:10).[2] Rather, the use of textual nomenclature to establish Pompeian room use constitutes an analogy predominantly between the archaeological remains in this southern Italian town and the fragments of textual evidence from other parts, and sometimes other periods, of the Roman world. Further, Reinhard Förtsch (1993:30–134) used excavated spaces, particularly those in Pompeii that had already been labeled with Vitruvian nomenclature, to elucidate the physical plans of Pliny's villas. In other words, he assumed that the Vitruvian nomenclature was actually part of the material record. Such analogy has also traditionally been used as the baseline data for developing understandings of Pompeian domestic life (see

Leach 1997:50). This analogical inference, particularly with texts that were written during a similar period, may indeed be a viable method for investigating behavior patterns. It would, however, be unscholarly to use such analogy to describe behavior in Pompeian houses in preference to investigating the full archaeological record there. Only in combination with a full assessment of the relationships among the structural, decorative, and contents remains of Pompeian domestic spaces—for the information that this material can provide regarding the activities that took place in these spaces—is it appropriate to investigate written sources for perspectives they may provide concerning interpretations of domestic behavior in Pompeian houses.

It is not the aim of this study to analyze the textual uses of room nomenclature in Roman houses. Eleanor Leach is currently carrying out a critical analysis of the information that this nomenclature provides on domestic behavior (see 1997). This chapter draws on her work and concentrates specifically on the relationships of the textual nomenclature and associated activities, as traditionally applied to rooms in Pompeian houses, to activities as identified through artifact distribution in the houses in this sample. The following discussion assesses the relationships between activities identified in the room types, as presented in chapter 5 (table 5.a), and those associated with the labels that have traditionally been applied to such rooms (for example, Mau 1899:241, Fig. 110; McKay 1977: Figs 8–10).

TYPE 1: MAIN ENTRANCEWAYS

The main entranceways from the street to the front hall of Pompeian houses are usually labeled *fauces* by modern scholars (for example, Shelton 1988:60, Figs. 1, 2; Clarke 1991:2; Descœudres et al. 1994:59; Berry 1997:188). Sometimes a divided entranceway is labeled as part *fauces* (or *ostium*) and part *vestibulum* (for example, Becker 1876:234–235, Plans A–B; Mau 1899:241–244, Fig. 110), or sometimes an architectural distinction is made between an entranceway labeled *fauces* and one labeled *vestibulum* (for example, reference to houses in North Africa: George 1997a:313).

Leach has demonstrated (1997:53–55) that the word *fauces* is "virtually never defined architecturally" in Latin texts and that it is more frequently used metaphorically. Vitruvius used it only once (6, 3.6), prescribing its proportions but not its location in the house plan (Leach 1993:26). Leach argued that the term *vestibula* has stronger architectural associations in the texts and was used in Roman literature to indicate a place at the front of the house where *clientes* waited before entering (see also Leach 1993:24–26; Nevett 1997:289–290). At the same time, she noted that most main entranceways to Pompeian houses were so narrow as to be inappropriate to accommodate such activities. She therefore postulated that a recognizable *vestibulum* was largely lacking in Pompeian houses and that practices in Pompeii may have been divergent from those recorded in the texts (Leach 1993:23).

As might be expected of a main entranceway, those in this sample were largely devoid of loose finds (table 5.1). Seating located outside of many of the Pompeian houses, including some 30 percent from this sample (see figure 5.1; figure 7.1), is often regarded as a provision for waiting clients (for example, de Vos and de Vos 1982:90). In this sample, fixed seating was not concentrated in the largest and most elaborate houses, which conceivably had more need for it (compare Wallace-Hadrill 1989). This association therefore seems to be an overinterpretation of the analogous relationship between the Pompeian evidence and the textual, which views these seats as being specifically for clients of the patron of the house. While clients may well have sat on them, others, including the house occupants, probably also made use of this relatively public facility. There seems insufficient evidence to identify the Latin label or labels that Pompeians would have used for this entranceway to their houses.

TYPE 2: ROOMS LEADING DIRECTLY OFF MAIN ENTRANCEWAYS

These usually small narrow rooms are often labeled *cellae ostiariae* by modern scholars, as are some rooms that flank the main entranceways but are entered from the front hall (that is, room type 4; for example, room 1 in the Casa del Menandro and room a in the Casa del Principe di Napoli. See Becker 1876:234, Plan A; Elia 1934:279; Fiorelli 1883:135; Maiuri 1933:36; Strocka 1984a:46; George 1997b:19 n. 19). Vitruvius (6, 7.1) used this term in his discussion of Greek houses. Petronius (29, 1) indicated that a so-labeled room could have been found just inside the entrance. However, the tone of his reference to the valuable contents of this room (37, 8) suggests rather that it was the last place they might be expected to be found, at least in large quantities.

The contents, fixtures, and decoration in type 2 rooms in this sample indicate a diversity of activities, including storage and seating, as located outside room type 1 (table 5.2). This archaeological evidence does not exclude type 2 rooms from being those of porters or doormen (*ostiarii*), but neither does it verify such a use. Generally speaking, the assemblages in these rooms were more utilitarian than Petronius' reference suggests. While the textual references alert us to the existence of such rooms in Roman houses, the evidence is insufficient to identify individual rooms in Pompeian houses as such. This labeling is therefore too positivist. It consists rather of a combination of an architectural type with limited textual analogy, rather than anything intrinsically evident in the archaeological remains. It is possible that a modern analogy of the butler's pantries or concierge's office (Perrot 1990:363–366), frequently located immediately inside the front door of nineteenth-century houses, also played a role in this interpretation.

TYPE 3: FRONT HALLS

Scholars invariably refer to the first court or front hall of Pompeian houses, usually encountered after passing through the main entrance from the street, as the *atrium*. Such labeling has given rise to the concept of the *"atrium* house" for the houses in Pompeii whose floor plan is like those discussed in this sample (for example, Evans 1984; Wallace-Hadrill 1997) and distinguishable from "non-*atrium* houses" (compare Nappo 1997: 93). This term's exploitation by

Renaissance architects, especially Palladio, and its application to a particular house form in Pompeii, means that it has become so entrenched in the study of the archaeological remains of Roman houses that scholars from Axel Boëthius and John Ward-Perkins (1970:72–76) to Andrew Wallace Hadrill (1997) have been debating the development of the *"atrium* house" as the "typical Roman house."

Vitruvius (6, 3.1–3) appears to use the terms *cavum aedium* and *atrium* interchangeably for covered or partially covered courtyards. He uses the term *atrium* more consistently for a specific space, particularly when referring to the rooms opening off it (6, 3.4–6). It was, however, the *cavum aedium* that he prescribed (6, 5.1) could be entered by uninvited visitors. Varro (*De ling. lat.* 5, 160–162) discussed the derivation of these two terms. He gave no hint as to the relationship between them, nor any information concerning the locations, forms, or functions of an *atrium*. He described the *cavum aedium* as having been a roofed, but open, internal space for communal use and surrounded by various different rooms (Leach 1997:57). The terms Varro used to describe the rooms around the *cavum aedium* were quite different from those Vitruvius used for the rooms surrounding the *atrium*. Pliny's Laurentine villa (*Ep.* 2, 17) had both an *atrium* and a *cavaedium*: first a dignified *atrium* and, beyond colonnades, a small partially roofed *cavaedium*. W. A. Becker, in his original plan of a Roman house, which was independent of influence from the Pompeian evidence but presumably followed Pliny's description (1876:234, Plan A), indicated that a large Roman house would have had a colonnaded *atrium* preceding the *cavum aedium*. I do not wish to debate the architectural form and development of what should or should not be labeled "the *atrium* house" on or off Italian soil.[3] Rather, I wish to examine the activities described in the ancient texts as taking place in an *atrium* or a *cavum aedium* and their relationships to the assemblages in the front halls of the houses in this sample.

The most commonly cited function for the *atrium* of a Roman house is the morning *salutatio* or visit to the owner of the house by dependents and clients (for example, Wiseman 1982:28–29; Clarke 1991:4; Leach 1993:23). Leach demonstrated that the *atrium* was the place for lobbying for political and social advantage (1997:58). Luxury and display furniture in this area has long been considered appropriate for such a function. It was noted, however, that such furniture was not a prerequisite for the front hall of Pompeian houses and, further, that it was not concentrated in this space or indeed in the largest and grandest houses in the sample.

Other activities associated with the *atrium* are the display of the *images*, ancestral masks (for example, Pliny *Nat. Hist.* 35, 2.6; Martial *Ep.* 2, 90; for further references, see Flower 1996:185 n. 2), and the worship of household deities. There is little reason to dispute that aediculae in front halls of Pompeian houses were household shrines where Lares, Penates, and the *genius* were likely to have been worshipped (Dwyer 1982:114; Orr 1978, 1988:294–295; Clarke 1991:9). However, actual shrines or *lararium* paintings were relatively rare in this sample and, indeed, textual references to the Penates often associated them with the rear parts of the house (see Nevett 1997:289). While no evidence of ancestral masks, or indeed any other type of ancestral portrait such as busts, was reported from this area in this sample, the latter appear to have been found in this location in other houses in Pompeii (for example, the Casa di Caecilius Iucundus).

In their dictionary of Greek and Latin terms, Daremberg and Saglio (1881: I, 363) refer to an *arca* containing household valuables being kept in the *atrium* of primitive houses. This association has become widely accepted (for example, Paoli 1958:62; Dwyer 1982:114; Armitt 1993:240; Descœudres et al. 1994:77). However, the textual references that Daremberg and Saglio, and also Pauly (1893–1963), cited (Servius *Ad Aen.* 1, 262 and 730; Varro *De Ling. lat.* 1, 5.128) do not indicate a location for the *arca*. While there is a significant pattern for storage containers in the front halls of these houses, most of these containers were upright cupboards; a smaller proportion were chests. Also, most of the chests were wooden. The type of metal chest illustrated by Daremberg and Saglio was found in only one

of the houses in the sample, the Casa dei Vettii (see Allison 1999b:60).

Livy (1, 57) referred to Lucretia and her maidens working wool "*in medio aedium*," and Asconius (*Milonianam* 38) considered the use of looms in the *atrium* more ceremonial than utilitarian by the mid-first century BC. The distribution of loomweights in the houses in this sample, however, indicates that the front hall of Pompeian houses was the principal area for cloth production towards the end of the first century. Both Virgil (*Aeneid* 7, 377–389) and Lucretius (4, 400–404) depicted children playing in the *atrium*. The boys in Virgil's reference were apparently playing with tops (Leach 1997:57). While no material evidence identifiable as children's toys was found in these front halls, or indeed in any of the assemblages in this study, these circumstances would not exclude the potential presence of children from this part of the house in Pompeii (see chapter 6). According to A. S. Wilkins (1907:94), Horace's comment (*Ep.* 1, 1.87) concerning the placement of the "*lectus genialis*" in the "*aula*" is a reference to the "marriage bed" having stood in the *atrium*. No evidence of bedding was found in the front halls in this sample, but it did occur in room type 7.

It has widely been assumed by modern scholars that by the time the Roman house had separate dining areas, as argued for most Pompeian houses, the *atrium* had become the waiting and reception area for friends and clients and a formal display area (for example, Becker 1876:250; Dwyer 1982:113–115), comparable perhaps with an entrance hall of an élite residence in the mid-nineteenth century (see Clark 1976:51, Figs. 1, 2). Such analogy draws on separate spheres' ideologies of the nineteenth century (see also Vickery 1993), which see marked distinctions among public, private, and service spaces (compare Wallace-Hadrill 1994:11; Thébert 1987:353–354; Dwyer 1991:29; see also Allison 1993:6). These textual references indicate that the *atrium* and the *cavum aedium* were the foci of a wide range of household activities, at least in the late Republic. All members of the household and outsiders must have made use of so-named spaces.

It has been acknowledged that it is difficult to identify different members of the household through artifact distribution. It is also extremely difficult to assess any temporal relationships among the activities as evidenced by the artifact distribution in front halls. Leach (1997:57) doubted the binary male/female temporal separation proposed by Laurence (see chapter 6). She did note that the Latin poets implied children might have played in the atrium when it was devoid of other occupants.

In summary, the artifact distribution indicates that the front hall had been the principal circulation and probable meeting area, accessible to all members of the household involved in a variety of domestic, industrial, and commercial activities. It was also one of the areas most accessible to outsiders. In these respects, it fits most comfortably with Varro's and Vitruvius' descriptions of a *cavum aedium*, or with descriptions of early *atria*. This may highlight that household behavior in Pompeii was not actually in accordance with that practiced in the capital or by élites during the first century AD.

TYPE 4: SMALL CLOSED ROOMS OFF FRONT HALLS

Pompeian houses often had a number of small narrow rooms on each side of the front hall. Modern scholars generally refer to rooms of this type as *cubicula* (for example, Jahn in Becker 1876:235, Plan B; McKay 1977:34; Strocka 1984a:20–21; Michel 1990:30; Clarke 1991:3, Fig. 1; Seiler 1992:25, 27). Vitruvius did not prescribe a label for such rooms, but Varro (*De ling. lat.* 5, 162) identified rooms around the *cavum aedium* as being useful for different purposes: *cellae* (storerooms), *penariae* (pantries), *cubicula* (sleeping rooms), or *cenacula* (dining rooms).

The current study shows that the most pronounced pattern for use of decorated, closed rooms around the front hall was for personal or private activities (for example, ablutions and needlework) and lighting equipment. This could include either the use or storage of items associated with these activities. Undecorated rooms of this type appear to have been used for more utilitarian storage. In general, both decorated and undecorated rooms indicated domestic storage,

including that of food, but with a marked lack of evidence for material associated with food preparation, eating, or sleeping. In these so-called *atrium cubicula* in the Casa di M. Lucretius, Dwyer reported (1982:115–116) quantities and types of finds seemingly not of sufficient quantity to indicate storage, but rather of personal activities similar to those observed in this study. He therefore concluded that the decorated rooms served as storerooms and that the family slept upstairs.

If the front hall could be identified as a *cavum aedium*, then these finds would confirm Varro's identification of the rooms around it, particularly the undecorated ones, as *cellae* or *penariae* but not as *cubicula* or *cenacula*. However, Varro gave no precise indication as to which structural and locational types had which functions. It is conceivable that his latter terms applied to other types of rooms in this area (for example, room type 6 was called a *cenaculum*). Varro was concerned with the origin of these terms rather than with the nomenclature and functions of his day.

Nevertheless, *cubiculum* has become the conventional term for this room type and has often been translated as "bedroom" (for example, Lytton 1834: Ch. 7; Mau 1899:255–256; McKay 1977: Fig. 8; Clarke 1991:12; compare Nevett 1997:283, 290–291).[4] Elia, in particular, considered the term *cubiculum* as synonymous with *bedroom* and used architectural and decorative characteristics to label rooms as such, both those around the front halls and those in the main garden areas in Pompeian houses (1932). These included thirteen Pompeian examples of rooms with First- and Second-Style decoration that consisted of a vaulted alcove with anteroom and correspondingly demarcated pavement and decoration (Elia 1932:399–411). She noted, however, that these decorative distinctions did not occur in rooms painted in the Fourth Style, which means that the very criteria by which she identified bedrooms were not extant in most Pompeian houses at the time of the eruption. Rather, she used the so-called bed recess to identify rooms as bedrooms of a later date. Adam also believed that the *cubiculum* or "*camera da letto*" could be recognized with certainty by its small dimensions and recess (1989a:237). This study shows that there is very little evidence to substantiate that such recesses were invariably used for beds; rather, they may have had a variety of uses (see chapter 4).

Given that the presence of a wall recess was no certain indication that a room contained a bed or couch (compare Riggsby 1997:42), actual sleeping evidence was comparatively rare in rooms of this type. If such rooms were indeed called *cubicula*, this scarcity might be explained by the lack of necessity to use a so-labeled room as a bedroom. As Nevett has emphasized (1997:283, 291), while some literary references to *cubicula* indicated that they could have contained a bed, others showed that activities in these spaces could cover a considerable range (see also Leach 1997:69–70; Riggsby 1997). As Nevett suggested, the word *cubiculum* was likely to have been a generic term and required qualifying to indicate its function, such as *cubiculum dormitorium* (Pliny *Nat. Hist.* 30, 52).

Textual evidence, such as that discussed by Nevett, Leach, and Riggsby, also emphasizes the likelihood that the modern concept of private and individual bedrooms did not exist in the Roman world. Indeed, the concept of numerous individual spaces set aside for sleeping seems to be a relatively recent phenomenon. We might instead consider that Pompeians slept wherever convenient, according to their status and interpersonal relationships, and to the season. Any bedding was likely to have been moved about as convenient (see Goldberg 1999:149–150). Elia's observation that it was not possible to distinguish separate locations for day or night sleeping would add weight to this proposition (1932: 417).[5]

More than 150 years ago, Johannes Overbeck suggested that the small closed rooms around the front hall of Pompeian houses were unlikely to have all had the same uses and the same names (1856:192). Their quantity should certainly suggest that their functions were also numerous. As Leach has pointed out, names such as *camera* and *conclave* were probably used for rooms of these types with variable uses (1997:

70). It should therefore be concluded that modern scholars should not be using this Latin terminology to determine the patterns of activities carried out in such rooms in Pompeian houses. Neither should the number of such rooms in a house be taken as a reliable indicator of the number of its occupants (compare Strocka 1984a:49–50, 1991:135–136; Ling 1997:132–144).

TYPE 5: OPEN-FRONTED ROOMS OFF THE SIDES OF FRONT HALLS

The open-fronted spaces off the sides of front halls are conventionally called *alae* by modern scholars. From Vitruvius' prescription (6, 3.4) that the width of *alae* should be proportionally related to the length of the *atrium*, scholars have long assumed that this was the nomenclature for rooms of this type in Pompeian houses (for example, Mau 1899:241 Fig. 110, 252–253; Paoli 1958:54–55; Dwyer 1982:31–32; Clarke 1991:6; Strocka 1991:32; Descœudres et al. 1994:85; Staub Gierow 1994:56, 61). Mau referred to a remark by Vitruvius that *alae* were used for the display of the portraits of ancestors (1899:252). It is probable that he was referring to Vitruvius' recommendation (6, 3.6) for the height at which *images* should be set (see also Tamm 1973:55). There is no actual mention of *alae* in this passage, and it is likely that Vitruvius was referring to a proportional relationship involving masks in the *atrium* (see Clarke 1991:6 n.10) or, conceivably, the *tablinum*.

This study indicates that this type of room in Pompeian houses, whether or not it was called an *ala*, was not used as a display area but had frequently been used for domestic storage during the final occupation phase. Leach noted that no other ancient author uses the term *alae* in this context (1997:53). She suggested that the term *exedra*, used by Quintilian in reference to spaces opening onto the *atrium*, may be a more suitable label for this spatial type (see Ling 1997:301). Given its frequent association with the intellectual life of public buildings (Leach 1997:61–62), however, this term might seem rather pretentious for a Pompeian household.

TYPE 6: MEDIUM/LARGE ROOMS OFF THE CORNERS OF FRONT HALLS

Rooms of this type 6 were usually long and narrow with a narrow doorway in one end of the long wall opening onto the front hall. They are generally labeled *triclinia* or dining rooms by modern scholars (for example, Mau 1899:253; Ehrhardt 1988:32; Michel 1990:36; Stemmer 1992:26; Peters et al. 1993:404; Descœudres et al. 1994:9, Fig. 6). Vitruvius recommended (6, 3.8) that *triclinia* should be twice as long as they are wide. Varro (*De ling. lat.* 5, 162) indicated that rooms for dining, called *cenacula*, were once found around the *cavum aedium*. Both Vitruvius (7, 4.4) and Varro also attest to a *triclinium hibernum* and a *hibernum*, respectively, which were used for dining in winter and were rather modest (see Tamm 1963:129). From this, it has been concluded that rooms of this type, in this location in Roman houses, functioned as winter dining rooms (for example, Richardson 1983: 63–64; Descœudres 1987:174, Fig. 10.13).

The term *triclinium* is widely used in the literary sources, which also indicate that the *triclinium* had a variety of different structural forms and no specific location (Leach 1997:67–68). Dunbabin argued (1996:67–68) that secure identification of rooms for dining is possible only when fittings such as masonry couches were present, or the floor design indicated the location of movable couches. However, the latter only suggests what the room had been designed for and does not necessarily have any bearing on its subsequent use. In fact, such patterned floors were relatively infrequent in the examples of this room type in this sample. As already noted, the artifact distribution in these rooms does not confirm their use as dining rooms and, hence, the labels of *triclinium* or *cenaculum*.

TYPE 7: OPEN ROOMS LEADING TO GARDENS OR OPEN-SIDED ROOMS OPPOSITE MAIN ENTRANCEWAYS

Type 7 rooms were usually located at the rear of the front hall and could often form a wide passageway leading from the front hall to the main garden. They are traditionally referred to by modern scholars as *tablina* (for example, Mau 1899, 249–252; Maiuri 1933:53 [hence Ling 1997:49]; Ehrhardt 1988:44; Michel 1990:34; Strocka 1991:33; Descœudres et al. 1994:93; George 1997a:305). This label is based on the recommendations of Vitruvius (6, 3.5) for a proportional relationship between the widths of the *tablinum* and of the *atrium*. As Leach has noted (1997:52–53), Festus also located the *tablinum* in the vicinity of the *atrium*.

Pliny (*Nat. Hist.* 35, 2.7) identified the *tabulinum* as a space filled with books of records and memorials of official careers. On the basis of this reference, it has frequently been assumed that this room type in Pompeian houses functioned as the office of the *paterfamilias* where the family archives and wealth were kept (for example, Mau 1899:252; Descœudres et al. 1994:93; George 1997a:305). Mau and Leach also noted textual references to the *tablinum* as having served as a summer dining room (see also Michel 1990:34). Mau argued, however, that this use occurred only during a period that predated the oldest houses in Pompeii (1899:251). From the decoration of this room type in the Casa di M. Lucretius and the Casa del Citarista, Dwyer (1982:116) concluded that these particular rooms served as *pinocothecae* or viewing frames to the garden.

Five of the rooms classified as type 7 in this sample had evidence of bedding and therefore could conceivably have been used for either sleeping or dining. In general, though, the contents of these rooms indicated more utilitarian storage, comparable to that in the front halls from which they led to the rear parts of the house. No evidence for any material that might be considered archival was recorded in these rooms, despite the fact that the majority of those with contents had wall decoration and therefore were the most likely to have had a formal function.

Leach noted that *tablinum* was a term that rarely occurred in the ancient sources and then only in "antiquarianizing contexts" (1997:52). It would seem that by AD 79 the function of such rooms in Pompeian houses, and possibly their labels, may have changed considerably.

TYPE 8: INTERNAL CORRIDORS

Type 8 corridors frequently led from the front hall, alongside room type 7, to the garden, but they also led from the front-hall/garden area to rooms located away from this main axis. Such internal corridors are sometimes referred to by modern scholars as *fauces* (for example, Becker 1876:234–235). As with the front entranceway (room type 1), this label is based on Vitruvius' use (6, 3.6) of this term in a proportional relationship to the *atrium*. Mau (1899:254) saw *fauces* as an erroneous term. More generally, these corridors are labeled *androncs* (Mau 1899:241, Fig. 110, 254; Paoli 1958:63; Strocka 1991:31; Staub Gierow 1994:29, 63; Ling 1997:50). Vitruvius commented (6, 7.5) on the use of this Greek term for passages between peristyles and visitors' quarters. Pliny (*Ep.* 2, 17) used it to indicate a passage between the walls of *cubicula* and the garden (see Paoli 1958:69 n. 23). Considering the obvious function of these corridors as passageways, artifact distribution is not particularly useful for assessing the validity of either term. Given the meaning of *andron* in Greek, any use of this term for corridors in Roman houses might conceivably have symbolized the intellectual pretensions of the writer (see de la Ruffinière du Prey 1994:8). It seems unlikely that this term was used widely among the inhabitants of Pompeian houses (see Richardson 1983:62).

TYPE 9: MAIN GARDENS, COLONNADED GARDENS, AND AMBULATORIES

The main garden area, which is usually located behind the front-hall area and often colonnaded or partially colonnaded, is generally referred to by modern scholars as the peristyle or pseudo-peristyle, from *peristylum* (for example, Becker 1876:234; Mau 1899:254–255; Maiuri 1933:74 [hence Ling 1997:59]; Strocka 1991:89; Seiler 1992:37; Descœudres et al. 1994:99, 133; Staub Gierow 1994:32, 66; Dickmann 1997). Vitruvius recommended (6, 3.7) that the *peristyla* lie crosswise, presumably to the *atrium*, and that they be wider than they are deep. In almost all Pompeian houses, the colonnaded garden actually lay

on the opposite orientation to Vitruvius' recommendation (see house plans in appendix A). *Peristylum* is again a Greek term. It has been assumed that, while the areas at the front of the house had Latin names, those in the rear of the house, both the colonnaded garden and its surrounding spaces, had Greek nomenclature (for example, Mau 1899:241; Paoli 1958:54–55). Leach (1997:59) found that such a distinction was unjustified and that the label *peristylum* was seldom mentioned by ancient authors other than Vitruvius. Again, the lack of Roman use of the term *peristylum* is probably a more valid testimony to its likely inappropriateness in Pompeian houses than any artifact distribution pattern, if indeed Pompeian houses can be classified as Roman houses.

When this open area was not fully peripteral (see figure 5.7), it is often called a *viridarium* by modern scholars (for example, Becker 1876:235; Jashemski 1979a:67, 187; Michel 1990:52; Staub Gierow 1994:32). This term occurred in a number of instances in the ancient literary sources (for example, Cicero *Atticus* 2, 3.2; Petronius 9; Suetonius *De Vita Caesarum*: *Tiberius* 60; Pliny *Nat. Hist.* 18, 2.2). In all these instances, with the possible exception of Pliny who alluded to its ornamental character, a *viridarium* appears to have been a fairly extensive garden or even a park. It would therefore again seem a rather pretentious term for the particular gardens for which it was used in Pompeii, which tend to be smaller than the fully peripteral ones.

Terms more widely used in the Latin sources were *porticus* or *ambulatio* (Leach 1997:59). The term *ambulatio* indicates the use of this space for strolling and was often associated with meditation and philosophical dispute (Dickmann 1997:123). The characteristics of a *porticus* that were often stressed were its spaciousness (for example, Cicero *Atticus* 3, 31.43; Vitruvius 5, 1) and its location for walking (Cicero *Atticus* 4, 16.4). Nevertheless, with a few exceptions (for example, Michel 1990:42; Strocka 1984a:24), the term *peristylum* or *viridarium* is preferred by modern scholars for Pompeian houses.

While the more structural and functional terms such as *porticus* and *ambulatio* seem more appropriate for these spaces in Pompeian houses, modern scholars tend to assume that a space with pleasing vistas for philosophical ponderings must be devoid of domestic paraphernalia. Such perspectives need not be projected into the Roman past. The artifact distribution witnessed in this sample does not therefore discount the suitability of these terms. While they are likely to have been applied to the colonnaded area, labels for the open space are more difficult to determine, although see the discussion below for room type 18.

Type 10: Medium/Large Closed Rooms off Gardens/Terraces without Good Views

These usually long and relatively narrow rooms, often located towards the corners of the main garden area, have been labeled by modern scholars as *triclinia* or referred to as dining rooms (for example, Mau 1898:22; Armitt 1993:239; Descœudres et al. 1994:111). This label is generally based on Vitruvius' recommendations (6, 3.8) concerning their proportions and spatial relationships with *exedrae*, *oeci*, and *pinacothecae*. Sometimes they have been further labeled as summer *triclinia* (for example, Descœudres 1987:174), based on Vitruvius' recommendations of dining areas for the different seasons (6, 4.2). Again, it should be stressed that there is no specific locational information in the literary sources for *triclinia*. Rather, the basis for the use of this term in Pompeii has been the room's proportions and ability to accommodate three dining couches, as well as any evidence for the latter in the decorative scheme (Foss 1994:91–94; Dunbabin 1996:68).

Type 10 rooms were relatively rare in Pompeii, as more frequently they were opened up to take the form of room type 11. This study shows that they tended to be empty but, in those that were not, the contents included food-preparation material and serving vessels rather than actual tableware. Only in two instances was there any suggestion that these rooms might have had dining furniture (compare Dell'Orto 1990:171). Thus, either these rooms were not used as dining

rooms, at least in their final occupation phase, or the type of material recorded in them was commonplace in formal dining rooms. This pattern is reminiscent of the similar long, narrow rooms off the front hall area (room type 6).

Type 11: Medium/Large Open-Fronted Rooms off Gardens/Terraces with Windows or Wide Entranceways Giving View of Garden or Lower Floor

Rooms of this type were similar to type 10 but generally more spacious and open (see figures 4.2 and 6.4). They could be located almost anywhere around the garden, on a terrace or a lower ground level with a commanding view, such as in Insula VIII 2. These rooms are variously labeled by modern scholars as *oeci* (for example, Mau 1899:259; Maiuri 1933:57, 160, 175; Strocka 1991:41, 44; Descœudres et al. 1994:109; Ling 1997:272, 301); *exedrae* (for example, Mau 1899:241, Fig. 110; Strocka 1991:35, 37; Seiler 1992:32; Descœudres et al. 1994:123); and *triclinia* (for example, Maiuri 1933:168; Strocka 1984a:26; 1991:38; Seiler 1992:62; Staub Gierow 1994:64). They are widely believed to have been dining rooms, the more spacious for large groups and for special occasions (see Mau 1899:259; Dwyer 1982:119).

Vitruvius specified the structure (6, 3.8–10) and proportions for an *oecus* but also recommended a northern aspect and garden view. Leach found (1997:60) that only one other Latin author used this term (Pliny *Nat. Hist.* 36, 60). As she argued, it was the grandeur with which the Vitruvian *oeci* inspired Renaissance architects that has given this term such currency in the study of Roman domestic architecture. There would seem little reason to assume that it belonged to the vocabulary of the Pompeian householder.

According to Vitruvius, *exedrae* were open spaces (7, 9.2) that should be of ample dimensions (6, 3.8). Cicero (*de Oratore* 3, 4.17) used this label for a place to which one could retire. Modern scholars often use it for rooms that are smaller than those they labeled *oeci* (for example, see Strocka 1991: compare 35, 37 with 41,

44). Again, Leach (1997:61–62) has drawn attention to the scarcity of this term in the ancient sources and to its use only by Roman aristocrats who felt the need to communicate their intellectuality. This term seems unlikely to have been in common usage in Pompeian houses. Jens-Arne Dickmann (1997:123) used Vitruvius' reference (6, 7.3) to this space in a Greek house to identify its location in Roman houses, a seemingly inappropriate cross-cultural approach given the complexity of the relationships between the two cultures' domestic practices.

Vitruvius' recommendations for *triclinia* (6, 3.8) indicate that they could also have been *exedrae* or *oeci*, which suggests that the former term was a functional one and the latter two were structural. Leach (1997:59) found that such a distinction generally occurred in the literary sources. Modern scholars, however, often apply the label *triclinium* to rooms of this type that are longer and narrower than those to which they applied the labels *exedra* or *oecus*.

According to Dwyer (1982:120), *triclinia* required elegant furniture, utensils, and serving ware, the latter objects being exhibited on sideboards or tables when not in use. From this study there would seem sufficient evidence to confirm that many rooms of this type in this sample were used for dining and, given the use of the above terms in the literature, *triclinium* would seem the most likely candidate as a label for this room type. However, the most predominant pattern is that these rooms had also been used to store equipment that was not necessarily fine tableware. The persistence of this latter pattern suggests that disrupted circumstances were not necessarily the cause for this activity. Again, as with the colonnaded garden, there is a need to break free from the modern concept that entertainment and intellectual pursuits were removed from the clutter of daily life.

TYPE 12: SMALL CLOSED ROOMS OFF GARDENS/TERRACES OR LOWER FLOORS

As with the small closed rooms around the front hall, to which rooms of this type were similar in form, type 12 rooms are also fre-

quently labeled *cubicula* by modern scholars (for example, Descœudres 1987:174, Fig. 10.13; Descœudres et al. 1994:103; Michel 1990:45, 50; Strocka 1991:42, 46, 48–49; Seiler 1992:49, 55, 59, 63; Ling 1997:271, 274). Again, this label has been used to indicate that the decorated rooms of this type functioned as bedrooms (Mau 1899:255). Elia suggested that such rooms were used for sleeping during the day (1932:417).

The analyses of assemblages from these rooms separated those that were decorated from those that were not. The contents of both suggest that such rooms were used for storage. Storage in the decorated examples was associated with personal activities but not actual sleeping. That in the undecorated rooms seems to indicate more permanent and utilitarian storage.

Leach has commented on the frequency with which the terms *triclinium* and *cubiculum* occur together in the literature (1997:67). As discussed above for room type 4, however, the frequent use of the term *cubiculum* in a variety of contexts suggests that it was not used to describe the function of a space. The only textual reference that provides any locational information for the term *cubiculum* is that of Varro (*De ling. lat.* 5, 162), who referred to such spaces around the *cavum aedium*.

Again, the concept of individualized bedrooms in the Roman world, which the term *cubiculum* has often been used to convey, would seem a projection of modern spatial/functional arrangements onto those of the past. At the same time, the concept of a sleeping space that could change according to climate and time of day is conceivable and validated by textual references. Whether or not the Pompeians labeled such a space a *cubiculum*, *camera*, or *conclave* (see Leach 1997:70), any application of these terms to Pompeian spaces does not provide evidence of function.

TYPE 13: SMALL OPEN-FRONTED AREAS OFF GARDENS/TERRACES OR LOWER FLOORS

Rooms of this type are also called *exedrae* by some modern scholars (for example, Maiuri

1933:89–121 [hence Ling 1997:274–275]; Strocka 1984a:29; Descœudres et al. 1994:9, Figs. 6, 104). Cicero (*de Oratore* 3, 4.17) indicated that an *exedra* was a place to which one could retire, Vitruvius (5, 11.2) alluded to its role in the intellectual activities in public buildings, and Varro (*R. R.* 3, 5.8) referred to birds being penned up in an *exedra* in a *peristylum*.

In this sample, type 13 rooms either lacked contents or contained material similar to that in the ambulatories of the colonnaded gardens. This suggests that they were a space into which the activities of these ambulatories may have extended. As discussed above, *exedra* was a rarely used structural term, taken from the Greek, and more frequently associated with public rather than residential buildings (Leach 1997:61–62). Again, as for room type 5, *exedra* seems a pretentious term for these small spaces in Pompeian houses.

TYPE 14: ROOMS WITH COOKING HEARTH OR ASSOCIATED ROOMS

Rooms of type 14 could be located anywhere in the house and are identified either by the presence of a built-in bench, which appears to be a cooking hearth, or by the room's apparent dependence on a room with a cooking hearth (figures 5.11, 5.23). Modern scholars sometimes employ the term *culina* to label rooms of this type in Pompeian houses (for example, Maiuri 1933:213; Stemmer 1992:34; Foss 1994:69). More frequently, however, they use modern terms such as kitchen (for example, Jahn in Becker 1876: Plan B; Descœudres 1987:174, Figs. 10.12–13; 1994:131; Ling 1997:278), *Küche* (for example, Ehrhardt 1988:36; Strocka 1991:53; Seiler 1992:68; Staub Gierow 1994:37) or *cucina* (for example, Maiuri 1933:214; Salza Prina Ricotti 1978/1980).

By using these modern terms to label this space, it is easy to assume that it performed a function similar to kitchens of the modern world. The fixtures and contents of type 14 rooms indicate, however, that one should be wary of paralleling this space with the large spaces dedicated to food preparation in serviced eighteenth- to early twentieth-century residences; the small mid-twentieth-century cooking spaces that were the domain of the housewife; or the large family kitchens that became more popular in many parts of the western world in the late twentieth century. The assemblages in this sample indicate that food preparation and some cooking could have been carried out in rooms of this type, but that cooking could also have been carried out in closer proximity to eating areas. Assemblages in rooms of this type also indicate a close relationship among food preparation, ablutions, and possibly religious practices within these spaces.

In this instance, the Latin term *culina* is probably more appropriate for type 14 rooms in Pompeian houses rather than for modern counterparts. Their fixtures and assemblages bear testimony to their specific function, and this term is often used in the literary sources for a structurally separate space for food preparation (see Horace, *Sat.* 1, 5.73; Petronius 2; Columella 1, 6.2; compare Foss 1994:69–74).

TYPE 15: LATRINES AS ENTIRE ROOMS

Rooms of this type are usually small and completely taken up with the fixture by which they are identified (see figure 5.13). They could be located in a variety of places within the house plan. The Latin nomenclature *latrina* or *lavatrina* (see Varro *De ling. lat.* 5, 118; Suetonius *De Vita Caesarum: Tiberius* 58) is sometimes used by modern scholars to label such rooms (for example, Jahn in Becker 1876:235, Plan B; Maiuri 1933:214; Stemmer 1992:35; Staub Gierow 1994:38), as is the derivative term *latrine* (for example, Descœudres and Sear 1987:13; Seiler 1992:52; 68; Ling 1997:319). This nomenclature would seem fairly noncontentious.

TYPE 16: OTHER ROOMS OUTSIDE FRONT-HALL/GARDEN COMPLEXES

Many houses in Pompeii had rooms or suites of rooms that were not part of the main front-hall/garden complex. The former were accessible from the latter, however, usually via an internal corridor. Such areas are often referred to by modern scholars as *rustic* or *service quarters* (for example, Maiuri 1933:186; Salza Prina Ricotti 1978/1980). While these scholars do not use textual nomenclature for this general area, Latin and Greek terms are often used for its components. The terms *apotheca* and *repositorium* are used to label spaces assumed to have been used for storage (for example, Maiuri 1933:204, 206; Strocka 1991:53). The term *cubiculum* is sometimes used on the assumption that so-labeled rooms had been the sleeping rooms of slaves or servants (for example, Ling 1997:35; Seiler 1992: 67). While references to sleeping quarters for slaves and freedmen are found in the texts (for example, Columella 1, 6; Cicero *Phil.* 2, 27; Pliny *Ep* 2, 17.9), they refer mainly to rural villas and the dwellings of the senatorial classes, where presumably there were more slaves than in Pompeian townhouses. There seems little reason to assume that the latter would have had rooms set aside for the sleeping and privacy of servants (see George 1997a: 317).

The assemblages in type 16 rooms indicate that they were not a coherent group. Nevertheless, their uses seem generally more utilitarian than similar rooms in the main axis of the house. While the terms *cubiculum*, *culina*, *stabulum*, *repositorium*, *apotheca*, and *posticum* may well be suitable for individual components of these areas in Pompeian houses, the apparent lack of Latin terminology that modern scholars could draw on for the concept of a service quarter should warn us to refrain from seeing these areas as separate service units comparable to those in large eighteenth- and nineteenth-century élite dwellings. Vitruvius referred to various apartments within the house as pertaining to particular industries (6, 4.2), but did not mention a service quarter (see also Columella 1, 6.9–10). His reference to *cellae familiaricae* (Vitruvius 6, 7.2) applies to Greek houses.

TYPE 17: STAIRWAYS

While stairways could often be located within another room in Pompeian houses, they also led directly from the front hall or garden to upper floors or to lower ground floors. Modern scholars tend to use modern terms for these (for

example, Ehrhardt 1988:40; Strocka 1991:26; Seiler 1992:37; Stemmer 1992:36). Use of the Latin term *scalae* has not been noted.

TYPE 18: SECONDARY INTERNAL GARDENS AND COURTYARDS, USUALLY NOT COLONNADED

Areas of this type did not generally open off the front hall or garden but were usually accessible indirectly from the front-hall/garden area through an internal corridor or some other type of room. Such spaces have been given a variety of textual labels by modern scholars, depending on their layout, decoration, and perceived function. For example, the terms *hortulus* or *hortus* are often applied to spaces that included gardens and seemed to be fairly informal and utilitarian (for example, Maiuri 1933:216; Descœudres et al. 1994:9), while smaller courtyards, often not cultivated, are labeled with the term *xystus* (for example, Maiuri 1927:38). De Franciscis (1988:18, 24) referred to the two covered areas at the front of the Casa di Julius Polybius as *atria*. However, Leach argued that area A in the Casa di Julius Polybius should be called a *vestibulum* (Leach 1993; see also Leach 1997:55).

Pliny uses the term *hortus* (*Ep.* 2, 17.15) to describe a garden full of fruit trees or a thick, rustic garden, whereas he uses the term *xystus* (*Ep.* 5, 6.16) for what seems to have been a more formal garden. Cicero (*Ad fam.* 1.9.20) referred to dining in a *hortus*. The term *hortulus* is used by ancient authors, such as Suetonius (*De Vita Caesarum: Nero* 50), Cicero (*de Orat.* 3, 63), and Seneca (*Ep.* 21, 10), to describe a garden as a peaceful and charming location and often as a public space. The distinctions made by scholars who labeled gardens in Pompeian houses is that a *hortus* or *hortulus* is seemingly less formal and more utilitarian than the main colonnaded garden, and a *xystus* is a courtyard or garden that appeared formal but was not colonnaded. This distinction seems unvalidated. Cicero's reference suggests rather that the last term could conceivably be suitable for the main garden area.

More frequently scholars use modern terms (for example, kitchen garden: Ling 1997:279;

173

yard: Ling 1997:319; *Lichthof*: Seiler 1992:63; *Bedienstetenatrium*: Fröhlich 1991:93; *cortile* or *cortiletto*: Maiuri 1927:38, 1933:204), perhaps because of the perceived difficulty of relating these excavated spaces to those discussed in the ancient literature. Both the assemblages and the layout of the areas classified as this type vary considerably but reveal their role as sources of light, water, and air, and the mixture of utilitarian and luxury contents are apparent. It is very probable that these areas had a variety of names. It is not necessary, however, to envisage that they were distinguished from the colonnaded gardens on the basis of nomenclature. Leach commented (1997:59) that the term *xystus*, while of Greek origin and more specialized, was used more frequently in the literature than *peristylum*. In fact, Pliny referred to a *xystus* that was in front of a *porticus*. The activities carried out in colonnaded gardens in houses that had no secondary garden or courtyard appear to have been little different from those carried out in courtyard areas of this type.

TYPE 19: SECONDARY ENTRANCES AND ENTRANCE COURTYARDS

This category refers to all entranceways to the house, excluding those that led directly to the front hall. Sometimes these secondary entrances are also labeled *fauces* by modern scholars (for example, Strocka 1991:64; Seiler 1992:66). As discussed above, this term does not seem appropriate. Past scholars have used the term *posticum* for these entranceways (for example, Jahn in Becker 1876:235, Plan B; Mau 1899:214, Figs. 110, 255; Maiuri 1933:201), although it is used infrequently in more recent works. The term *posticum* is used in ancient texts for the back entrance or back part of the house (for example, Horace, *Ep.* 1, 5.31; Plautus, *Most* 3, 3.27). Given that such entranceways in Pompeii were sometimes decorated, the impression that they served as an inferior rear entrance should be avoided.

TYPE 20: ROOMS AT THE FRONT OF HOUSE, OPEN TO THE STREET

Rooms or spaces of type 20 had a wide entrance to the street and were often located to one side of the main entrance, with a narrow entrance in the back wall leading to the main part of the house. The term *taberna* has been applied to rooms of this type by modern scholars (for example, de Franciscis 1988:18; Stemmer 1992:36; Descœudres et al. 1994:9, Fig. 6). Generally, this term was used in ancient texts to refer to a separate shop or workshop (for example, Martial *Ep.* 1, 117.10; Varro *De ling. lat.* 8, 55). Its use has been attested in Pompeii (Pirson 1997:168), although seemingly as a separate establishment with accommodation rather than as the types of rooms discussed here (compare Purcell 1995:329). The fixtures and assemblages in type 20 rooms in this sample did not set them apart from the residential part of the house. While there may be many reasons for this, the evidence is insubstantial to identify them as commercial spaces.

TYPE 21: BATH AREAS

Certain suites of rooms in Pompeian houses are identified as bath areas on the basis of architectural criteria. For the different spaces within these suites, modern scholars variously use the terms *apodyterium* (Sogliano 1896:430; Della Corte 1916:31; Maiuri 1933:139), *apodyterium-frigidarium* (Strocka 1991:55), *frigidarium* (Mau 1887:134), *tepidarium* (Mau 1893:53; Maiuri 1933:139; Strocka 1991:56; Ling 1997:276), *caldarium* (Mau 1887:134; 1893:53; Della Corte 1916:31; Maiuri 1933:142; Strocka 1991:58; Ling 1997:276), and *laconicum* (Ling 1997:277). Vitruvius recommended the sequence *caldarium–tepidarium–frigidarium* for public bath complexes (5, 10.1). While he recommended that the heated chambers be vaulted, he also advised (5, 10.5) that a domed *laconicum* should adjoin the *tepidarium*. Pliny (*Ep.* 5, 6.25) described *balineae* in his villa in Tuscany, which consisted of an *apodyterium* preceding a *frigidarium*, in turn preceding a medium room and a *caldarium*. While the *balineum* in his Laurentine villa (*Ep.* 2, 17) had a *frigidarium*, the adjacent spaces consisted of an *unctorium*, a furnace, two *cellae*, and a *calida piscina*.

As mentioned in chapter 5, there was little in the way of loose finds in these spaces in this sample to validate their function as bath-suites.

Rather, the architecture is used to identify their overall role as a bath complex. For example, Mau's (1887:133) identification of room 6 in the Casa di Giuseppe II as an *apodyterium* or a *tepidarium* appears to be based on his attempt to associate this bath complex with the sequence prescribed by Vitruvius rather than from anything visible in the physical remains.

There was also a lack of actual baths in these rooms to conform to the functions described by the labels, although the Casa delle Nozze d'Argento had a pool in the nearby garden area. It is therefore extremely difficult to distinguish, for example, whether one room was a *caldarium, laconicum,* or *unctorium,* or whether another was an *apodyterium, frigidarium,* or *tepidarium.* It is conceivable that some rooms performed more than one function, either contemporaneously or according to the season. The application of specific Latin nomenclature to the components of bath complexes in private housing in Pompeii should be treated with caution.

TYPE 22: UPPER FLOORS

Remains of upper-story rooms are sometimes evident in Pompeian houses, but more frequently their former presence is attested by stairways leading upward from the ground floor. Previous research on the upper stories of Pompeian houses was often concerned with the existence of a dining room in this area, or perceived it as a separate living space. The former is usually based on modern scholars' application of the term *cenaculum* either to a single room or to the whole area (for example, Mau 1899:267–270; Maiuri 1927:34–35; McKay 1977:80; Sutherland 1990). In turn, this application is based on Varro's definition (*De ling. lat.* 5, 162) of a *cenaculum* as a dining room that had been moved upstairs. The term *cenaculum* is also attested in Pompeii (see Pirson 1997:168–169). While it may have referred to the upper floor here, such an assumption is based on Varro's definition rather than on anything evident in the inscription. The inscription indicated only that the *cenaculum* was a rentable area within the Insula Arriana Polliana. This *insula* comprised a number of separate establishments on the ground floor. The only evidence of upper-story rooms apparent in the ground plan (Pirson 1997: Fig. 1) is that they were attached to ground-floor establishments and were not separate dwellings (see Pirson 1997:168).

The contents of the upper-floor areas in this study give no indication that dining prevailed there. This may not be surprising, as the dining equipment may have habitually been stored on the ground floor. Generally the finds indicated a pattern of activities similar to those on the lower floors, although perhaps more limited. The evidence would seem insubstantial to assume that Pompeians had referred to this area as a *cenaculum.*

CONCLUSIONS

Studies of spatial function in Roman houses have been obsessed with marrying textual nomenclature for room types to the structural and decorative evidence of excavated spaces in order first to designate and then to analyze the activities carried out in these spaces (Wallace-Hadrill 1994:6). Textual nomenclature from certain ancient authors has been allied with anecdotal information from others to gain insights into the spatial division of household activities in Pompeii. This very combination of architectural and textual remains, often in an uncritical or even unconscious association with modern analogy, has created the impression that we are very familiar with Pompeian, and hence Roman, domestic life. As Leach has demonstrated, this is often an oversimplification of the relationship among diverse forms of data (see also Jameson 1990: 92–93 for Greek houses).

The great wealth of textual and architectural material remains from the Roman world is continuously being reworked by different scholars from different perspectives. The full data set of the archaeological material has, however, been largely ignored. Material from archaeological sites has been excavated out of its architectural contexts and used for specialist studies of pottery, glass, metal, and so forth (see Allison 1997a).

There seems to be a belief that to include a contextual study of all this material would only bring further complications to an already complicated area of study—a gross oversight and a limitation of the available evidence, particularly if we are indeed concerned with the organization of households and household space in the Roman world. A quarter of a century ago, Brigitta Tamm wrote of the need to abandon "old points of departure in the discussion about Roman houses . . . and concentrate on other material instead" (1973:55). Nevertheless, scholars continue to believe that a lack of fit between textually and artifactually defined use of space is a result of the unreliability of the archaeological record. It is more meaningful to take a critical approach to the relationships between textual references, with their various perspectives and agendas, and the totality of archaeological records.

In the first instance, the textual information that we often employ to assess room use should be treated with more caution. Not only is it largely written for agendas other than to inform us about domestic life, but it is also written by a predominantly aristocratic male élite with little concern for the majority of the occupants of a house (see, for example, Gower 1993:2). Thus, studies of the material remains of Roman domestic space have tended to concentrate on the houses of the wealthy, which offer material that compares better with textual sources (for example, McKay 1977:30–79; Wallace-Hadrill 1994). The few studies that have looked at seemingly lower-status housing (for example, Packer 1975:133–142; McKay 1977:80–99; Nappo 1997; Pirson 1997) have also interpreted the architectural remains from the perspective provided by the textual evidence.

This study shows that through an analysis of the distribution of artifact assemblages, assumed room use that was identified by combining textual and architectural evidence does not always apply in Pompeian houses, especially not in smaller dwellings where a multifunctional use of space may have been more prevalent. Ancient authors such as Vitruvius make us only too aware that buildings tended to be constructed within strict, often very traditional, parameters. While there would always be a certain amount of traditional use of space in such structures, social change and fashion often move too quickly for the buildings to be knocked down and rebuilt to respond to new needs. Extant architectural remains of a Roman house may give us an insight into how an architect or builder, or a building tradition, intended such a building to function. Its use, and the labels describing that use, are likely to change considerably over time. We need only examine, for example, our own reuse of nineteenth-century and earlier twentieth-century houses to see how rapidly such functional change can occur, and the labeling of spaces change, without altering a building's structure.

There has recently been a growing awareness of the need for a more critical approach to the use of vocabulary in the study of domestic space in Pompeii (Laurence 1995:313). There is still a fundamental assumption that it is principally through textual references that we can gain a more enlightened understanding of life in such contexts. The issue here would seem to be that because literary-trained scholars are turning to the archaeological remains with text-driven questions, they will always be frustrated with the inability of archaeology to provide the answers they need without recourse to textual analogy. The previous two chapters indicated the extent to which the archaeological evidence can provide information on spatial distribution of household activities. It remains to question the roots of any variability and to take an even more critical approach to the context of textual inference and then to its conceivable relationship with Pompeian archaeological remains. The work of scholars such as Wallace-Hadrill, Nevett, Leach, and Riggsby is important in this regard.

For example, Leach questioned the relationship between specific labels and specific domestic activities and highlighted the multiple purposes of rooms in Roman houses. A problem for studies that concentrate on a particular architecturally or textually labeled room type (for example, Foss 1994; Dickmann 1997) is that the studies tend to overplay the role of that specific spatial type in the daily running of the household and to identify separate spaces too readily according to a particular function. It seems more valid to assess the interrelationships of the various components of the house.

Leach has also argued that long-held beliefs about a separation of the parts of a Roman house into those with Greek-named spaces and those with Latin-named spaces are unfounded. Rather, such beliefs stem from an overreliance on Vitruvian terminology, which has been used as a type of Linnaean classification system by modern scholars. The apparent conflicting use of certain terms by Vitruvius and Varro should heighten our awareness of a kind of real-estate-agent-speak in which writers such as Vitruvius and Pliny seem to indulge.

In summary, the employment of Latin labels as a conventional system for discussing the excavated spaces of Roman houses is indeed helpful (for example, Peters et al. 1993:403; see also Dickmann 1999: esp. 23–39), particularly when scholarly works on Pompeii cover a range of modern languages. However, the continued use of this Latinization should be viewed as a convention only. This convention should not be used to validate the identification of the physical remains and the activities that took place there through textual descriptions of specific domestic behavior. It should not form a starting point for writing social history.

Studies that combine textual evidence from the Roman capital with architectural evidence from its provinces to assess the use of space in Roman houses also run the risk of producing a prescriptive, architectural history rather than a truly social history. Leach has argued that there is good reason to protest "the dominance of literary evidence in interpreting the function of domestic spaces in Pompeii" (1997:50). Such a process presents Pompeii as an analogy or adjunct of Rome. Indeed, relationships between Greek and Latin terms for parts of houses in former Magna Graecia may well have been fundamentally different from those in the Roman capital.

This analysis suggests that there are, to date, no secure labels for most spaces in Pompeian houses. Until further evidence can substantiate the use of any text-based nomenclature, scholars should be more critical in their use of so-labeled spaces for the substantiation of spatially related domestic activities. In these last three chapters, it has been possible only to touch on current debates concerned with room use in Roman houses, many of which are grounded in the Pompeian evidence. Some of the principal issues have been highlighted, however, to demonstrate that such studies would benefit from paying more attention, where possible, to artifact distribution in excavated spaces in Pompeii and elsewhere in the Roman world.

NOTES

1. Terms for domestic spaces used by Pliny and included in the discussion in this chapter are not included in the glossary because I do not wish to give the impression that their meanings are well understood.

2. Laurence (1995) has misrepresented the argument in the work being reviewed (that is, Allison 1993:6–7).

3. For example, Yvon Thébert argued (1987:325–326) that the peristyled courts in houses in Roman North Africa were not called *atria* because they were different in location, form, and function from the Pompeian front halls and did not conform to the Vitruvian ideal. He acknowledged that limited furnishings were uncovered in these spaces. He has followed the general assumption that Pompeian front halls provided the archetype for *atria*, that Vitruvius provided the dictionary for what people of the Roman world called the parts of their houses, and that anything divergent from that form must have had another label (see Allison 2001).

4. For example, where Maiuri (1927:26) refers to room f in the Casa del Sacerdos Amandus as a *cubiculum*, Foss (1994:251) has translated this as bedroom.

5. Elia (1932:420) purported to discuss a room in House II 7,2. This would appear to be an error, as the room illustrated is room 1 in the Casa del Sacello Iliaco.

Figure 8.1 North wall of room e showing hole to room f, Casa dei Ceii

8.

Conditions Before and After the Eruption in AD 79

THE PREVIOUS CHAPTERS DEMONSTRATE that this study revealed consistent distribution patterns of less easily moved artifacts or collections of artifacts in Pompeian house samples, which might be termed "systemic house-floor assemblages" (Schiffer 1985:18, 38). These distribution patterns can provide information concerning patterns for the habitual spatial distribution of activities within these houses. Other less pervasive distribution patterns within these assemblages are likely to have resulted from disrupted living conditions, possibly caused by seismic and volcanic activity. It is also possible that some of these patterns may have resulted from post-abandonment disturbance.

As discussed in chapter 2, most Pompeian research has been dominated by an assumption that only one earthquake occurred in the period AD 62 to AD 79 that could have disrupted Pompeian life. If the "upper layer" (Jongman 1988:56) of the site of Pompeii showed a town in a state of disruption, with people living in shelters (Dell'Orto in Conticello et al. 1990:188) following the devastation caused by such an earthquake (see Zanker 1988:4), then the "house-floor assemblages" would not have been as orderly as the New Archaeologists have presumed (for example, Schiffer 1985:18). If such observed pre-abandonment disruption and damaged or altered structure and decoration can indeed be given a fixed date, either that of an earthquake in AD 62 or that of the eruption in AD 79, then one might also expect this study to reveal prevalent and uniform distribution patterns of house contents that can be attributed to either one of these disasters. These distribution patterns should show consistent relationships between the state of structural and decorative repair and the apparently disrupted distribution. If such re-

lationships are not obvious, then one might argue that much pre-abandonment damage and disruption cannot be given an absolute date of AD 62 but could be attributed instead to ongoing disturbance, possibly caused by further episodic seismic activity between AD 62 and AD 79. Recent reassessments of the textual and volcanological evidence, as discussed in chapter 2, have indicated the likelihood of such ongoing disturbance and that assumptions of a single-time horizon for the last seventeen years of Pompeii's occupancy are not necessarily valid.

The present analysis of household assemblage patterns has commenced from the premise that the most prevalent patterns indicate habitual room use. Therefore, any deviation from this, such as the utilitarian use of formally decorated rooms, formal use of undecorated rooms, or the reoccupation of incompletely decorated rooms, is likely to document altered or deteriorated living conditions during disturbance in these final years. An assessment of pre-eruption disturbance to an assumed state of normality must also be cognizant of any post-eruption disturbance to what has widely been considered by non-specialists to have been a pristine volcanic deposit.

POST-ERUPTION DISTURBANCE

As highlighted in chapter 2, previous investigators have often been too quick to attribute the absence of expected contents, assumed to have been of value to intruders, to post-eruption activity. A more critical assessment of the relationship between the archaeological conditions of Pompeian houses and any post-eruption disturbance is needed. The data in this study and its patterning allow for such an assessment.

179

The most likely evidence for post-eruption disturbance consists of reports of disturbance to the volcanic deposit. Holes cut through the walls of houses are also reputedly evidence for post-eruption intrusion. These holes were variously located from floor level to more than 2 m above the floor, and they ranged in size from 0.5 x 0.5 m to more than 1 x 2 m. In most cases they were patched after excavation, presumably to consolidate the wall and preserve any wall decoration (figure 8.1). Sometimes they were left open (for example, a hole between room 19 and corridor L in the Casa del Menandro; see figure 2.10). Only rarely was the volcanic deposit left in situ (for example, in a hole between front halls A' and A" in the Casa dell'Efebo; figure 8.2). The excavators recorded signs of previous disturbance in parts of House VIII 2,29–30 (*Giornale degli Scavi di Pompei* A,VI,3:8), including the discovery of a modern lamp. The present study found no direct correlation between the quantity and classes of material in a room, these holes, and disturbance of the volcanic deposit. For example, in the front-hall area of the Casa del Menandro, where finds were scarce, there was a relative lack of holes compared with rooms in the rest of house where such holes were more apparent. Evidence of disturbance to the volcanic deposit was recorded in room HH in the Casa di Julius Polybius, and yet the room contained undisturbed

finds on the pavement level. In the Casa dei Quadretti Teatrali and House VI 15,5, the only observable holes in the walls were in the areas where the most finds were reported.

It is important to assess what information the evidence of disturbance provides concerning the nature and date of the disturbance. It also should not be assumed that every case is the same. As discussed in chapter 2, previous scholars noted that the hole in the wall in room 19 of the Casa del Menandro and those in the Casa di Obellius Firmus (Trevelyan 1976: Fig. 70) were likely to have been made by fugitives seeking to escape from the eruption rather than by post-eruption intruders. In this study, the holes in the entranceway of the Casa del Sacerdos Amandus were conceivably also associated with the skeletons found in this corridor. These individuals included a child and possibly a woman. While evidence for disturbance to the volcanic deposit was noted during the excavation of other areas of this *insula*, none was recorded in the entranceway or in room h, which was linked to the corridor by one of these holes. On the contrary, room h (the kitchen) had what appears to have been the most complete inventory in the whole house, in situ on the hearth.

In room f in the Casa dei Ceii, two large holes in the south and east walls (figures 8.1 and 8.3) were identified by Della Corte (1913:250) as

Figure 8.2 South wall of front hall A" showing hole through to front hall A', with volcanic deposit in situ, Casa dell'Efebo

Figure 8.3 Hole in east wall of room f, Casa dei Ceii.

those made by ancient intruders. The hole in the east wall had plaster on its lower side, indicating it had originally been a window. The people making the hole may have located the window first and cut from the Casa dei Ceii's side through to the Casa del Criptoportico, suggesting that they were familiar with the layout of the house. The report in the *Giornali degli Scavi di Pompei* (A,VI,6:254) that the finds from this room were in a volcanic deposit that had been disturbed by those who made the hole. This implies that they were unlikely to have been fugitives trying to escape the eruption. The finds from nearby corridor k may have been dragged there by these people. If so, then the hoe found in this corridor may well have belonged to post-eruption activity. In balance, this case could conceivably have been one of disturbance not long after the eruption, possibly caused by the owners, who would have known the location of the window.

There are other examples, however, where those who made the holes were not familiar with the house plan. In room e of House I 7,19, the second hole in the southern end of the east wall cannot have penetrated the wall because it was below the ground level of the Casa dell'Efebo garden on the other side. This evidence suggests that at least this hole was not made by fugitives or inhabitants returning to collect their valuables, either of whom would have been familiar with the layout of the house. Similarly, in room n of the Casa di Trebius Valens there were holes in the east and west walls. The one in the west wall was the result of an attempt to penetrate to room p. However, as the latter room was at a significantly higher level, the resulting hole was probably impassible. It was therefore unlikely to have been made by anyone who knew the layout of the house. This also applies to the hole in the north wall of room 10 in the Casa degli Amanti, which would have led to the soil beneath room 22 and the garden of the Casa del Menandro.

Room c of the Casa del Principe di Napoli had two holes in the north wall and one in the south, all towards the east end. The dispersal of the bones of a skeleton found here (*Giornale degli Scavi di Pompei* A,VI,3:210) suggests that this individual had been disturbed some time after burial and decay. Consequently, any disturbance was unlikely to have been related to salvage or plundering activity immediately after the eruption but would have occurred at some later date. The Casa degli Amorini Dorati had two separate groups of different-sized holes across the north wall of room O: larger ones at floor level, and smaller ones some 2 m above the floor. This situation suggested to Seiler (conversation with author in the field, 1989) that there might have been two phases of disturbance in this house. Skeletons found in area v of House VIII 2,28 may have been occupants of this house who, with their valuables, had taken refuge in this area during the final eruption. Observed disturbance to the volcanic deposit suggests, however, that they could equally have been post-eruption intruders.

Besides possible evidence for post-depositional human disturbance, there was also evidence of what was apparently natural disturbance to the volcanic stratigraphy. The hole in the north wall of front hall A" in the Casa dell'Efebo (Fig. 8.2) must have been overlooked by the excavators and restorers, who generally cleared away the volcanic deposit that would have documented any disturbance and then patched the wall with modern cement.[1] The visible section of the deposit in this hole appears to show waterlaid stratigraphy. This stratigraphy suggests that natural processes, beyond the expected decay of organic material, may have caused a certain amount of disturbance to and mixing of not only the volcanic deposit but also the house contents.

Thus, holes in the walls or reported mixed deposits were not necessarily directly related to post-eruption intrusion. They certainly cannot all be attributed to the returning inhabitants. If some of these holes can be shown to be evidence of post-eruption activity, it can also be shown that the intruders did not generally remove all portable artifacts from the disturbed rooms. It is therefore invalid to assume that the absence, or partial absence, of room contents indicates post-eruption disturbance. In cases of consistent absence of material or absence of certain classes of expected material, one must consider whether this absence indicates pre-eruption activity.

PRE-ERUPTION DISTURBANCE

Hoarding

The "upper layer" of household activities prior to the eruption, identifiable through the material remains of Pompeian houses, was likely to reflect those activities that took place during the

eruption. One such behavior pattern is the hoarding or relocation of possessions to a safer place. Belongings considered valuable are likely to have been moved from open areas such as gardens to covered or roofed areas or from upper- or ground-level areas to spaces below ground.

The most likely evidence for such activity is the location of collections of jewelry, coins, and bronze and silver vessels in areas that seem unlikely to have been habitual storage areas for this type of material. Assemblages that include such collections were discovered in a total of fourteen rooms in ten of the houses in this sample (table 8.1). Possibly four of these assemblages predominantly comprised such valuable and easily movable material: that in the underground area entered from the entranceway VIII 2,27; room v of House VIII 2,28; and possibly in rooms e and u in the Casa di Trebius Valens. These assemblages more commonly also included utilitarian material, building material, broken sculpture, or furniture. For example, in the underground room B in the Casa del Menandro, fittings from the *compluvium* in front hall b, as well as a sundial and numerous other utilitarian artifacts (figure 8.4), were found with silver and bronze tableware, gold jewelry, and coins (figure 8.5). It seems improbable that these items would have been hoarded during the throes of an eruption or moved during post-eruption disturbance. Nevertheless, this material had evidently been collected together and stored in this underground room. The association of utilitarian with seemingly more valuable material renders it inappropriate, therefore, to ascribe this assemblage, wholly and securely, to hoarding during the final eruption. It might have been associated, at least partially, with an earlier disruption in or disturbance to the daily activities in the house. In the Casa di Julius Polybius, room EE seems to have been reused for dining after its decoration had been left incomplete. All manner of household material, including bronze vessels and lighting equipment, were then stored there, although not necessarily all at the same time (figure 1.3). This again implies that any change of plan and the deposition of the assemblage were

Table 8.1 Hoarded material

House	Room	Type	Small valuables*	Large valuables**
Casa di Julius Polybius	EE	11	•	•
Casa della Venere in Bikini	2	3	•	•
	7	7		•
Casa del Menandro	8	7		•
	c	9		•
	B	16	•	•
	35	16	•	
	41	3		•
	43	4	•	•
House I 10,8	8	4		•
	9	8		•
	12	12	•	
Casa dei Quadretti Teatrali	b	3	•	
House I 6,8–9	d	7		•
	i	9		•
Casa dell'Efebo	A'	3		•
	15	7		•
	17	11		•
Casa dei Ceii	g	12	•	
	i	14		•
Casa di Trebius Valens	e	4	•	
	x	9		•
	u	12	•	
Casa del Sacello Iliaco	f	7	•	
Casa della Ara Massima	I	6		•
	F	5		•?
Casa degli Amorini Dorati	D	4		•
	Y	16		•
Casa di M. Lucretius Fronto	13	11		•
	15	12		•
	20	12		•
Casa del Principe di Napoli	c	4		•
Casa dei Vettii	r	11		•
	w	14		•
Casa delle Nozze d'Argento	b	2		•
House VIII 2,14–16	cc	5		•
House VIII 2,26	VIII 2,27	19	•	
House VIII 2,28	k	17	•	•
	r	4		•
	v	16	•	
Casa di Giuseppe II	c	4		•
	i'	12		•

* Including jewelry, coins, and silver and bronze vessels   ** Includes statuary and luxury furniture

Figure 8.4 View of north side of room B, showing platform with building material, amphorae, and a sundial, and indicating position of the chest containing silver, Casa del Menandro (Maiuri 1933: Fig. 102)

Figure 8.5 Collection of bronze, silver, and glass vessels (inv. nos 4685–86, 4688–89, 4722–23) found near south wall of room B, Casa del Menandro

not caused by a single event but were related to ongoing disturbance.

Besides jewelry and precious metal items, the relocation of bronze and marble statuary and luxury furniture (for example, marble tables and marble or bronze basins) to covered areas is also a likely activity during an eruption. Such items probably originated from the open parts of the house (see Dwyer 1982:121), such as the front-hall or garden areas. An example was a statue of Venus found in a cupboard in the Casa della Venere in Bikini. This type of relocation seems to have occurred in a total of thirty-two to thirty-three rooms in seventeen houses. There were also examples of furniture and sculpture seemingly displaced within a room, such as a bronze

Figure 8.6 Labrum and *casseruole* in southwest corner of front hall, Casa del
Menandro. *Pompeii photo archive neg. D103384*

labrum in the southwest corner of front hall b of
the Casa del Menandro (figure 8.6), a base for
which was never recovered, and a marble *labrum*
found in two separate pieces in front hall b of
the Casa dei Ceii. In only one case, in room EE of
the Casa di Julius Polybius, was the statuary or
furniture complete rather than fragmentary. It is
arguable that the fragmentary nature of much of
this material was the result of damage during
the eruption or post-eruption disturbance. Fragmentary sculpture and garden furniture has,
however, been found in undisturbed deposits
(for example, in room B and hall 41 in the Casa
del Menandro). There were also instances where
parts of the same piece were recovered from
widely separated parts of the house. For example, parts of a Priapus fountain statue were
found in rooms r and w in the Casa dei Vettii
(figure 8.7), parts of a bronze Ephebus were
found in room 15 and front hall A' in the Casa
dell'Efebo, and parts of another bronze male
statue were found in rooms k and r in House
VIII 2,28. These circumstances cannot be attributed to eruption damage and are difficult to ascribe either to post-eruption activity or to urgent
hoarding during the eruption. In the Casa dei
Vettii, in particular, complete statuary and marble furniture was left standing in the garden,

while the fragmentary pieces had been removed
to covered areas. This example implies removal
perhaps for later restoration rather than removal
during an eruption or by post-eruption intruders. Similarly, the removal of the base of a statue
from a public location and its placement upside-
down in the ambulatory of the garden of the
Casa di Trebius Valens does not seem to be a
likely activity during the final eruption (figure
8.8).

It is therefore conceivable that furnishings
may have been salvaged during or after previous disruptions. As this type of activity was observed in more than half the houses in the
sample, it can be regarded as a significant pattern. In the Casa del Menandro, the Casa
dell'Efebo, the Casa dei Vettii, and the Casa di
Trebius Valens, it occurred after the initiation of
one, if not more, Fourth-Style decorative programs.

It has formerly been thought that such valued possessions also included wall paintings.
Room q of the Casa dei Vettii had been decorated in the Fourth Style, but the central panels
were missing at the time of excavation (figure
8.9). Mau considered (1896:63) that they had
been removed by occupants returning to the
house after the eruption. He noted that the panel

Figure 8.7 Remains of Priapus statue as found in kitchen w, Casa dei Vettii. *Pompeii photo archive neg. D80461*

Figure 8.8 Statue base found upside-down in east ambulatory of garden x, Casa di Trebius Valens (Warscher 1948: vol. 5, 553 no. 26)

from the north wall had been fixed with iron brackets, suggesting it may have been a separate panel that had previously been removed from an older decoration and reinstalled during the redecoration of the house. This assumes a certain amount of antiquarianism on the part of Pompeians. The panel in room d of the same house also had such brackets, but its plastered and painted surfaces indicated that it had been executed at the same time as, and as part of, the rest of the wall decoration. It had not been a separate insertion. The brackets may have acted as stabilizers. It is possible that the brackets in room q had also served some stabilizing function and were not an indication of the portability of these panels. The assumption that these panels had a higher value to Pompeians than the rest of decoration would seem to be accrediting them with the same value systems as the eighteenth- and nineteenth-century excavators (see Allison 1997b).

In conclusion, much of the evident hoarding in Pompeian houses cannot be securely attributed to the brief time of the final eruption. If, conversely, it is attributed uniformly on traditional chronologies to the earthquake of AD 62, then the Fourth-Style decoration with which it was often associated must pre-date AD 62. Such conclusions would be extremely problematic, however, for houses like the Casa del Menandro and the Casa dei Vettii because this would date several phases of Fourth-Style decoration, with their subsequent repair, all prior to AD 62.

Figure 8.9 Missing central panel, east wall of room q, Casa dei Vettii

Building Activity

The evidence in the previous section highlights the unreliability of fixed chronologies. If at the time of the eruption the houses of the town were indeed still being repaired after earthquake damage in AD 62, then one of the most likely patterns of activity we should expect to find is that of building restoration, evidenced by the presence of building material. It is also probable that building material might have been kept in certain areas for some time, whether or not repair was actually being carried out. While building material was recorded in four secondary and entrance courtyards, one cannot assume that the storage of this material indicates that actual building work was being undertaken at the time of the eruption (table 8.2). One can only conclude that the occupants had intended to carry out repairs at some stage prior to this date. In any event, the material would have caused some disruption to the functioning of the household.

More acute disruption was likely to have occurred when such material was deposited in the formal areas of the house or in places where routine domestic activities were carried out. Building material was reported in twelve to fifteen areas that had either wall or floor decoration or other formal furbishments (for example, formal gardens). This material may have been placed in these locations because redecoration was underway in the vicinity at the time of the eruption (figure 8.10). In six of these cases, however, domestic material was associated with this building material: room 3 in the Casa del Menandro; room 10 in House I 10,8; room 14 in the Casa dei Quadretti Teatrali; garden 23 in the Casa dell'Efebo; room e in House I 7,19; and room c in the Casa del Sacello Iliaco. Some of these rooms seem to have had incomplete Fourth-Style decoration (table 8.3). Strocka (1984b) has shown that the refurbishing of room c in the Casa del Sacello Iliaco had been abandoned and that the room had subsequently been reused, presumably to store domestic material. This may also have been the situation for the other areas, implying that after they were partially renovated or used to store building material, these rooms were used later for domestic activity or domestic storage,

187

Table 8.2 Locations of building material causing disruption

House	Room	Room type	Building material in secondary and entrance courts	Building material in formal areas
Casa di Julius Polybius	A	19	•	
	C	19	•	
Casa del Menandro	3	6		• ?
	23	13		•
	44	18	•	
House I 10,8	10	11		•
Casa di Stallius Eros	5	4		•
	7	10		•
Casa dei Quadretti Teatrali	14	12		•
Casa dell'Efebo	23	9		•
House I 7, 19	b	6		•
	e	11		•
	k	10		•
Casa del Sacello Iliaco	c	6		•
	m	9		• ?
	s	18	•	
House VI 15,5	g	5		•
	h	11		•
Casa delle Nozze d'Argento	2	18		• ?

Figure 8.10 Northeast area of garden m showing pile of gypsum, Casa del Sacello Iliaco

Table 8.3 Damage, repair, and alteration to houses with Fourth-Style decoration

House	Room	Room type	Incomplete/damaged 4th Style with domestic contents	Damaged and repaired 4th Style with domestic contents	Defaced/altered 4th Style	Completed 4th Style with building material	4th Style with building or industrial material	Post-4th-Style aediculae
Casa di Julius Polybius	A	19	•					
	Y	4					• ?	
	UU	4					• ?	
	N	3					• ?	
	AA	12			• ?			
Casa della Venere in Bikini	1	1			•			
Casa del Menandro	b	3						•
	23	13				•		
	18	11	•					
	43	4			•			
	46–49	21			•			
House I 10,8	3	4					• ?	
	8	4			•			
	10	11					•	
Casa degli Amanti	7	4					•	
Casa di Stallius Eros	13	9			•			
Casa dei Quadretti Teatrali	5	4	• ?					
Casa dei Ceii	g	12			•			
Casa del Sacello Iliaco	c	6	•					
	d	4	•	•				
	e	5	•					
	h	4	• ?					
	l	4	•					
House VI 16,26	M	9					• ?	
Casa della Ara Massima	B	3				•		
	F	5		•				
	G	6		•				
Casa degli Amorini Dorati	B	3		• ?				
	G	11		•				
Casa di M. Lucretius Fronto	13	11	• ?					
	20	12					•	
Casa del Principe di Napoli	c	4		•				
	k	11		•				

Continued on next page

Table 8.3 Damage, repair, and alteration to houses with Fourth-Style decoration (continued)

House	Room	Room type	Incomplete/ damaged 4th Style with domestic contents	Damaged and repaired 4th Style with domestic contents	Defaced /altered 4th Style	Completed 4th Style with building material	4th Style with building or industrial material	Post-4th-Style aediculae
Casa dei Vettii	c	3		•				
	h	5		•				
Casa delle Nozze d'Argento	n	11	•					
House VIII 2,28	d	3						•
Casa di Giuseppe II	c	4		•				
	d'	14			•			
	k	4			•			
	m	4			•		•	
	n	17			•			
	f	16					•	
	f"	16					•	
House VIII 2,29–30	f	4			•			
	k	5						•

conceivably when the reconstruction program was abandoned. In garden 23 of the Casa dell'Efebo, room 10 of House I 10,8, and room 14 of the Casa dei Quadretti Teatrali, this abandonment of reconstruction and resumption of domestic activity occurred after these areas had been decorated, or partially decorated, in the Fourth Style. Even if the building material had been brought in to repair damage caused by the AD 62 earthquake, the evident ongoing alteration and disruption to living conditions could not all have been dated to this event.

As discussed in chapter 2, a general argument has been made that the Fourth Style was in vogue only after the AD 62 earthquake (see also Mielsch 1981). Therefore, incomplete Fourth-Style decoration has been considered a sign of redecoration activity interrupted by the eruption. In more recent years, scholars have paid more attention to the possibility that the Fourth Style may have developed prior to AD 62. Their arguments are usually based on the assumption that any damage to or state of incompleteness of such decoration is attributable to the recorded earthquake of AD 62 (for example, de Vos 1982;

Strocka 1984a:35–39, 1984b; Thomas 1995; Ling 1995). In combination, these arguments present only two possible scenarios: incomplete Fourth-Style decoration was interrupted by either (1) the AD 79 eruption or (2) the AD 62 earthquake. In the first scenario (and in the second if no further disruption or change of plan had occurred), the contents of such a room or area were likely to have been associated with repair activity. This study indicates that there were at least seven, and possibly up to ten, examples of rooms in a total of six houses with incomplete or damaged Fourth-Style decoration and with contents that were domestic rather than related to building and decoration activity. This sample also included further examples of incomplete Fourth-Style decoration in Region VIII (for example, room d in House VIII 2,29–30), but, because of the poor recording of this area, the state of the decoration and the presence of room contents were not always documented.

The sample included nine to ten examples of rooms with damaged and subsequently repaired Fourth-Style decorations and domestic assemblages that seemed to document reoccupation after cursory repair. Sometimes these assemblages included seemingly relocated or salvaged material (for example, room c in the Casa del Principe di Napoli and room c in the Casa di Giuseppe II). There were also twelve to thirteen areas where the room's structure had been altered after its Fourth-Style decoration or whose Fourth-Style decoration had been defaced, often to convert a decorated room into a storage area (for example, with shelving). In entranceway 1 to the Casa della Venere in Bikini, the Fourth-Style decoration had been defaced with graffiti before it was finished.

Two other rooms appear to have completed Fourth-Style decoration but also contained building material. The uses of yet another seven to twelve rooms with Fourth-Style decoration appear to have been altered, presumably from a formal function, by the presence of building material, tools, or other industrial/commercial paraphernalia. Assemblages in other rooms hinted at alteration or downgrading that post-dated their Fourth-Style decoration. However, these assemblages are unlikely to document hoarding activity during the final eruption because of the fragmentary state or utilitarian nature of some of the contents (for example, room e in the Casa della Nozze d'Argento).

Other rooms may also fit into these categories of disruption through building and repair activities. Their absence here is not necessarily because they would not fit the conditions but rather because their decoration and contents were not sufficiently recorded. This sample also included three examples of *lararium* aediculae that were erected in front halls after the latter had been decorated in the Fourth Style. Such functional alterations suggest that general changes in the use of different parts of the house, or even in the religious practices of the occupants, were likely to have occurred after the initiation of Fourth-Style decoration.

Strocka has argued (1984b) that cursory repair and reuse of rooms with incomplete Fourth-Style decoration indicates that the decoration must have been executed prior to AD 62. He has frequently used stylistic analysis to substantiate his arguments for the chronological relation-ships of these paintings (for example, Strocka 1995). The tight time frame of the period in question and the limitations of our knowledge of the workforce organization required for executing the paintings (see, for example, Allison 1995b) throw some doubt on the suitability of such analyses for dating purposes. In this sample, more than half the houses from the Region I area, all but one of the houses in Regions V to VI, and—despite the poor standard of recording in this area—three in Region VIII showed another occupation phase after that for which the Fourth-Style decoration was intended. If it is argued that all these post-Fourth-Style alterations were attributable to disruption or makeshift conditions caused by the AD 62 earthquake, then it would seem from this sample that little substantial rebuilding and redecoration had actually been carried out after that earthquake. On this premise, all that happened was that parts of the town had merely been patched up and downgraded.

The premise that all damage and subsequent repair to Pompeian houses was attributable to a single earthquake is unsatisfactory because many of the houses in the sample had evidence of more than one phase of disruption and alteration (for example, the Casa del Sacello Iliaco and the Casa dei Vettii in particular). There was evidence, both in public and private buildings, that restoration programs had indeed been carried out after AD 62. The complete redecoration of the Casa della Caccia Antica can be dated after AD 71 (Allison 1991a:144–154; Allison and Sear 2002:84), and the planned restoration of the Temple of Isis post-dated an earthquake, reputedly that of AD 62 (de Vos and de Vos 1982:73; compare Allison 1999c).

In summary, it is not appropriate to view all these alterations as the result of the one disruption that we happen to know about because of the written evidence. This study uses artifact distribution to produce patterns of apparently disrupted or makeshift conditions that are more likely to document ongoing alteration and downgrading than a fixed point in time. Thus, in addition to the more critical perspectives of textual and volcanological evidence discussed in chapter 2, these patterns further stress the improbability of the traditional and widely held view that AD 62 provides a blanket date for restoration and redecoration in Pompeian houses. Absolute dating can only be achieved where evidence is available, such as that of the coin impressions in the decoration of the front hall of the Casa della Caccia Antica. Damage, repair, alteration, and abandonment could have occurred at various times in the last decades of Pompeii.

Ongoing Disruption and State of Occupancy

Thus, rather than basing the chronology and assessment of the conditions of the final decades of Pompeii on the assumption that all alteration, disruption, incomplete repair, or abandonment was attributable to the absolute dates of either the AD 62 earthquake or the AD 79 eruption, it would seem more appropriate to summarize the possible relative chronologies commencing with what might be seen as the latest pre-eruption activity in Pompeii.

With the exception of some collections of valuables, none of the assemblages discussed in the preceding two sections can be definitively ascribed to activities during the final eruption. To identify the latest pre-eruption activity, one must look for evidence that shows that the houses were indeed occupied at the time of the eruption. The most obvious evidence is the presence of human skeletons, as recorded in fifteen houses—half the houses in the sample and including four of the seven houses in Region VIII (table 8.4). While it is possible that a number of occupants may have escaped during the eruption, we cannot say for certain that the skeletons found in the houses during excavation were those of the original occupants, particularly skeletons found in the upper levels of the volcanic deposit. It is conceivable that fugitives may have taken refuge in other houses during their flight. Nevertheless, generally speaking, the presence of these skeletons implies some occupancy of the immediate residential area at the time of the eruption.

Additional evidence for late-phase occupancy is that of operating kitchens. Kitchen utensils are unlikely to have been packed up and hoarded during the final eruption. Such material is unlikely to have been attractive to post-eruption intruders, with the possible exception of some bronze vessels. Therefore, a quantity and range of movable kitchen utensils recorded in rooms identified as kitchens suggests that the house was occupied at the time of the eruption. This seems to have been the case in ten houses in the sample. While room w in the Casa dei Vettii also had broken statuary that indicated some disruption (see figure 8.7), a considerable number of cooking utensils were left in this kitchen, suggesting that it may have been operating fairly late in the history of the house (see figure 5.11). While kitchen utensils were also recorded in other kitchens in the sample (see table 5.14b), the latter tended to have a smaller quantity and range than in these ten houses. Thus, about a third of the houses in the sample have evidence that suggests their kitchens were operational at the time of the eruption.[2] A general concordance between houses with skeletons and houses with seemingly operating kitchens is notable. The exceptions are mainly those houses where the skeletons were found in the upper levels of the deposit, or those in Region VIII where little attention was paid to mundane finds. More obvious exceptions are House I 7,19 and the Casa di Trebius Valens which had skeletons but no evidence of a functioning kitchen. In the Casa del Sacello Iliaco and the Casa dei Vettii, there were utensils in the kitchen but no skeletons. While apparent kitchen utensils were reported in room i in House I 7,19, it has also been observed that this particular house had been in a considerable state of disruption and that the individuals may have come from another house (that is, the Casa dell'Efebo or the Casa di Paquius Proculus [I, 7,1]). Broken statuary found in the kitchen of the Casa dei Vettii suggests that, despite the presence of cooking apparatus, the room's usual function may have been disrupted prior to the eruption.

From the combined evidence of skeletons and kitchen utensils, it might be hypothesized that the Casa di Julius Polybius, the Casa del Fabbro, the Casa del Sacerdos Amandus, the Casa di Trebius Valens, the Casa di M. Lucretius Fronto, the Casa

Table 8.4 Evidence for ongoing disruption

House	Room/Area	Human skeletons	In situ kitchen utensils	Coarse/incomplete decoration*	Other coarsely plastered rooms	Downgraded/abandoned entertainment areas	Inoperative bath-suites
Casa di Julius Polybius	Nk		•				
	GG	•					
	HH	•					
Casa della Venere in Bikini	9		•?				
Casa del Menandro	19	•					
	52		•?				
	L	•					
	43	•					
	46–49						•
Casa del Fabbro	7				•		
	9	•					
	11		•				
	8–12					•	
House I 10,8	4			•			
	9–12					•	
Casa degli Amanti	UF(8)	•					
Casa dei Quadretti Teatrali	6			•			
	11			•			
	11–16					•	
House I 6, 8–9	e–i					•	
Casa di Stallius Eros	6				•		
Casa del Sacerdos Amandus	a	•					
	h		•				
	i		•				
	n			•			
Casa dell'Efebo	13			•			
	23					•	
	UF	•					
House I 7,19	u	•					
	a	•					
	r	•					
	q			•			
Casa di Trebius Valens	q, y						•
	x	•					
	UF	•					
Casa dei Ceii	d			•			
Casa del Sacello Iliaco	c					•	
	f			•		•	
	n		•				
	m–r					•	

Continued on next page

Table 8.4 Evidence for ongoing disruption (continued)

House	Room/ Area	Human skeletons	In situ kitchen utensils	Coarse/ incomplete decoration*	Other coarsely plastered rooms	Downgraded/ abandoned entertainment areas	Inoperative bath-suites
House VI 16,26	C			•			
	T			•			
	M–S					•	
Casa degli Amorini Dorati	UF	•					
Casa di M. Lucretius Fronto	14	•					
	10–16					•	
	18		•				
Casa del Principe di Napoli	c	•					
	h		•				
House VI 15,5	b				•		
	h					•	
	u–v					•	
Casa dei Vettii	w		•				
Casa delle Nozze d'Argento	2					•	
	5					•	
	t–v						•
House VIII 2,14–16	ee				•		
	UF	•					
House VIII 2,28	v	•					
Casa di Giuseppe II	b					•	
	d					•	
	n				•		
	v–z					•?	
	LF	•					
	3	•					
	6–8						•
House VIII 2,34	c					•	
	LF	•				•?	
House VIII 2,29–30	q				•		
House VIII 5,9	d		•				
	f				•		

* With domestic contents

del Principe di Napoli, House VIII 5,9, and possibly the Casa del Menandro, House I 7,19, the Casa del Sacello Iliaco, and the Casa dei Vettii all showed more recent pre-eruption occupancy than the rest of the houses in the sample.

Even so, it is apparent in all these houses that some aspects of the occupancy had deteriorated and possibly had been reduced prior to the final eruption. For example, rooms in four of these houses are included in the list of ten areas with coarse plaster, often reputedly incomplete decoration, and with domestic contents. Either this coarse plaster was the actual intended decoration or there had been a change of attitude that caused the occupiers to leave the decoration incomplete and to reuse the room.

Another six rooms were referred to in the excavation reports as having been coarsely finished. It is not always possible to ascertain whether this referred to white service plaster, incomplete plastering, or even the lack of plaster. It is also difficult to assess whether many rooms and areas that have not received protective roofing since excavation, and whose walls appear coarsely plastered today, were so originally or once had painted decoration. Most of these six rooms were of type 7. The formal and entertainment areas of some twelve houses in the sample seem to have been either downgraded or abandoned prior to the final eruption. Also, the bath-suites in four of the houses were apparently inoperative at the time of the eruption, although many had already been decorated in the Fourth Style.

This may all seem rather confused, and no doubt it probably was. The general impression is that there is no consistent pattern of disruption and abandonment across the houses in this sample. Putting aside Adam's statement (1989b:461) that today it is impossible to compile a list of houses effectively inhabited in AD 79, it might be possible to present an impression of their comparative conditions (table 8.5). Houses such as the Casa della Ara Massima, the Casa degli Amorini Dorati, and the Casa dei Vettii appear to have been flourishing, presumably at the beginning of the Fourth-Style period. There is no evidence that the Casa degli Amorini Dorati was

Table 8.5 Individual houses showing evidence of late occupancy and alteration

House	Late occupancy	Flourishing*	Altered**	Abandoned entertainment area**	Commercial conversion**
Casa di Julius Polybius	•				•
Casa del Menandro	• ?				
Casa del Fabbro	•				•
Casa dei Quadretti Teatrali				•	
Casa del Sacerdos Amandus	•				
Casa dell'Efebo				•	
House I 7,19	• ?				
Casa di Trebius Valens	•				
Casa del Sacello Iliaco	• ?				
Casa della Ara Massima		•	•		
Casa degli Amorini Dorati		•			
Casa di M. Lucretius Fronto	•			•	
Casa del Principe di Napoli	•				
Casa dei Vettii	• ?	•			
House VIII 2,14–16					•
House VIII 5,9	•				

* During Fourth Style   ** After Fourth Style

actually occupied at the time of the eruption. The occupational material in the Casa della Ara Massima suggests alteration of the spatial distribution of activities or downgrading after its Fourth-Style decoration. The entertainment areas of houses such as the Casa dei Quadretti Teatrali, the Casa dell'Efebo, and the Casa di M. Lucretius Fronto seem to have been abandoned sometime after they received at least part of their Fourth-Style decoration but prior to the final eruption. Other houses, such as the Casa di Julius Polybius, the Casa del Fabbro, and House VIII 2,14–16, seem to have been converted for more commercial/industrial activity, often after their decoration in the Fourth Style. Attributing all this alteration and downgrading and other evidence of subsequent disruption (for example, area A in the Casa di Julius Polybius) to damage caused by the AD 62 earthquake would require dating practically all the Fourth Style to before AD 62. While much might be consistent with the ordinary ongoing conditions of change in these houses, it is also conceivable that some of the disruption and overall deteriorated conditions is attributable to ongoing seismic activities throughout the period AD 62 to AD 79.

DISCUSSION

The use of this sample to interpret the living conditions in Pompeii in its last decades demonstrates that these final years and the abandonment process were more complex and involved more piecemeal changes than has been widely assumed. The evidence for relative chronologies within the houses in this study suggests that on more than one occasion in this period, the Pompeians had to relocate sculpture, furniture, and possibly other valuables; to repair structure and decoration; and to rearrange their living spaces, conceivably because of damage and disruption caused by recurrent, possibly seismic, factors.

Some scholars have noted instances of statuary being relocated from public contexts, reputedly in the years after the AD 62 earthquake (for example, D'Arms 1988:60; Zanker 1988:42). Such relocations were not necessarily a direct result

either of one earthquake or of an official program. When Vesuvius erupted in AD 79, according to Ward-Perkins and Claridge, only "a handful of private houses had been completely restored" after damage caused in AD 62 (1980:13). While the present sample may not be representative, it is noteworthy that, unless the Fourth-Style decoration in the garden of the Casa di Stallius Eros can be dated before AD 62, all the houses showed some occupation after some disruption, but not all showed occupation at the time of the eruption.

Maiuri (1942:113) observed that at the time of the eruption, many houses in Region VI Insulae 15–16 were still in ruins resulting from the AD 62 earthquake. In contrast, Gioacchino Francesco La Torre (1988:86) observed that the houses best restored after this earthquake were in Regions VI and VII. The examples from these regions chosen for this study all indicated disruption or damage that can be dated after their Fourth-Style decoration. La Torre (1988:86) also observed that, for many of the houses in Region VIII, restoration work had not begun and some had been abandoned and relegated to sources for salvaged materials (see Maiuri 1942:138, 160). Hence, he noted, the main concentration of commercial activity was in zones where houses had been restored most quickly and most completely. This contradicts Noack and Lehmann-Hartleben (1936:157). The evidence from the current study suggests that some of the houses in Region VIII (for example, House VIII 2,28, House VIII 2,29–30, and the Casa di Giuseppe II) had been repaired, downgraded, altered for commercial activity, or abandoned only after they received their Fourth-Style decoration. La Torre concluded (1988:78) that 36 percent of the town's buildings had been shops, which indicated its commercial character, especially in its last phase after the earthquake. This reasoning seems to be based on the designation of spaces as commercial and artisanal but yet lacks validation or even any assessment of whether they were all functioning at the same time. For example, it is apparent that a bakery had been a late installation in the Casa del Labirinto (Strocka 1991:94), but the one in the Casa degli Casti

196

Amanti appears to have been undergoing repair (Varone 1989:233). Cerulli-Irelli (1977a:56) noted that the lamp workshop (I 22,2–3) had been inoperative on the day of the eruption. Likewise, Annecchino (1977a:106–107) noted that the pottery industry in the vicinity of the *Palaestra Grande* (II 3,7) had been transferred elsewhere prior to the eruption.

Adam (1989b:472) observed social and economic changes that he related to the earthquake of AD 62. He concluded that many houses had been transformed into commercial establishments and workshop localities, and that many Pompeians had abandoned their ruined dwellings, apparently not intending to return. He noted that it had not been an epoch of prosperity, and that there had been numerous changing fortunes. He also noted that public monuments had not had the same priority for restoration as private houses. While all these observations seem valid, the current study has shown that one cannot assume that all this alteration, downgrading, and abandonment was necessarily attributable to one earthquake and to one phase of restoration. The variety of patterns fits much better with a model in which the Pompeians experienced ongoing disruption. A likely factor would have been seismic activity leading up to the final eruption, of which the AD 62 earthquake was a well-heeded warning. The precise impact of such ongoing seismic activity on the size and nature of the population of Pompeii at the time of the eruption is difficult to gauge. It has been argued (for example, Maiuri 1933:11–16; Dexter 1975:283) that many of the wealthy had left Pompeii prior to the eruption, leaving only a small staff, or a "faithful retainer," to mind their houses. It can be reasonably argued, however, that much of the activity reputedly carried out by such staff (for example, in room 43 in the Casa del Menandro and peristyle x in the Casa di Trebius Valens) seems rather to have been that of salvagers collecting and recycling the abandoned valuables and fixtures of those who had already left the town because of ongoing disruption, perhaps even the threat of disaster. The removal of monuments from a public location hints at a possible breakdown of civic pride and interest or a need to remove the monuments to a safer, private place. If one accepts the evidence of active political life in the years after the AD 62 earthquake (see Mouristen 1988:32–33; Franklin 1980:61–69, 124), then this decline of civic life might have been later, conceivably the result of further disruption and possibly social disorder.

The assumption that most Pompeians escaped during the eruption is largely based on the paucity of excavated victims. There is no proof that some of the abandonment or escape, as suggested by Maiuri and Dexter, had not occurred earlier. There is likewise no evidence to attribute abandonment to conditions resulting from the AD 62 earthquake. As noted above, many of the apparently abandoned and partially abandoned houses had been decorated in the Fourth Style, sometimes in several different phases. It is therefore possible that the inhabitants had drifted away from the town during these years of disruption. It is also conceivable that the eighty-seven skeletons excavated in the thirty houses of this sample are in fact representative of the population density at the time of the eruption. Estimates of the population that the town may once have supported (see Jongman 1988:110) are likely to be irrelevant in calculating the size of the actual population at the time of the eruption.

It has often been acknowledged that the social conditions in Pompeii's last years were turbulent to some degree (D'Arms 1988:61). It is not acceptable, however, to assume that this turbulence was the result of a single, but catastrophic, recorded earthquake. It is equally possible that deteriorating conditions were caused by continued disruption. The date of AD 62 may serve as a *terminus post quem* for much of the observed structural and decorative repair or evidence of disrupted living conditions. Such alterations must first be shown to have been the result of damage caused by seismic activity and not of general renovations or adaptations. Also, it needs to be demonstrated that the alterations occurred as a single distinct phase. In many houses, several phases of alteration and deterioration could be observed.

The period between AD 62 and AD 79 cannot be viewed as a static interim phase between two major events, with all the damage ascribed to one event and all the repair deriving from it. Rather, the process seems to have been more complex. Ordinary domestic change and ongoing disturbance of some kind produced varying patterns of damage, repair, changing room use, and deterioration in Pompeian houses (Allison 1995c).[3]

NOTES

1. I am grateful to Wolfgang Ehrhardt for drawing my attention to this hole in the Casa dell 'Efebo.

2. Foss commented that any observed absence of cooking ware was because the material would normally have been stored somewhere other than the kitchen area (1994:60-61). This is undoubtedly possible. In this sample, cooking and food-preparation material appears to have occurred relatively rarely in storage (see table 6.1b). In contrast, this type of material was certainly evident in the kitchens of more than one-third of this sample at the time of the eruption. In any event, this analysis concentrates on the presence and comparative presence of this material rather than its absence.

3. Recent scholars are now moving away from the single earthquake concept and presenting more flexible and less essentially text-driven interpretations of their observations (for example, De Simone 1995; Jacobelli 1995; Seiler 1995; Fulford and Wallace-Hadrill 1998:135–136).

Figure 9.1 View of Pompeii and Mt. Vesuvius from Porta Nocera

9.

Conclusions

CONDITIONS IN POMPEII AT THE TIME of the eruption are not as well understood and researched as popular belief would have it. Scholars in different branches of archaeology have quite diverse views on the available information regarding these conditions and the state of knowledge about them.

Paul Zanker (1988:41), for example, wrote *"Pompeji war 79 n.Chr trotz aller Anstrengungen der vergangenen Jahre an vielen Stellen noch immer eine zerstörte Stadt. Die Pompejaner blieben nach dem Erdbeben sich selbst überlassen. . ."* [Despite all efforts in the preceding years, Pompeii was still, in many places, a destroyed town in AD 79. After the earthquake the Pompeians were left to their own devices] (my translation). Zanker's comment suggests that the town would have deteriorated away from a pristine index of some supposedly normal relationship among social life, space, and archaeological debris. Disturbance of the actual deposit, indicative of reuse of the site, would be expected. By contrast, Schiffer wrote that "The good state of preservation afforded by the catastrophic abandonment of Pompeii has become a yardstick of legendary proportions for assessing the evidence surviving elsewhere" (1987:237), and "the real Pompeii premise . . . is that one can analyze house-floor assemblages *as if* they were systemic inventories—unmodified by formation processes" (1985:38). Both these scholars are manifestly referring to the same archaeological remains of Pompeii that related to its final occupation phase prior to the AD 79 eruption of Mt. Vesuvius. Zanker reached his conclusions largely from studies of the architecture, decoration, and epigraphy. The premise discussed by Schiffer was purportedly based on actual "house-floor assemblages," a difficult undertaking since there has been no prior comprehensive study of the distribution and associations of the loose finds,

that is, the household inventories that provide the most precise evidence of the final state of the town. Had either of these scholars been able to refer to a systematic investigation of the contents of Pompeian houses or even undertaken such a task themselves, their individual perceptions of what constituted the final occupation phase might have been less divergent.

This study has attempted such an investigation. First, the contents of thirty Pompeian houses were collated, material most likely to represent the latest activity in these houses before their individual abandonment at whatever date during the last decades. These collated data provide a valuable research tool for any significant study of the site. Second, these data was used to analyze both the spatial distribution of household activities and the living conditions during the later occupation phases. Assemblages were assessed in the light of the excavation and recording methods, possible post-eruption disturbance, their relationship to the structure and decoration of the room or space, and the use of space as assumed from textual nomenclature. Through this study it has become apparent that neither Schiffer's nor Zanker's views of the last days of Pompeii allowed for the complexity of these remains.

Predominant distribution patterns demonstrate how some of the Pompeian rooms had been used. These patterns did not necessarily conform to the activities assigned to these room types by their textual, particularly Vitruvian, nomenclature. It must either be concluded that the nomenclature is incorrect or that room use in Pompeian houses was not equivalent to that of aristocratic houses in or near Rome. This analysis also demonstrates that separation of activity areas primarily on the basis of modern analogy gives a biased view of how a Pompeian house would have been organized and how activities—domestic and industrial/commercial, utilitarian and formal—would have been distributed throughout the various spaces. Once the principal patterns of room use have been identified, other less pervasive patterns show more clearly the dislocation of artifacts during disrupted circumstances. The occurrence of a number of phases of dislocation in many individual houses demonstrates that this spectrum of disruption could in no way be limited to a simple choice between the AD 62 earthquake and the AD 79 eruption.

In effect, the distribution patterns indicate that Pompeian remains were affected by the very criteria from which Schiffer (1985:24) and other New Archaeologists believed the site had been sealed. Not only had the house-floor assemblages suffered considerable post-eruption disturbance, but the concept of the period AD 62 to AD 79 as a time horizon—shared by other scholars besides Zanker—proved misleading. The overlaying of these patterns shows that it is invalid to use the earthquake of AD 62 as a fixed date for all the evident damage, repair, alteration, or deterioration in these houses and the eruption of AD 79 as a date for abandonment. On the contrary, the contents and their relationship to the structures indicate the ongoing activity and changing conditions that one might expect at any settlement site.

This study demonstrates that an assessment of the material remains of an historical period site, based on available literary sources rather than incorporating a genuinely archaeological perspective, is particularly vulnerable to distortion. Studies of Roman room function that employ Pompeii to illustrate the written evidence have tended to ignore, or rearrange, contents that were either not mentioned in this literature or did not fit its perspective. Masonry and wall-painting chronologies, which have relied on the recorded events of AD 62 or AD 79 to date evident damage, repair, or partial completion in Pompeii, have ignored not only the possibility of unrecorded seismic events or changes of attitude that might have caused this disruption, but also the part played by the house contents in the final

occupancy of houses in the Vesuvian towns. It is clear from this study that the archaeological evidence must be allowed to speak with its own voice (see Dyson 1981:11). If that evidence then appears to diverge from expectations, one must consider whether this is a divergence from preconceived ideas of normality or a distortion arising from disruption to recognizable habitual activity (see Binford 1981:200).

Pompeii might indeed give "the ancient historian the nearest thing to a time-capsule" (Jongman 1988:55), but life in Pompeii cannot be seen to have been *"bruscamente interrotta, come un film che si ferma, durante la proiezione"* [suddenly interrupted, like a film that stops during the projection] (my translation) (Augusti 1967:15). Pompeii is not "only an ideal for one interested in events, specific behaviors and event-centered 'history'" (Binford 1981:205). It affirms Schiffer's theories on formation processes of the archaeological record. However, not only are "most sites . . . not like little Pompeiis" (Schiffer 1985:38). Pompeii itself does not conform to the eponymous ideal. Schiffer's goal of seeking to understand the past in ethnographic terms must be a forlorn hope. Not even Pompeii itself, with its abrupt demise, contained the instantaneously frozen state (Will 1979:34) from which one could even hope to achieve Schiffer's goal.[1] The Pompeii Premise, however understood by Robert Ascher (1961:324), Lewis Binford (1981), or Michael Schiffer (1985:18), has not and cannot be founded on the instance of Pompeii as an epitome. What the evidence does affirm, however, is Binford's point that to speak of distortion by the activities of people redepositing cultural material is inappropriate. The actual condition of the cultural assemblage is informative about what happened to the occupants of Pompeii during the last decades. It is not, however, distorted evidence because it is not a divergence from some pristine former state of social pattern in which we ought to be more interested.

Even a site that experiences a sudden climatic or geomorphic termination, arresting the process of its cultural formation, has already been formed by cultural and environmental metamorphoses, as Schiffer's analyses would generally lead one to expect. Within the "systemic house-floor assemblages" are intermingled accretions of activities resulting from ongoing change and physical deterioration. Instead of being the archetypal site of the "frozen moment," the excavations of Pompeii demonstrate the variability and complexity that exist even in the archaeological record of a reputedly single moment. It is not an archetype of the single moment. Rather, it is an archetype of the detailed information of social life that is available if we pay attention to change, redeposition, and deterioration. An eruption unquestionably provides the "frozen moment" of popular mythology. The material has already been mixed, however, and an at least partial thaw, in the form of both environmental and cultural post-depositional activity, comes quickly afterward. A new premise could be stated: historical time capsules may exist, but their archaeological identity is defined by both past and future continuous activity—even at Pompeii.

To clarify the relative chronology of events in Pompeii prior to AD 79, scholars also need to work backwards from the later to the earlier parts of the archaeological sequence. Chronological analyses of Pompeii have traditionally commenced from the establishment of a building and worked towards AD 79. The story of Pompeii has therefore been formulated using procedures appropriate to the history of extant settlements (for example, above-ground medieval towns) rather than to an excavated archaeological site. A more general archaeological practice for creating a relative chronology is to start from the top layer and work down. In Pompeii, the most immediate level, after the volcanic debris has been removed, is that of the house-floor assemblages, evidence that has largely been ignored. Once these assemblages, their interrelationships, their relationships to the structures and to the volcanic deposits, have been more clearly understood, it may be easier to investigate the chronologies of the buildings and their decoration.

This study highlights the kinds of house contents discovered in a sample of houses, of one particular architectural type, from one Roman town in southern Italy. The patterns isolated here are specifically relevant to this group of houses, to this town, and to the circumstances under which the artifacts were deposited. Similar investigations of other house types in this town and of houses at other Roman sites may throw more light on the potential universality of some of these patterns, as will a more rigorous assessment of the relationships of these patterns to patterns of household activity identified in ancient texts. The degree of correspondence between these assemblages and the activities ascribed to archaeological spaces through textual nomenclature should be taken to emphasize the need for reinvestigation of the validity of this ascription and for a more critical assessment of the interpretative procedures through which ancient texts are used to assign activities to spaces in Roman houses. It should also highlight that the kinds of information we can glean from archaeological data are often very different from those we can glean from written texts. Neither is more valid than the other. They are just different, and the relationship between them is often difficult to grasp.

NOTE

1. "Frozen" is a curious term to use for a city that met its end through burial by volcanic ash and molten lava.

Appendix A
Plans of the Houses

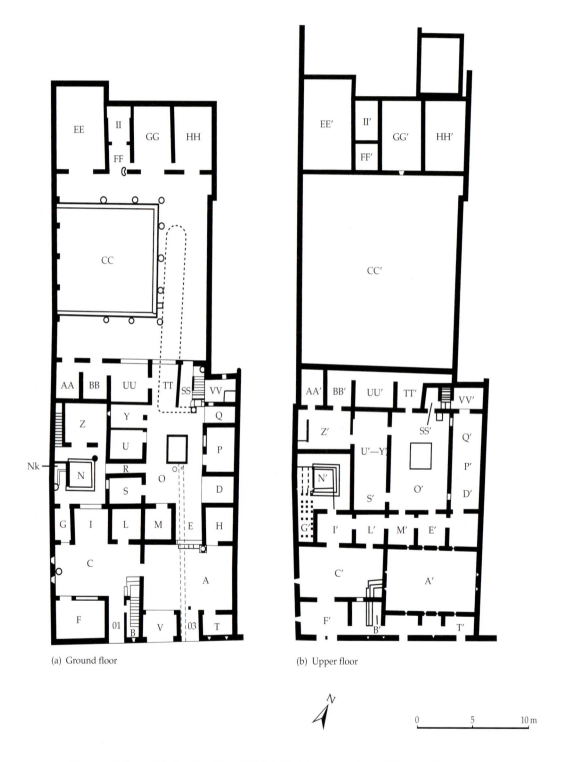

(a) Ground floor   (b) Upper floor

Figure A.1 Casa di Julius Polybius (IX 13, 1–3): (a) ground floor; (b) upper floor

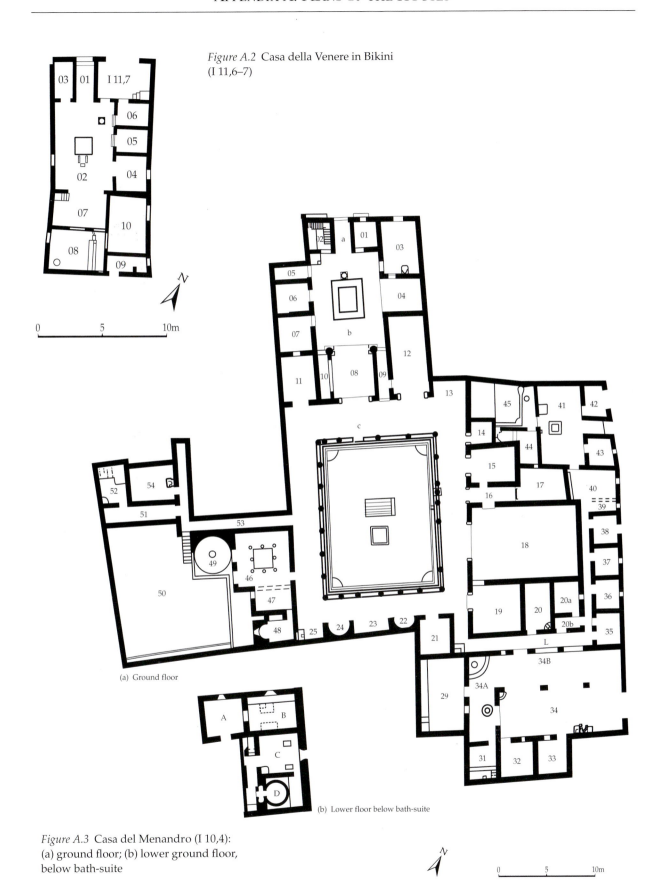

Figure A.2 Casa della Venere in Bikini
(I 11,6–7)

(a) Ground floor

(b) Lower floor below bath-suite

Figure A.3 Casa del Menandro (I 10,4):
(a) ground floor; (b) lower ground floor,
below bath-suite

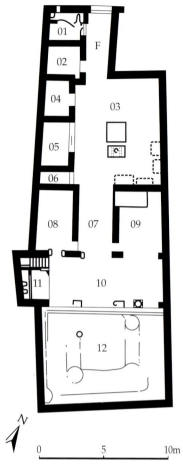

Figure A.4 Casa del Fabbro (I 10,7)

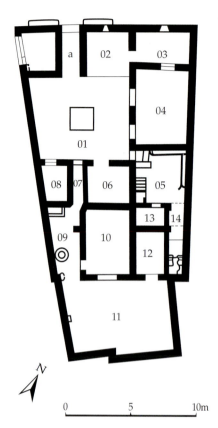

Figure A.5 House I 10,8

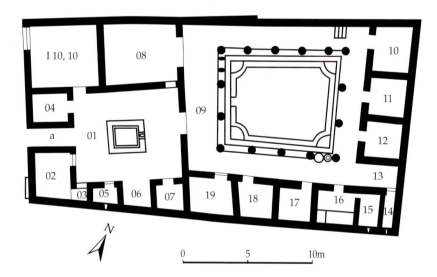

Figure A.6 Casa degli Amanti (I 10,11)

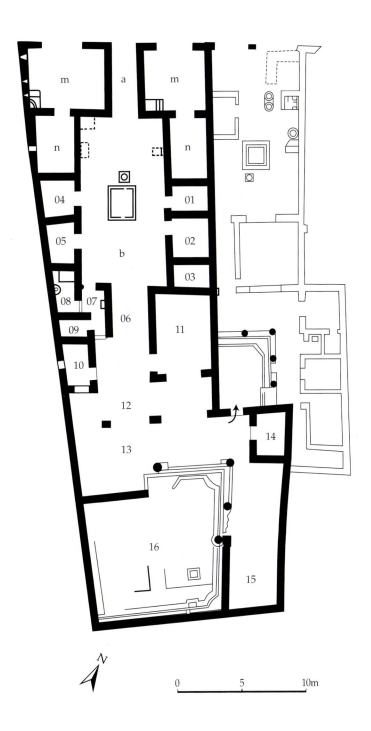

Figure A.7 Casa dei Quadretti Teatrali (I 6,11)

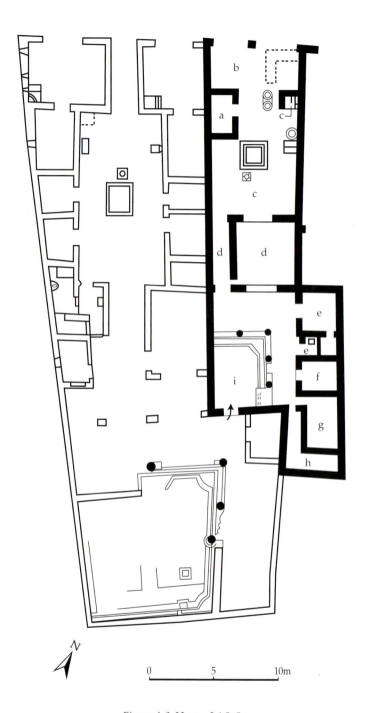

Figure A.8 House I 6,8–9

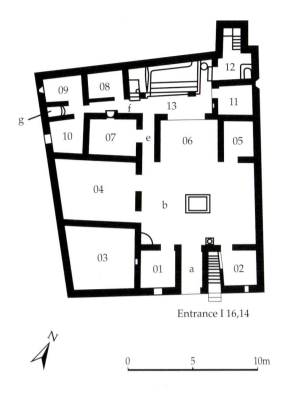

Entrance I 16,14

N

0   5   10m

Figure A.9 Casa di Stallius Eros (I 6,13)

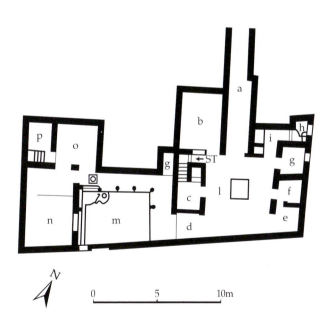

N

0   5   10m

Figure A.10 Casa del Sacerdos Amandus (I 7,7)

209

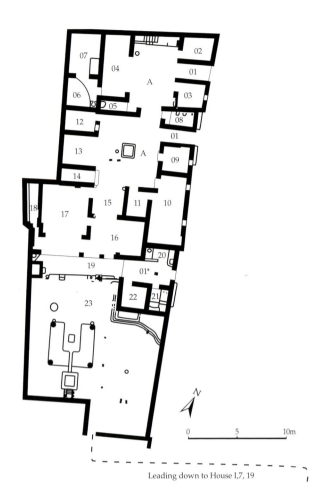

Figure A.11 Casa dell'Efebo (I 7,10–12)

Leading down to House I,7, 19

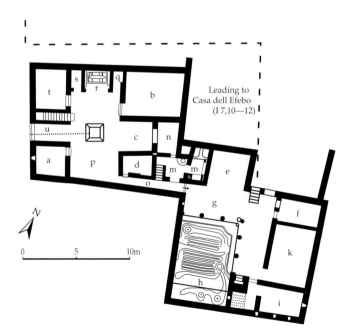

Leading to
Casa dell Efebo
(I 7,10—12)

Figure A.12 House I 7,19

210

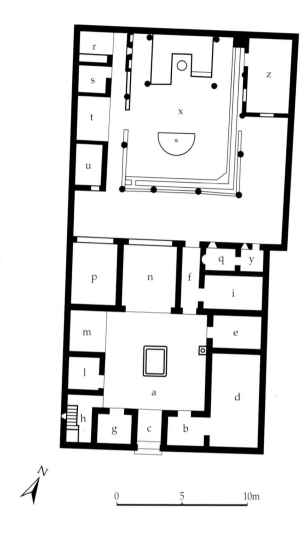

Figure A.13 Casa di Trebius Valens (III 2,1)

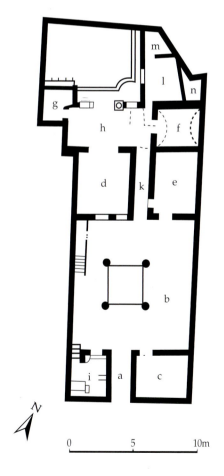

Figure A.14 Casa dei Ceii (I 6,15)

211

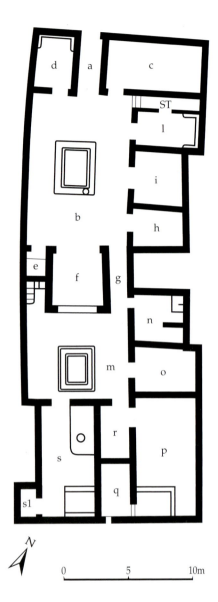

Figure A.15 Casa del Sacello Iliaco (I 6,4)

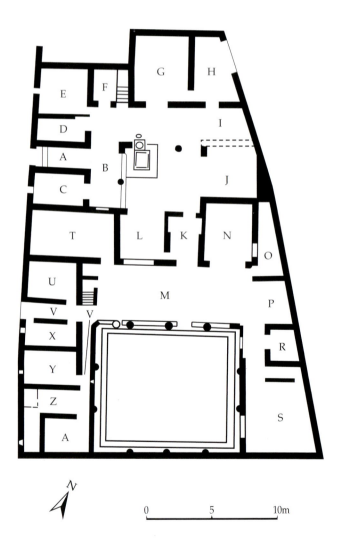

Figure A.16 House VI 16,26

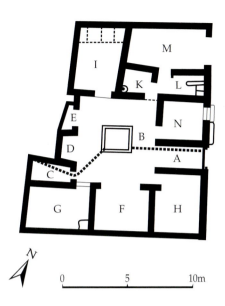

Figure A.17 Casa della Ara Massima (VI 16,15)

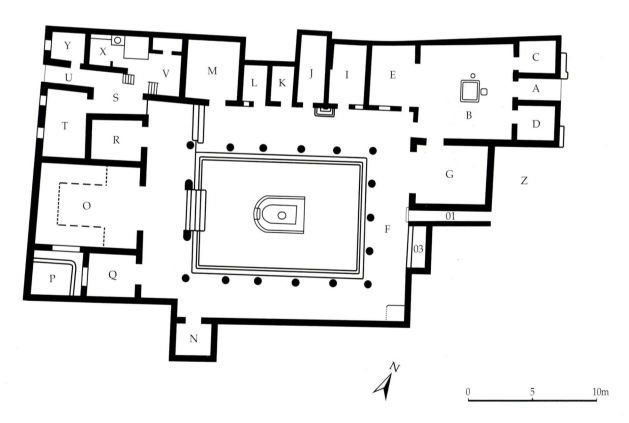

Figure A.18 Casa degli Amorini Dorati (VI 16,7)

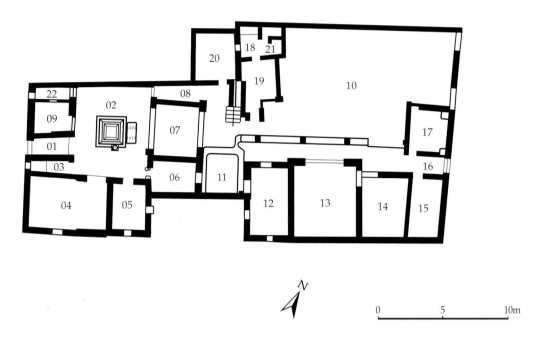

Figure A.19 Casa di M. Lucretius Fronto (V 4, a)

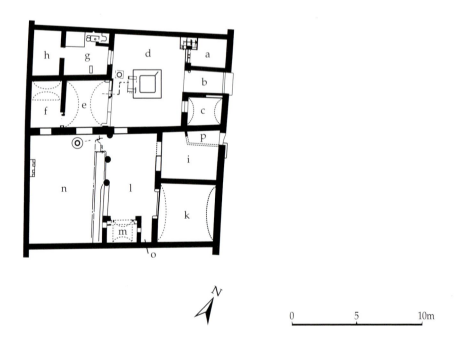

Figure A.20 Casa del Principe di Napoli (VI 15,7–8)

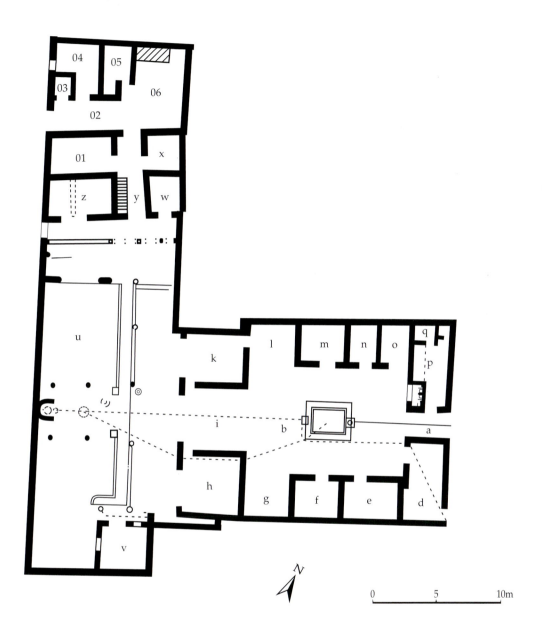

Figure A.21 House VI 15,5

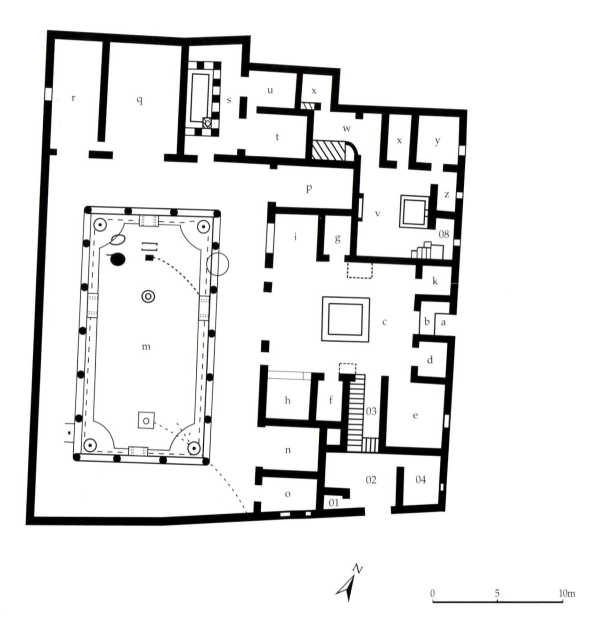

Figure A.22 Casa dei Vettii (VI 15,1)

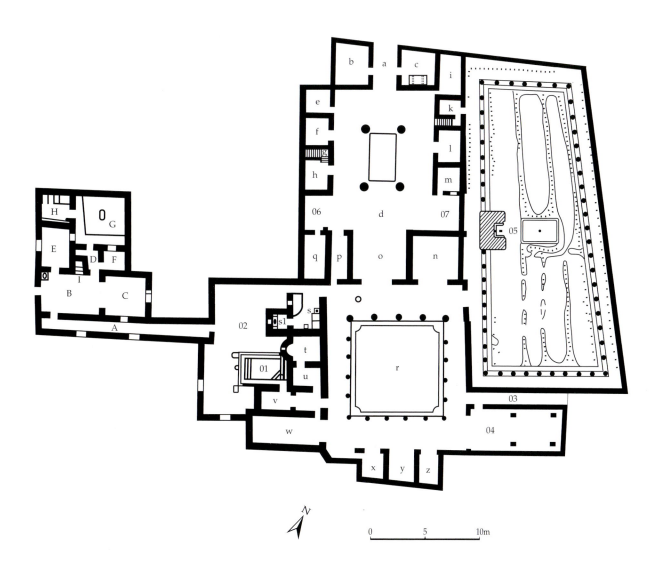

Figure A.23 Casa delle Nozze d'Argento (V 2,1)

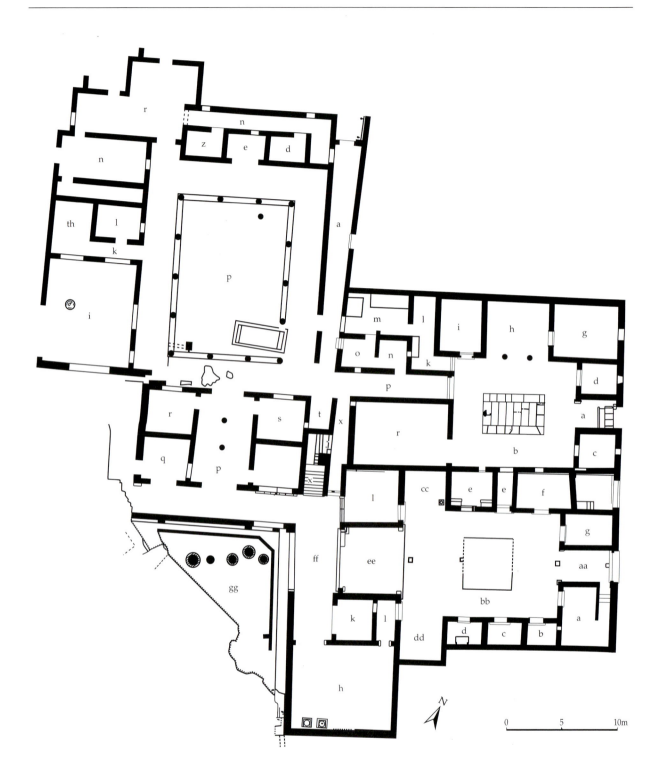

Figure A.24 House VIII 2,14–16

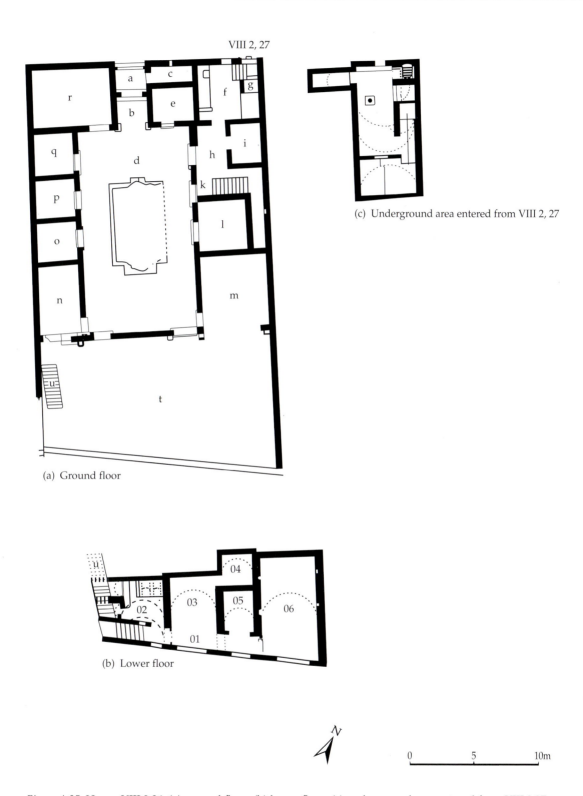

VIII 2, 27

(c) Underground area entered from VIII 2, 27

(a) Ground floor

(b) Lower floor

N

0   5   10m

Figure A.25 House VIII 2,26: (a) ground floor; (b) lower floor; (c) underground area entered from VIII 2,27

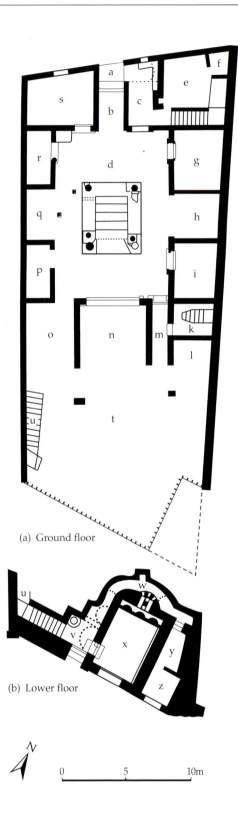

(a) Ground floor

(b) Lower floor

Figure A.26 House VIII 2,28: (a) ground floor; (b) lower floor

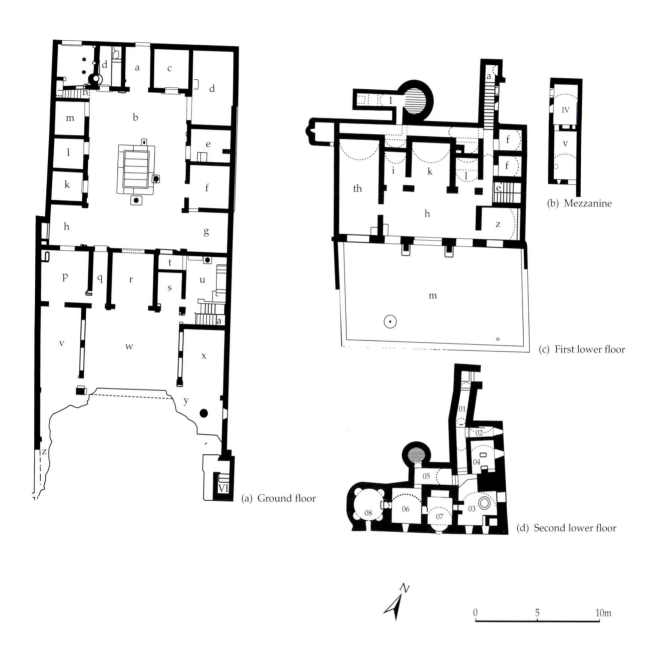

(a) Ground floor

(b) Mezzanine

(c) First lower floor

(d) Second lower floor

Figure A.27 Casa di Giuseppe II (VIII 2,39): (a) ground floor; (b) mezzanine; (c) first lower floor; (d) second lower floor

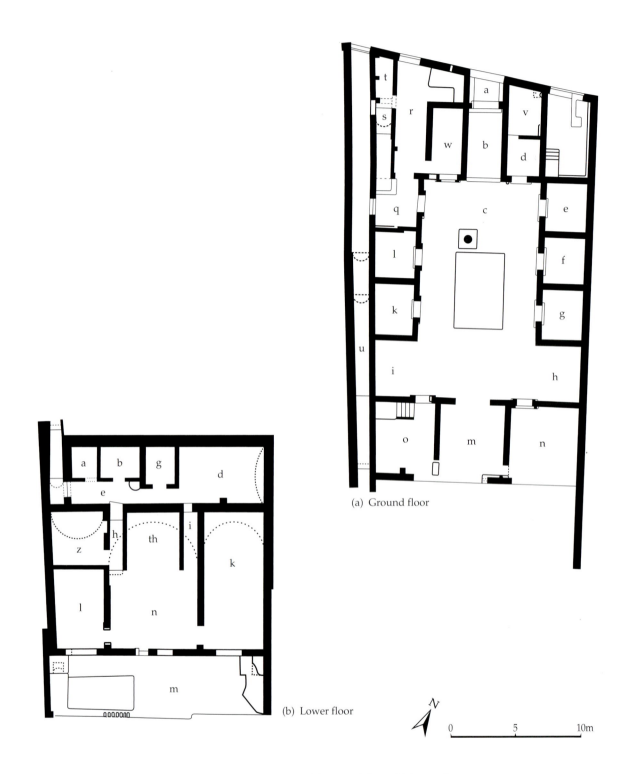

(a) Ground floor

(b) Lower floor

N

0   5   10m

Figure A.28 House VIII 2,34: (a) ground floor; (b) lower floor

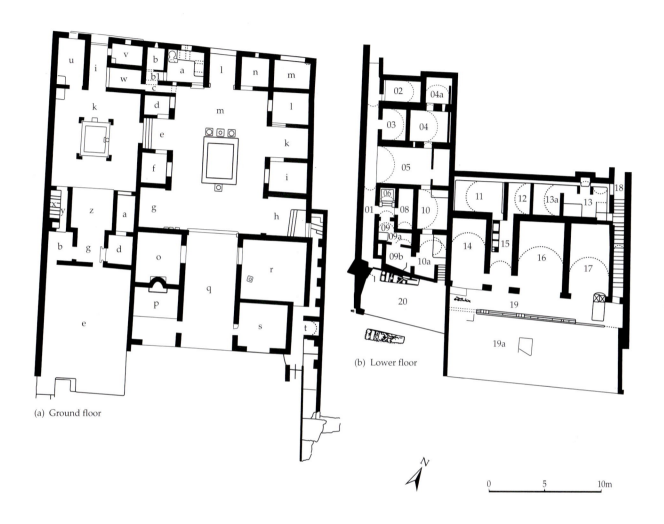

(a) Ground floor

(b) Lower floor

Figure A.29 House VIII 2,29–30: (a) ground floor; (b) lower floor

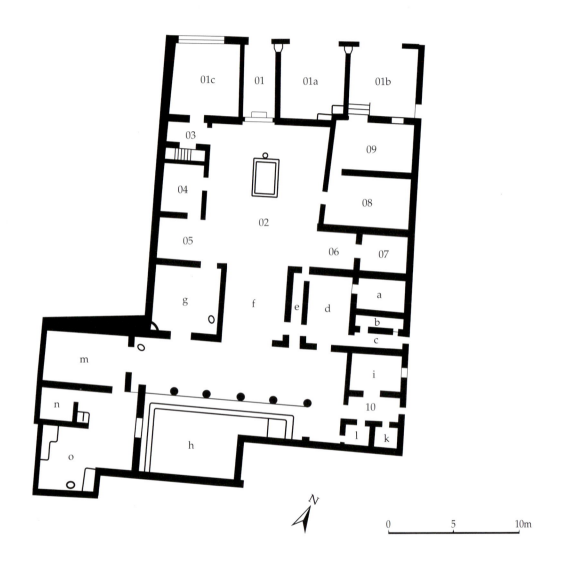

Figure A.30 House VIII 5,9

Bibliography

The following bibliography includes all references that appear in this volume and on the companion website.

Adam, J.-P.

1984　*La construction romaine: Materiaux et technique.* Paris: Picard.

1986　Observations techniques sur les suites du séisme de 62 à Pompéi. In *Tremblement de terre, éruptions volcaniques et vie des hommes dans la campanie antique,* edited by C. A. Livadie, 67–87. Naples: Centre Jean Bérard.

1989a　L'edilizia privata: Pompei e il suo agro, In *I terramoti prima del Mille in Italia e nell'area mediterranea,* edited by E. Guidaboni, 224–243. Bologna: SGA Storia–Geofisica–Ambiente.

1989b　Osservazione tecniche sugli effetti del terramotto di Pompei del 62 d.C. In *I terramoti prima del Mille in Italia e nell'area mediterranea,* edited by E. Guidaboni, 460–474. Bologna: Storia–Geofisica –Ambiente.

Adams, W. H.

1987　Review. *Historical Archaeology* 21.1:105–107.

Allison, P. M.

1989　Painter–workshops in Pompeii. *Boreas: Münster Beiträge zur Archäologie* 12:111–118.

1991a　The wall-paintings of the Casa della Caccia Antica in Pompeii. Master's thesis, University of Sydney, 1986. Ann Arbor: University Microfilms 1344571.

1991b　"Workshops" and "patternbooks." In *Akten des 4. Internationalen Kolloquiums zur römischen Wandmalerei in Köln, Sept. 1989. Kölner Jahrbuch für Vor– und Frühgeschichte* 24:79–84.

1992a　The relationship between wall-decoration and room type in Pompeian houses: A case study of the Casa della Caccia Antica. *Journal of Roman Archaeology* 5: 235–249.

1992b　Artefact assemblages: Not the Pompeii Premise. In *Papers of the Fourth Conference of Italian Archaeology,* edited by E. Herring, R. Whitehouse, and J. Wilkins, vol. 3.1: 49–56. London: Accordia Research Centre.

1992c　Review. *Journal of Roman Studies* 82:274.

1993　How do we identify the use of space in Roman housing? In *Functional and spatial analysis of wall painting: Proceedings of the 5th International Congress of Ancient Wall Painting, Amsterdam 1992,* edited by E. Moormann, 4–11. Annual Papers on Classical Archaeology Supplement 3. Leiden: Bulletin antieke beschaving.

1994a　The distribution of Pompeian house contents and its significance. Ph.D. dissertation, University of Sydney, 1992. Ann Arbor: University Microfilms 9400463.

1994b　Issues of data exchange and accessibility: Pompeii. In *Methods in the Mountains: Proceedings of the International Union of the Pre– and Protohistoric Sciences Commission IV Meeting–Data Management, Mathematical Methods and Computing in Archaeology,* edited by I. Johnson, 35–41. University of Sydney Archaeological Methods Series, No. 2. Sydney: Prehistory and Historical Archaeology, University of Sydney.

1994c　Room use in Pompeian houses. In *Pompeii revisited: The life and death of a Roman town,* J.-P. Descoeudres et al., 82–89. Special volume. Sydney: Mediterranean Archaeology.

1995a　House contents in Pompeii: Data collection and interpretative procedures for a reappraisal of Roman domestic life and site formation processes. *Journal of European Archaeology* 3.1:145–176.

1995b　Painter-workshops or decorator's teams? *Mededelingen van het Nederlands Instituut te Rome, Antiquity* 54:98–108.

1995c　On-going seismic activity and its effect on living conditions in Pompeii in the last decades. In *Archäologie und seismologie: La regione vesuviana dal 62 al 79 d.C.: problemi archeologici e sismologici,* edited by T. Fröhlich and L. Jacobelli. Deutsches Archäologisches Institut Rom, Soprintendenza Archeologica di Pompei, Osservatorio Vesuviano, 183–190. Munich: Biering and Brinkman.

1996   The Pompeii comprise: The consuming evidence. In *Archaeology, ideology and method: Inter-Academy Seminar on Current Archaeological Research 1993,* edited by K. Gulliver, W. Ernst, and F. Scriba, 97–106. Rome: Canadian Academic Centre in Italy.

1997a   Why do excavation reports have finds' catalogues? In *Not so much a pot, more a way of life: Current approaches to artefact analysis in archaeology,* edited by C. G. Cumberpatch and P. W. Blinkhorn, 77–84. Monograph 83. Oxford: Oxbow.

1997b   Subject matter and meaning in the paintings of the Casa della Caccia Antica in Pompeii. In *I temi figurati nella pittura parietale antica (IV sec. a.C.–IV sec. d. C),* Atti del VI Convegno Internazionale sulla Pittura Parietale Antica, edited by D. Scagliarini Corlàita, 19–24. Bologna: University Press.

1997c   Roman households: An archaeological perspective. In *Roman urbanism: Beyond the consumer city,* edited by H. Parkins, 112–146. London: Routledge.

1997d   Artefact distribution and spatial function in Pompeian houses. In *The Roman family in Italy: Status, sentiment and space,* edited by B. Rawson and P. Weaver, 321–354. Oxford: Clarendon Press.

1999a   Introduction. In *The archaeology of household activities,* edited by P. M. Allison, 1–18. London: Routledge.

1999b   Labels for ladles: Interpreting the material culture from Roman households. In *The archaeology of household activities,* edited by P. M. Allison, 57–77. London: Routledge.

1999c   Pompeian epigraphy as archaeological evidence. In *Beryllanea: Essays in Honour of Professor Beryl Rawson,* presented February 1999, 136-144. Sydney.

2001   Using the material and written sources: Turn of the millennium approaches to Roman domestic space. *American Journal of Archaeology* 105:1–28.

2002   Recurring tremors: The continuing impact of the AD 79 eruption of Mt. Vesuvius. In *Natural disasters and cultural change,* edited by R. Torrence and J. Grattan. London and New York: Routledge.

n.d.   *The Insula del Menandro in Pompeii III: The finds and their contexts.*Oxford: Clarendon Press. Forthcoming.

Allison, P. M., and F. Sear

2002   *The Casa della Caccia Antica.* Häuser in Pompeji 11. Münich: Hirmer.

Ames, K. L.

1982   Meaning in artefacts: Hall furnishings in Victorian America. In *Material culture studies in America,* edited by T. J. Schlereth, 206–221. Nashville: American Association for State and Local History.

Andersson, E. B.

1990   Fountains and the Roman dwelling. *Jahrbuch des Deutschen Archäologischen Instituts Archäologischen Instituts* 105:207–236.

Andreau, J.

1973a   Remarques sur la societé. *Dialoghi di Archeologia* 7:213–254.

1973b   Histoire des séismes et histoire économique: Le tremblement de terre de Pompéi (62 ap. J.–C.). *Annales Économies Sociétes Civilisations* 28.1:369–395.

Annecchino, M.

1977a   Suppellettile fittile da cucina di Pompei. In *L'instrumentum domesticum di Ercolano e Pompei,* by A. Carandini et al., 105–120. Rome: L'Erma di Bretschneider.

1977b   Fritillus, un piccolo vaso di terracotta. *Cronache Pompeiani* 3:198–213.

Anonymous

1890   Pompei—Giornale degli scavi compilato dai soprastanti. *Notizie degli Scavi di Antichità*: 290–291, 327–328.

1891   Pompei—Giornale degli scavi compilato dai soprastanti. *Notizie degli Scavi di Antichità*: 36–37, 59–60, 133–134, 168–169, 292.

1892   Pompei—Giornale degli scavi redatto dai soprastanti. *Notizie degli Scavi di Antichità*: 29–31, 100, 121, 202–204, 238–239, 274–275, 318, 350, 481–483.

1895   Pompei—Giornale degli scavi redatto dagli assistenti. *Notizie degli Scavi di Antichità:* 31–34, 47, 84, 108–109, 207, 233–234, 251, 352–353, 474.

1896   Pompei—Giornale degli scavi redatto dei soprastanti. *Notizie degli Scavi di Antichità:* 104, 167-168, 204, 227–230, 372–373, 473–475, 532–536.

Archer, W.

1990   The paintings in the alae of the Casa dei Vettii and the definition of the Fourth Pompeian style. *American Journal of Archaeology* 94:95–123.

1994   The maturing of the Fourth Style: The Casa della Nozze d'Argento at Pompeii. *Journal of Roman Archaeology* 7:129–215.

Armitt, M.

1991   La Case della Venere in Bikini. Unpublished Ph.D. dissertation, University of Adelaide.

1993   La Casa della Venere in Bikini (1 11, 6–7). In *Ercolano 1738–1988: 250 anni di ricerca archeologica, Atti del Convegno Internazionale Ravello–Ercolano–Napoli–Pompei (30 ottobre–5 novembre),* edited by L. Franchi dell'Orto, 237–241. Rome: L'Erma di Bretschneider.

Arthur, P.

1989   Archeologica e terramoti a Napoli. In *I terramoti prima del Mille in Italia e nell'area mediterranea,* edited by E. Guidaboni, 501–506. Bologna: Storia–Geofisica –Ambiente.

Ascher, R.

1961   Analogy in archaeological interpretation. *Southwestern Journal of Anthropology* 17:317–325.

Asconius, Q. Pediani

    Orationum Ciceronis Quinque Enarratio. Oxford: Caledonian Press (4th edition 1962).

Atkinson, D.

1914   A hoard of Samian ware from Pompeii. *Journal of Roman Studies* 4:26–64.

Atkinson, T. D., et al.

1904   *Excavations at Phylakopi in Melos.* British School at Rome. London: MacMillan.

Augusti, S.

1967   *I colori pompeiani.* Rome: De Luca.

Ault, B.

1994   Classical houses and households: An architectural and artifactual case study from Haleis, Greece. Ph.D. dissertation, Indiana University. Ann Arbor: University Microfilms 9518532.

Ault, B., and L. Nevett

1999   Digging houses: Archaeologies of Classical and Hellenistic Greek domestic assemblages. In *The archaeology of household activities,* edited by P. M. Allison, 43–56. London: Routledge.

Barbet, A.

1985   *La peinture murale romaine: Les styles décoratif pompéiens.* Paris: Picard.

Barbet, A., and C. Allag

1972   Techniques de préparations des parois dans la peinture romaine. *Mélanges de l'École française de Rome* 84:935–1069.

Bartman, E.

1991   Sculptural collecting and display in the private realm. In *Roman art in the private sphere: New perspectives on the architecture and decor of the domus, villa and insula,* edited by E. Gazda, 71–88. Ann Arbor: University of Michigan Press.

Bastet, F. L.

1975   Forschungen im Haus des M. Lucretius Fronto. In *Neue Forschungen in Pompeji,* edited by B. Andreae and H. Kyrieleis, 193–197. Recklinghausen: Aurel Bongers.

Bastet, F. L., and M. de Vos

1979   *Proposto per una classificazione del terzo stile pompeiano.* Gravenhage: Staatsuitgeverij.

Bechi, G.

1834   Relazione degli scavi di Pompei. *Real Museo Borbonico* X:1–7.

Becker, W. A.

1876   Excursus I, Scene I, The Roman House. In *Roman scenes at the time of Augustus,* 5th edition, 231–280. London: Longmans, Green and Co.

Bernstein, F.

1988   Pompeian women and the programmata. In *Studia Pompeiana & Classica: In honour of Wilhelmina F. Jashemski,* edited by R. I. Curtius, 1–18. New York: Caratzas.

Berry, J.
1997   Household artefacts: Towards a re–inter-
        pretation of Roman domestic space. In
        *Domestic space in the Roman world: Pompeii
        and beyond*, edited by R. Laurence and A. F.
        Wallace–Hadrill, 183–196. Supplementary
        series no. 22. Portsmouth, RI: Journal of
        Roman Archaeology.

Binford, L. R.
1981   Behavioral archaeology and the "Pompeii
        premise." *Journal of Anthropological
        Research* 37:195–208.

Bishop, M.
1988   Cavalry equipment of the Roman army in
        the first century AD. In *Military equipment
        and the identity of Roman soldiers, Proceed-
        ings of the Fourth Roman Military Conference,*
        edited by J. C. Coulton, 67–195. Oxford:
        British Archaeological Reports.

Blong, R. J.
1984   *Volcanic hazards: A source book on the effects
        of eruptions.* Sydney: Academic Press.

Boëthius, A., and J. B. Ward-Perkins
1970   *Etruscan and Roman architecture.* Middlesex:
        Harmondsworth, Pelican Books.

Bon, S. E., and R. Jones, eds.
1997   *Sequence and space in Pompeii.* Monograph
        77. Oxford: Oxbow Books.

Bon, S. E., R. Jones, B. Kurchin, and D. J. Robinson
1997   The context of the House of the Surgeon:
        Investigations in Insula VI, 1 at Pompeii.
        In *Sequence and space in Pompeii,* edited by
        S. E. Bon and R. Jones, 32–49. Monogragh
        77. Oxford: Oxbow Books.

Borriello, M. R., M. Lista, U. Pappalardo, V. Sampa-
        olo, and C. Ziviello
1986   *Le Collezione del Museo Nazionale di Napoli (i
        mosaici, le pitture, gli oggetti di uso quotidi-
        ano, gli argento ecc).* Naples: De Luca.

Boyce, G. K.
1937   *Corpus of the lararia of Pompeii.* Rome: Mem-
        oirs of the American Academy in Rome 14.

Bragantini, I., M. de Vos, F. Parise Badoni, and V.
        Sampaolo
1980   *Pitture e Pavimenti di Pompei, Repertorio
        della fotografie de Gabinetto Fotografico Nazio-
        nale* I. Rome: Ministero beni culturale e

ambientali, Istituto centrale per il catalogo
e la documentazione.

1983   *Pitture e Pavimenti di Pompei, Repertorio
        della fotografie de Gabinetto Fotografico Nazio-
        nale* II. Rome: Ministero beni culturale e
        ambientali, Istituto centrale per il catalogo
        e la documentazione.

1986   *Pitture e Pavimenti di Pompei, Repertorio
        della fotografie de Gabinetto Fotografico Nazio-
        nale* III. Rome: Ministero beni culturale e
        ambientali, Istituto centrale per il catalogo
        e la documentazione.

Brett, G.
1968   *Dinner is served: A history of dining in
        England 1400–1900.* London: Rupert Hart-
        Davis.

Brunsting, H.
1975   Forschungen im Garten des M. Lucretius
        Fronto. In *Neue Forschungen in Pompeji,*
        edited by B. Andreae and H. Kyrieleis,
        198–199. Recklinghausen: Aurel Bongers.

Bryson, N.
1983   *Vision and painting: The logic of the gaze.*
        London: MacMillan.

Cahill, N.
2002   *Household and city organization at Olynthus.*
        New Haven: Yale University Press.

Callender, M. H.
1965   *Roman amphorae.* London: Oxford Univer-
        sity Press.

Carafa, P., and M. T. D'Alessio
1995–96 Lo scavo nella casa di "Giuseppe II" (VIII,
        2, 38–39) e nel portico occidentale del foro
        triangolare a Pompei, Rapporto prelim-
        inare. *Rivisti di Studi Pompeiani* 7:137–152.

Carandini, A.
1984   *Settefinestre una villa schiavista nell'Etruria
        romana* I–III. Milan: Panini.

Carandini, A., M. Annecchino, A. M. Bisi Ingrassia,
        et al.
1977   *L'instrumentum domesticum di Ercolano e
        Pompei.* Rome: L'Erma di Bretschneider.

Carandini, A., D. Manacorda, C. Panella, C. Pav-
        olini, E. Papi, and P. Carafa
1996   Per lo studio della Insulae di Pompei.
        Archaeologica Classica 48:321–327.

Carrington, R. C.

1933   Notes on the building materials of Pompeii. *Journal of Roman Studies* 23:125–138.

Castiglione Morelli del Franco, N.

1982   Le orificerie della casa di C. Giulio Polibio. In *La regione sotterrata dal Vesuvio. Studi e prospettive, Atti del convegno internazionale 11–15 novembre 1979*, 789–808. Naples: Università degli Studi di Napoli.

1983   Le lucerne della casa di Giulio Polibio a Pompei. *Pompeii Herculaneum Stabiae* 1:213–258.

Castiglione Morelli del Franco, N., and R. Vitale

1989   L'Insula 8 della Regio I: Un campione d'indagine socio-economica, *Rivista di Studi Pompeiani* 3:185–221.

Castrén, P.

1975   *Ordo Populusque pompeianus: Polity and society in Roman Pompeii.* Acta Instituti Romani Finlandiae 8. Rome: Bardi.

Cerulli Irelli, G.

1975   Intorno al problema della rinascita di Pompei. In *Neue Forschungen in Pompeji*, edited by B. Andreae and H. Kyrieleis, 291–298. Recklinghausen: Aurel Bongers.

1977a   Officina di lucerne frittili a Pompei. In *L'instrumentum domesticum di Ercolano e Pompei*, by A. Carandini et al., 53–72. Rome: L'Erma di Bretschneider.

1977b   L'attività archeologica nelle province di Napoli e Caserta–Locri Epizefiri. In *Atti del 17. Convegno di Studi sulla Magna Grecia, Taranto 1976*, 755–816. Taranto: Istituto per la storia e l'archeologia della Magna Grecia.

1990   Der letzten pompejanische Stil. In *Pompejanische Wandmalerei*, by G. Cerulli Irelli, et al., 233–238. Zürich: Belser Verlag.

Cicero

Ad Atticum. Translated by E. O. Winsted, 1912–18. London: William Heinemann; Cambridge, Mass.: Harvard University Press.

Epistulae ad familiares. Translated by W. Glynn Williams, 1965. London: William Heinemann; Cambridge, Mass.: Harvard University Press.

De Oratore. Translated by H. Rackham, 1960. London: William Heinemann; Cambridge, Mass.: Harvard University Press.

Philippicae. Translated by W. C. A. Ker, 1926. London: William Heinemann; Cambridge, Mass.: Harvard University Press.

Ciolek–Torello, R. S.

1984   An alternative model of room function from Grasshopper Pueblo, Arizona. In *Intrasite spatial analysis in archaeology*, edited by H. J. Hietala, 127–153. New York: Cambridge University Press.

Cioni, R., and R. Vecci

1988   Stratigrafia delle successioni piroclastiche vesuviane nella zona di Terzigno: La grande cava di Pozzelle. *Rivista di Studi Pompeiani* 2:119–126.

Ciprotti, P.

1964   Der letzte Tag von Pompeji. *Altertum* 10:40–54.

Clark Jr., C. E.

1976   Domestic architecture as an index to social history: The romantic revival and the cult of domesticity in America, 1840–1870. *Journal of Interdisciplinary History* 7.1:33–56.

Clarke, J. R.

1991   *The houses of Roman Italy, 100 BC–AD 250: Ritual, space and decoration.* Los Angeles: University of California Press.

Columella

De re rustica. Books 1–6. Translated by H. B. Ash, 1949. London: William Heinemann; Cambridge, Mass.: Harvard University Press.

Conkey, M. W., and J. D. Spector

1984   Archaeology and the study of gender. *Advances in Archaeological Method and Theory* 7:1–38.

Conticello, B., et al.

1990   *Rediscovering Pompeii. Exhibition by IBM-Italia.* Rome: L'Erma di Bretschneider.

Copony, R.

1987   Fortes Fortuna Iuvat. Fiktion und Realität im 1. Vesuvbrief des Jüngeren Plinius VI, 16. *Grazer Beitrage* 14:215–229.

Corlàita Scargliarini, D.

1974–76   Spazio e decorazione nella pittura pompeiana. *Palladio* 24–26:3–44.

Crook, J. A.

1992 Women in Roman succession. In *The family in ancient Rome: New perspectives*, 2nd edition, edited by B. Rawson, 58–82. London: Routledge.

Crummy, N.

1983 *The Roman small finds from excavations in Colchester 1971–1979*. Colchester: Colchester Archaeological Trust.

Cubberley, A. L., J. A. Lloyd, and P. C. Roberts

1988 Testa and Clibani: Baking covers in classical Italy. *Papers of the British School at Rome* 56:98–119.

Curtius, L.

1972 *Die Wandmalerei Pompejis*. 2nd edition. Darmstadt: Wissenschaftliche Buchgesellschaft.

Daremberg, Ch., and E. Saglio

1877–1919 *Dictionnaire des antiquités grecques et romaines d'après les textes et les monuments:* I.1 (1881, third edition); I.2 (1887); II.1 (1892); II.2 (1896); III.1 (1900); III.2 (1904); IV.1 (1907); IV.2 (1908); V (1919). Paris: Librairie Hachette.

D'Arms, J. H.

1988 Pompeii and Rome in the Augustan age and beyond: The eminence of the Gens Holconia. In *Studia Pompeiana & Classica in honour of Wilhelmina F. Jashemski*, edited by R. Curtius, 51–74. New York: Caratzas.

Davey, N., and R. Ling

1982 *Wall-painting in Roman Britain*. London: Society for the Promotion of Roman Studies.

Daviau, M.

1993 *Houses and their furnishings in Bronze Age Palestine: Domestic activity areas and artefact distribution in the Middle and Late Bronze Ages*. Journal for the Study of the Old Testament, Series supplement 143. Sheffield: Sheffield Academic Press.

David, N.

1971 The Fulani compound and the archaeologist. *World Archaeology* 3.1:111–131.

De Caro, S.

1978 Attività archeologica, *Pompei. Cronache Pompeiani* 4:230–231.

1987 The sculptures of the Villa of Poppaea at Oplontis: A preliminary report. In *Ancient Roman Villa Gardens*, edited by E. B. MacDougall. Washington, D.C.: Dumbarton Oaks Research Library and Collections.

1990 Review. *Gnomon* 62.2:152–161.

De Carolis, E.

1987 Due lucerne di bronzo provenienti da Oplontis. *Rivisti di Studi Pompeiani* 1:81–84.

De Franciscis, A.

1975 Notiziario. *Cronache Pompeiani* 1:247.

1975–76 *Fasti archaeologici*: no. 11940.

1988 La Casa di C. Iulius Polybius. *Rivisti di Studi Pompeiani* 2:14–34.

De la Bédoyère, G.

1989 *The finds of Roman Britain*. London: Batsford.

De la Ruffinière du Prey, P.

1994 *The Villas of Pliny from antiquity to posterity*. Chicago and London: University of Chicago Press.

Della Corte, M.

1911 Pompei—Scavi eseguiti durante il mese di settembre. *Notizie degli Scavi di Antichità*, Series 5, No. 8:349–351.

1912 Pompei—Continuazione dello scavo di Via dell'Abbondanza. *Notizie degli Scavi di Antichità*, Series 5, No. 9:135–148, 174–192, 215–224, 246–259, 351–356, 401-408, 442–449, 476–480.

1913 Pompei—Continuazione dello scavo di Via dell'Abbondanza. *Notizie degli Scavi di Antichità*, Series 5, No. 10:28–35, 55–64, 82–85, 141–148, 188–192, 220-224, 249–256, 356–360, 411–416.

1914 Pompei—Continuazione dello scavo di Via dell'Abbondanza. *Notizie degli Scavi di Antichità*, Series 5, No. 11:74–80, 255-256, 291–296.

1915 Pompei—Continuazione dello scavo di Via dell'Abbondanza. *Notizie degli Scavi di Antichità*, Series 5, No. 12:342–345, 420–425.

1916 Pompei—Continuazione dello scavo di Via dell'Abbondanza. *Notizie degli Scavi di Antichità*, Series 5, No. 13:30–35, 151–158.

1919 Pompei—Continuazione della esplorazione nella predetta Abbondanza. Scavi esegueti nel mese di ottobre 1915. *Notizie degli Scavi di Antichità,* Series 5, No. 16:420–425.

1965 *Case ed Abitanti.* 3rd edition. Naples: Fausto Fiorentino.

Delibrias, G., G. M. Di Paola, M. Rosi, and R. Santacroce

1979 La storia eruttiva del complesso vulcanico Somma Vesuvio ricostruita dalle successioni piroclastiche del Monte Somma. *Rendiconti Società Italiana di Mineralogia e Petrologia* 35.1:411–438.

Dell'Orto, F.

1990 Catalogo: L'arredamento, furnishings. In *Rediscovering Pompeii,* by B. Conticello, et al., 170–185. Rome: L'Erma di Bretschneider.

Den Boersterd, M. H. P.

1956 *The bronze vessels in the Rijksmuseum* xxi. Dep. van Onderwigs, Kunsten en Wetenschappen 31. Nijmegen.

Descœudres, J.-P.

1987 Rome and Roman art. In *The enduring past: Archaeology of the ancient world for Australians,* edited by A. Cremin, 164–209. Sydney: University of New South Wales Press.

Descœudres, J.-P., and F. Sear

1987 The Australian expedition to Pompeii. *Rivista di Studi Pompeiani* 1:11–36.

Descœudres, J.-P., et al.

1994 *Pompeii revisited: The life and death of a Roman town.* Special volume. Sydney: Mediterranean Archaeology.

De Simone, A.

1995 I terramoti precedenti l'eruzione. Nuove attestazione da recenti scavi. *Archäologie und seismologie: La regione vesuviana dal 62 al 79 d.C., problemi archeologici e sismologici,* edited by T. Fröhlich and L. Jacobelli. Deutsches Archäologisches Institut Rom, Soprintendenza Archeologica di Pompei, Osservatorio Vesuviano, 37-43. Munich: Biering and Brinkmann.

Dessau, H.

1962 *Inscriptiones Latinae Selectae* I–III. Dublin and Zurich: Wiedmann.

De Vos, A., and M. de Vos

1982 *Pompei Ercolano Stabia.* Rome: Guide archeologica Laterza.

De Vos, M.

1977 Primo stile figurato e maturo quarto stile negli scarichi provenienti dalle macerie del terramoto del 62 d.c. a Pompei. *Mededelingen van het Nederlands Instituut te Rome, Antiquity* 39:29–47.

1982 La casa di Ganimede in Pompei VII 13,4. Pavimenti e pitture: Terzo e quarto stile negli scarichi trovati sotto i pavimenti. *Mitteilungen des Deutschen Archäologischen Instituts, Römische Abteilung* 89:315–352.

Dexter, C. E.

1975 The Casa di Cecilio Giocondo in Pompeii. Ph.D. dissertation, Duke University. Ann Arbor: University Microfilms 7510696.

Dickmann, J.-A.

1997 The peristyle and the transformation of domestic space. In *Domestic space in the Roman world: Pompeii and beyond,* edited by R. Laurence and A. F. Wallace-Hadrill, 121–136. Supplementary series no. 22. Portsmouth, RI: Journal of Roman Archaeology.

1999 *Domus frequentata.* Munich: Pfeil.

Dio Cassius

Roman history. Books 61–70. Translated by E. Cary, 1995. London: William Heinemann; Cambridge, Mass.: Harvard University Press.

Diodorus of Sicily

Bibliotheca Historia. Translated by C. H. Oldfather, 1933–1967. London: William Heineman; Cambridge, Mass.: Harvard University Press.

Dixon, S.

2001 *Reading Roman Women: Sources, genres and real life.* London: Duckworth.

Dobbins, J. J.

1994 Problems of chronology, decoration, and urban design in the forum at Pompeii. *American Journal of Archaeology* 98:629–694.

Douglas, M., and B. Isherwood

1979 *The world of goods.* London: Allen Lane.

Drummer, A.

1994 Villa: Untersuchungen zum Bedeutungen zum Bedeutungswandel eines Motivs in römischer Bildkunst und Literatur. Ph.D. dissertation, Ludwig-Maximilians-Universität, Munich.

Duch, G. A.

1966 Note complementaire sur la technique de l'analyse succinct des mortier "tuileau" romain. *Actes de Ve Colloque international d'études gauloises, celtique e protoceltique. Samarobriva Ambianorum 28–30 août*, Celticum XV, 269–275. Rennes.

Duff, J. W., and A. M. Duff

1982 *Minor Latin poets in two volumes*. London: William Heineman; Cambridge: Harvard University Press.

Dunbabin, K.

1991 Triclinium and Stibadium. In *Dining in a classical context*, edited by W. J. Slater, 121–148. Ann Arbor: University of Michigan Press.

1996 Convivial spaces: Dining and entertainment in the Roman villa. *Journal of Roman Archaeology* 9:66–80.

Dwyer, E.

1982 *Pompeian domestic sculpture: A study of five Pompeian houses and their contents*. Rome: Giorgio Bretschneider.

1991 The Pompeian atrium house in theory and practice. In *Roman art in the private sphere: New perspectives on the architecture and decor of the domus, villa and insula*, edited by E. Gazda, 25–48. Ann Arbor: University of Michigan Press.

Dybkjaer-Larsen, J.

1982 The water-towers in Pompeii. *Analecta Romana Instituti Danici* 2:41–67.

Dyson, S. L.

1981 A classical archaeologist's response to the "New Archaeology." *Bulletin of the American School of Oriental Research* 242:7–13.

1989 The role of ideology and institutions in shaping Classical Archaeology in the nineteenth and twentieth centuries. In *Tracing archaeology's past: The historiography of archaeology*, edited by A. L. Christenson, 127–135. Carbondale and Edwardsville: Southern Illinois University Press.

Ehrhardt, W.

1987 *Stilgeschichte Untersuchungen an römischen Wandmalereien von der Späten Republik bis zur Zeit Neros*. Mainz am Rhein: Philip von Zabern.

1988 *Casa dell'Orso, Häuser in Pompeji* 2. Munich: Hirmer.

Elia, O.

1932 I cubiculi nelle case di Pompei. *Historia* 4, 3:394–421.

1934 Pompei: Relazione sullo scavo dell'Insula X della Regio I. *Notizie degli Scavi di Antichità*: 264–344.

Ellis, S.

2000 *Roman housing*. London: Duckworth.

Eschebach, H.

1970 *Städtebauliche Entwicklungen des antiken Pompeji*. Rome: Mitteilungen des Deutschen Archäologischen Instituts, Römische Abteilung Erganzungsheft 17.

Eschebach, H., and L. Eschebach

1995 *Pompeji vom 7. Jahrhundert v. Chr. bis 79 n. Chr.* Cologne: Böhlau.

Evans, E. M.

1984 The atrium complex in the houses in Pompeii. Ph.D. dissertation, Birmingham University, British Library Microfilms.

Evans, J. K.

1991 *War, women and children in Ancient Rome*. London: Routledge.

Finley, M.

1985 *Ancient history: Evidence and models*. London: Chatto and Windus.

Fiorelli, G.

1873 *Gli Scavi di Pompei dal 1861–1872*. Naples: Tipografia Italiana nel Liceo V. Emmanuele.

1860–64 ed. *Pompeianorum Antiquitatum Historia* I–III. Naples.

1881 Notizie degli Scavi—Pompei. *Notizie degli Scavi di Antichità*, Series 3, No. 7:195–197, 216, 248, 300–302.

1883 Notizie degli Scavi—Pompei. *Notizie degli Scavi di Antichità*: 135–136, 175–176, 215–216, 346–349, 375–376, 424–426.

1884   Pompei—Relazione del prof. A. Sogliano, sopra gli scavi eseguiti nel dicembre 1884. *Notizie degli Scavi di Antichità:* 396–397, 432.

1885   Pompei—Rapporto del prof. G. de Petra sui rinvenimenti fatti durante 1885. *Notizie degli Scavi di Antichità:* 163–164 (Sogliano), 225–258 (Sogliano), 532–539 (Sogliano).

Flower, H.

1996   *Ancestor masks and aristocratic power in Roman culture.* Oxford: Clarendon Press.

Förtsch, R.

1993   *Archäologischer Kommentar zu den Villenbriefen des jüngeren Plinius.* Mainz am Rhein: Philip von Zabern.

Foss, P.

1994   Kitchens and dining rooms at Pompeii: The spatial and social relationship of cooking to eating in the Roman household. Ph.D. dissertation, University of Michigan. Ann Arbor: University Microfilms 9513356.

1997   Watchful lares: Roman household organization and the rituals of cooking and dining. In *Domestic space in the Roman world: Pompeii and beyond,* edited by R. Laurence and A. Wallace-Hadrill, 196–218. Supplementary series no. 22. Portsmouth, RI: Journal of Roman Archaeology.

Franklin Jr., J. L.

1980   *Pompeii: The electoral programmata, campaigns and politics, AD 71–79.* Papers and Monographs of the American Academy in Rome 28. Rome: American Academy in Rome.

1990   *Pompeii: The "Casa del Marinaio" and its history.* Soprintendenza archeologica di Pompei monograph 3. Rome: L'Erma di Bretschneider.

Fremersdorf, F.

1940   Römische Scharnierbänder aus Bein. In *Serta Hoffilleriana: Commentationes Gratulatorias Victori Hoffiller Sexagenario Obtulerunt Collegae Amici Discipuli Ad XI Kal Mar MCMXXXVII,* 321–337. Zagreb: Zaklada Tiskare Narodnih Novina.

Frere, S.

1972   *Verulamium Excavations* 1. Report of the Research Committee of the Society of Antiquaries of London, No. 28. Oxford: Society of Antiquaries.

Fröhlich, T.

1991   *Lararien und Fassadenbilder in der Vesuvstädten: Untersuchungen zur "Volkstümlichen" Pompejanischen Malerei.* Römisch Abteilung Erganzungsheft 32. Mainz: Philip von Zabern.

1995   La Porta di Ercolano a Pompei e la cronologia dell'opus vittatum mixtum. In *Archäologie und seismologie: La regione vesuviana dal 62 al 79 d.C., problemi archeologici e sismologici,* edited by T. Fröhlich and L. Jacobelli. Deutsches Archäologisches Institut Rom, Soprintendenza Archeologica di Pompei, Osservatorio Vesuviano, 153–159. Munich: Biering and Brinkmann.

Fröhlich, T., and L. Jacobelli, eds.

1995   *Archaölogie und seismologie: La regione vesuviana dal 62 al 79 d.C., problemi archeologici e sismologici.* Deutsches Archäologisches Institut Rom, Soprintendenza Archeologica di Pompei, Osservatorio Vesuviano. Munich: Biering and Brinkmann.

Fulford, M., and A. Wallace-Hadrill

1998   Unpeeling Pompeii. *Antiquity* 72, No. 275:128–145.

Gaitzsch, W.

1980   *Eiserne römische Werkzeuge, Studien zur römischen Werkzeugkunde in Italien und den nördlichen provinzen des Imperiums Romanum.* International Series 78(i). Oxford: British Archaeological Reports.

Gardner, J. F.

1991   *Women in Roman law and society.* Bloomington: Indiana University Press.

Gardner, J. F., and T. Wiedemann

1991   *The Roman household: A sourcebook.* London: Routledge.

George, M.

1997a   Repopulating the Roman house. In *The Roman family in Italy: Status, sentiment and space,* edited by B. Rawson and P. Weaver, 299–319. Oxford: Clarendon Press.

1997b   Servus and Domus: The slave in the Roman house. In *Domestic space in the Roman World: Pompeii and beyond,* edited by R. Laurence and A. F. Wallace-Hadrill, 15–

24. Supplementary series no. 22. Portsmouth, RI: Journal of Roman Archaeology.

1998 Elements of the peristyle in Campanian atria. *Journal of Roman Archaeology* 11:82–100.

Gibbs, S. L.

1976 *Greek and Roman sundials.* Yale Studies in the History of Science and Medicine 11. New Haven: Yale University Press.

Giordano, C.

1974 Inscrizione graffite e dipinte nella Casa di C. Guilio Polibio. *Rendiconti della Accademia di Archeologi, Lettere e Belle Arti* 49:21–28.

Giornali degli Scavi di Pompei

n.d. Unpublished excavation reports held in the archives of the Soprintendenza archeologica di Pompei and of the Soprintendenza archeologica di Napoli.

Gnoli, R.

1971 *Marmora Romana.* Rome: Edizioni dell'Elefante.

Goldberg, M.

1999 Spatial and behavioral negotiation in Classical Athenian city houses. In *The archaeology of household activities*, edited by P. M. Allison, 142–161. London: Routledge.

Gower, E.

1993 *The loaded table: Representations of food in Roman literature.* Oxford: Clarendon Press.

Gralfs, B.

1988 *Metallverarbeitende Produktionsstätten in Pompeji.* International Series 433. Oxford: British Archaeological Reports.

Grant, M.

1971 *Cities of Vesuvius: Pompeii and Herculaneum.* London: Wiederman and Nicholson.

Guadagno, G.

1995 Documenti epigrafici ercolanesi relativi ad un terramoto. In *Archäologie und seismologie: La regione vesuviana dal 62 al 79 d.C., problemi archeologici e sismologici*, edited by T. Fröhlich, and L. Jacobelli. Deutsches Archäologisches Institut Rom, Soprintendenza Archeologica di Pompei, Osservatorio Vesuviano, 131–135. Munich: Biering and Brinkmann.

Harris, W. V.

1993 *The inscribed economy: Production and distribution in the Roman Empire in the light of instrumentum domesticum: The proceedings of a conference held at the American Academy in Rome on 10-11 January 1992.* Supplementary series no. 6. Ann Arbor, MI: Journal of Roman Archaeology.

Horace

Epistulae. Edited by A. S. Wilkins, 1907. London: MacMillan.

Satirae. Edited by A. Palmer, 1899. London: MacMillan.

Isings, C.

1957 *Roman glass from dated finds.* Groningen: J. B. Wolters.

Jacobelli, L.

1995 I terramoti fra il 62 e il 79 nell'area vesuviana: Le ragioni di un convegno. In *Archäologie und seismologie: La regione vesuviana dal 62 al 79 d.C., problemi archeologici e sismologici*, edited by T. Fröhlich and L. Jacobelli. Deutsches Archäologisches Institut Rom, Soprintendenza Archeologica di Pompei, Osservatorio Vesuviano, 17–21. Munich: Biering and Brinkmann.

Jacobi, L.

1897 *Das Römerkastell Saalburg bei Homburg.* Homburg: L. Jacobi.

Jameson, M. H.

1990 Domestic space in the Greek city state. In *Domestic architecture and the use of space*, edited by S. Kent, 92–113. Cambridge: Cambridge University Press.

Jansen, G. C. M.

1991 Water systems and sanitation in the houses of Herculaneum. *Mededelingen van het Nederlands Instituut te Rome, Antiquity* 50:145–172.

1997 Private toilets at Pompeii: Appearance and operations. In *Sequence and space in Pompeii*, edited by S. E. Bon and R. Jones, 121–134. Monograph 77. Oxford: Oxbow Books.

Jashemski, W. F.

1979a *The gardens of Pompeii, Herculaneum and the villas destroyed by Vesuvius.* New York and New Rochelle: Caratzas.

1979b Pompeii and Mount Vesuvius, AD 79. In *Volcanic activity and human ecology,* edited by P. D. Sheets and D. K. Grayson, 587–622. New York: Academic Press.

1993 *The gardens of Pompeii, Herculaneum and villas destroyed by Vesuvius* II (Appendices). New York: Caratzas.

Jongman, W. M.

1988 *The economy and society of Pompeii.* Amsterdam: Gieben.

Juvenal

Satires. Edited by J. D. Duff, 1970. Cambridge: Cambridge University Press.

Kampen, N. B.

1996 *Sexuality in ancient art: Near East, Greece and Italy.* Cambridge: Cambridge University Press.

Kanowski, M. G.

1984 *Containers of Classical Greece: A handbook of shapes.* Brisbane: University of Queensland.

Kent, S., ed.

1990 *Domestic architecture and the use of space.* Cambridge: Cambridge University Press.

Kockel, V.

1986 Archäologische Funde und Forschungen in den Vesuvstädten II. *Archäologischer Anzeiger* 22:443–581.

La Torre, G. F.

1988 Gli impianti commerciali ed artigianali nel tessuto urbano di Pompei. In *Pompei. L'informatica al servizio di una città antica,* 73–102. Rome: L'Erma di Bretschneider.

Laidlaw, A.

1985 *The First Style in Pompeii: Painting and architecture.* Rome: L'Erma di Bretschneider.

Lane, T., and J. Serle

1990 *Australians at home: A documentary history of Australian domestic interiors from 1788 to 1914.* Melbourne: Oxford University Press.

Laurence, R.

1994 *Roman Pompeii: Space and society.* London and New York: Routledge.

1995 Review. *Journal of Roman Studies* 85:313–314.

1997 Space and text. In *Domestic space in the Roman world: Pompeii and beyond,* edited by R. Laurence and A. F. Wallace-Hadrill, 7–14. Supplementary series no. 22. Portsmouth, RI: Journal of Roman Archaeology.

Laurence, R., and A. F. Wallace-Hadrill, eds.

1997 *Domestic space in the Roman world: Pompeii and beyond.* Supplementary series no. 22. Portsmouth, RI: Journal of Roman Archaeology.

Lazer, E.

1997 Human skeletal remains in the Casa del Menandro . In *The insula of the Menander at Pompeii I: The structures,* by R. Ling, Appendix F, 342–343. Oxford: Clarendon Press.

Leach, E. W.

1993 The entrance room in the House of Iulius Polybius and the nature of the Roman vestibulum. In *Functional and spatial analysis of wall painting: Proceedings of the 5th International Congress of Ancient Wall Painting, Amsterdam 1992,* edited by E. Moormann, 23–33. Annual papers in Classical Archaeology Supplement 3. Leiden: Bulletin Antieke Beschaving.

1997 Oecus on Ibycus: Investigating the vocabulary of the Roman house. In *Sequence and space in Pompeii,* edited by S. E. Bon and R. Jones, 50–72. Monograph 77. Oxford: Oxbow Books.

Ling, R.

1983a The Insula of the Menander at Pompeii: Interim report. *Antiquaries Journal* 63.1:34–57.

1983b The baths of the Casa del Menandro at Pompeii. *Pompeii Herculaneum Stabiae* 1:49–60.

1989 Review. *Burlington Magazine* 131:153.

1991 *Roman painting.* Cambridge: Cambridge University Press.

1995 Earthquake damage in Pompeii I 10: One earthquake or two. In *Archäologie und seismologie: La regione vesuviana dal 62 al 79 d.C., problemi archeologici e sismologici,* edited by T. Fröhlich and L. Jacobelli. Deutsches Archäologisches Institut Rom, Soprintendenza Archeologica di Pompei, Osservatorio Vesuviano, 201–209. Munich: Biering and Brinkman.

1997 *The Insula of the Menander at Pompeii I: The structures.* Oxford: Clarendon Press.

Lirer, L., R. Munno, P. Petrosino, and A. Vinci

1993 Tephrostratigraphy of the AD 79 pyroclastic deposits in perivolcanic areas of Mt. Vesuvio (Italy). *Journal of Volcanology and Geothermal Research* 58:133–149.

Lirer, L., T. Pescatore, B. Booth, and G. P. L. Walker

1973 Two Plinian pumice-fall deposits from Somma-Vesuvius, Italy. *Geological Society of America Bulletin* 84 (March): 759–772.

Livadie, C. A., ed.

1986 *Tremblement de terre, éruptions volcaniques et vie des hommes dans la campanie antique.* Naples: Centre Jean Bérard.

Livy

Historiarum Romanarum. Books 1–2. Translated by B. O. Foster, 1988. London: William Heinemann; Cambridge: Harvard University Press.

Lucretius

De rerum natura 4. Translated by J. Godwin, 1986. Warminster: Aris and Phillips.

Lytton, Bulwer–, Lord

1834 *The last days of Pompeii.* (First published in 1834).

McKay, A. G.

1977 *Houses, villas and palaces in the Roman world.* Southampton: Thames and Hudson (reprint).

Maiuri, A.

1925 L'Efebo di Via dell'Abbondanza a Pompei. *Bollettino d'Arte del Ministero della Pubblica Istruzione* Series II, 5:337–353.

1927 Pompei—Relazione sui lavori di scavo dal marzo 1924 al marzo 1926. *Notizie degli Scavi di Antichità,* Series 6, No. 3:3–83.

1929 Pompei—Relazione sui lavori di scavo dall'aprile 1926 al dicembre 1927. *Notizie degli Scavi di Antichità,* Series 6, No. 5:354–476.

1933 *La Casa del Menandro e il suo Tesoro di Argenteria.* Rome: La Libreria dello Stato.

1942 *L'Ultima Fase Edilizia di Pompei.* Rome: Istituto di Studi Romani.

1958 *Ercolano: i nuovi scavi (1927–1958).* Rome: Poligrafico dello Stato.

Martial

Epigrammata. Translated by W. C. A. Ker, 1957. London: William Heinemann; Cambridge: Harvard University Press.

Marturano, A., and V. Rinaldis

1995 Il terramoto del 62 d.C.: eventi carico de responsibilità. In *Archäologie und seismologie: La regione vesuviana dal 62 al 79 d.C., problemi archeologici e sismologici,* edited by T. Fröhlich, and L. Jacobelli. Deutsches Archäologisches Institut Rom, Soprintendenza Archeologica di Pompei, Osservatorio Vesuviano, 131–135. Munich: Biering and Brinkmann.

Mattäus, H.

1984 Untersuchungen zür Gerate - und Werkzeugformen aus der Umgebung von Pompei, zu ost-mediterran-hellenistisch Tradition im römischen Handwerk Kaiserzeit. *Bericht der Römisch-Germanischen Kommission* 65:73–150.

Mau, A.

1882 *Geschichte der decorativen Wandmalerei in Pompeji.* Berlin: Reimer.

1883 Scavi di Pompei. *Bulletino dell'Instituto di Corrispondenza archaeologica* 1:52–56, 71–83, 125–133, 143–155, 170–177.

1884 Scavi di Pompei. *Bulletino dell'Instituto di Corrispondenza archaeologica* 1:210–216.

1885 Scavi di Pompei. *Bulletino dell'Instituto di Corrispondenza archaeologica* 1:85–95.

1886 Scavi di Pompei 1884–85. *Mitteilungen des Deutschen Archäologischen Instituts, Römische Abteilung* 1:141–157.

1887 Scavi di Pompei 1885–86. *Mitteilungen des Deutschen Archäologischen Instituts, Römische Abteilung* 2:110–138.

1888 Scavi di Pompei 1886–88. *Mitteilungen des Deutschen Archäologischen Instituts, Römische Abteilung* 3:181–207.

1892 Scavi di Pompei. *Mitteilungen des Deutschen Archäologischen Instituts, Römische Abteilung* 7:3–25.

1893 Scavi di Pompei 1891–92. *Mitteilungen des Deutschen Archäologischen Instituts, Römische Abteilung* 8:3–61.

1896 Scavi di Pompei 1894–95. *Mitteilungen des Deutschen Archäologischen Instituts, Römische Abteilung* 11:3–97.

1898   Insula VI,15. *Mitteilungen des Deutschen Archäologischen Instituts, Römische Abteilung* 13:3–59.

1899   *Pompeii: Its life and art.* Translated by F. W. Kelsey. London: MacMillan.

1901   Ausgrabungen vom Pompeji. *Mitteilungen des Deutschen Archäologischen Instituts, Römische Abteilung* 16:283–365.

Mazois, F.
1812   *Les ruines de Pompéi.* Paris.

Michel, D.
1980   Pompejanische Gartenmalerei. In *Tainia, Festschrift für Roland Hampe,* edited by H. Cahn and E. Simon, 373–404. Mainz am Rhein: Philip von Zabern.

1990   *Casa dei Cei,* Häuser in Pompeji 3. Munich: Hirmer.

Mielsch, H.
1981   Funde und Forschungen zur Wandmalerei der Prinzipatszeit von 1945 bis 1975 mit einem Nachtrag 1980. *Aufstieg und Neidergang der römischen Welt II, Principat* 12.2:157–264.

1988   Review. *Göttingische Gelehrte Anzeiger* 240:90–130.

Miller, D.
1985   *Artefacts as categories: A study of ceramic variability in Central India.* Cambridge: Cambridge University Press.

1995   *Acknowledging consumption: A review of new studies.* London and New York: Routledge.

Millette, D. M.
1999   Textual imaginations: Vitruvius in archaeological [re]constructions. *Assemblage* 3. Online journal, available from *www.shef.ac.uk/~assem/3/.*

Ministero per i Beni Culturali e Ambientali,
1989   *Notiziario VI,* 26.

Mols, S. T. A. M.
1999   *Wooden furniture in Herculaneum: Form, technique and function.* Amsterdam: Gieben.

Moormann, E., ed.
1993   *Functional and spatial analysis of wall painting: Proceedings of the Fifth International Congress on Ancient Wall Painting, Amsterdam 1992.* Annual Papers on Classical Archaeology Supplement 3. Leiden: Bulletin antieke beschaving.

Morel, J. P.
1979   La ceramica e il vetro. In *Pompei 79,* edited by F. Zevi, 241–264. Naples: Gaitano Macchiaroli.

Mouritsen, H.
1988   *Elections, magistrates and the municipal elite: Studies in Pompeian epigraphy.* Analecta Romana Instituti Danici Supplement 5. Rome.

1990   A note on Pompeian epigraphy and social structure. *Classica et Mediaevalia* 41:131–149.

Nappo, S.
1997   The urban transformation at Pompeii in the late third and early second centuries BC. In *Domestic space in the Roman world: Pompeii and beyond,* edited by R. Laurence and A. F. Wallace-Hadrill, 91–120. Supplementary series no. 22. Portsmouth, RI: Journal of Roman Archaeology.

Neudecker, R.
1988   *Die Skulpturen-Austattung römischer Villen in Italien.* Mainz: P. von Zabern.

Neumann, K.
1996   *Rabaul. Yu Swit Moa Yet: Surviving the 1994 Volcanic Eruption.* Oxford: Oxford University Press.

Nevett, L.
1997   Perceptions of domestic space in Roman Italy. In *The Roman family in Italy: Status, sentiment and space,* edited by B. Rawson and P. Weaver, 281–298. Oxford: Clarendon Press.

1999   *House and society in the Ancient Greek world.* Cambridge: Cambridge University Press.

Noack, F., and K. Lehmann-Hartleben
1936   *Baugeschichtliche Untersuchungen am Stadtrand von Pompeji, Denkmäler antike Architekture.* Bd. 2. Berlin and Leipzig: Walter de Gruyter and Co.

Nuber, H. U.
1972   Kanne und Griffschale. Ihr Gebrauch in taglichen Leben und die Biegabe in Grabern der römischen Kaiserzeit. *Bericht der Römisch-Germanischen Kommission* 53. Frankfurt am Main.

Oliva Auricchio, M.

1966-78 Giornali degli Scavi I–IX. Unpublished manuscripts. Archives of the Soprintendenza archeologica di Pompei.

Orr, D. G.

1978 Roman domestic religion: The evidence of the household shrine. *Aufstieg und Niedergang der römischen Welt II Principat* 16.2:1557–1591.

1988 Learning from Lararia: Notes on household shrines in Pompeii. In *Studia Pompeiana & Classica: in honour of Wilhelmina F. Jashemski*, edited by R. I. Curtius, 293–303. New York: Caratzas.

Overbeck, J.

1856 *Pompeji in seinen Gebäuden, Alterthümern und Kunstwerken für Kunst- und Alterthumsfreunde*. Leipzig: Wilhelm Englemann.

Packer, J. E.

1975 Middle and lower class housing in Pompeii and Herculaneum: A preliminary report. In *Neue Forschungen in Pompeji*, edited by B. Andreae and H. Kyrieleis, 133–142. Recklinghausen: Aurel Bongers.

Panella, C.

1977 Anfore Tripolitane a Pompei. In *L'instrumentum domesticum di Ercolano e Pompei*, edited by A. Carandini et al., 135–149. Rome: L'Erma di Bretschneider.

Paoli, U.

1958 *Rome: Its people, life and customs*. Aberdeen: Longmans.

Pappalardo, U.

1990 L'eruzione pliniana del Vesuvio nel 79 d.C: Ercolano. In *Volcanology and archaeology. Pact 25*, edited by C. A. Livadie and F. Widermann, 197–215. Strasbourg: Council of Europe.

Parker Pearson, M.

1998 The beginning of wisdom. *Antiquity* 72, No. 277:680–686.

Parkin, T. G.

1994 Review. *Journal of Roman Studies* 84:178–185.

1997 Out of sight, out of mind: Elderly members of the Roman family. In *The Roman family in Italy: Status, sentiment and space*, edited

by B. Rawson and P. Weaver, 123–148. Oxford: Clarendon Press.

Parslow, C.

1990 Review. *American Journal of Archaeology* 94:512–513.

Pauly, A. F. von

Paulys Realencyclopädie der classichen Altertumswissenschaft. Stuttgart: A. Druckmüller.

Peacock, D. P. S., and D. F. Williams

1986 *Amphorae and the Roman economy: An introductory guide*. London and New York: Longman.

Pernice, E.

1900 Bronzen aus Boscoreale. *Archäologischer Anzeiger* 15:177–198.

1938 *Pavimenti und figürliche Mosaiken, Die hellenistiche Kunst in Pompeji* 5. Berlin: Walter de Gruyter.

Perrot, M.

1990 *A history of private life IV: From the fires of revolution to the Great War*. London and Cambridge, Mass.: Harvard University Press.

Pesando, F.

1997 *Domus: Edilizia privata e società pompeiana fra III e I secolo a.C.* Rome: L'Erma di Bretschneider.

Peters, W. J.

1977 La composizione delle parete dipinte nella Casa dei Vettii a Pompei. *Mededelingen van het Nederlands Instituut te Rome, Antiquity* 39:95–128.

Peters, W. J., E. M. Moormann, T. L. Heres, H. Brusting, and S. L. Wynia

1993 *La Casa di Marcus Lucretius Fronto a Pompei e le sue pitture*. Amsterdam: Thesis Publishers.

Petronius

Satyricon. Cena Trimalcionus. Translated by R. Bracht Branham and D. Kinney, 1996. Berkeley: University of California.

Pinon, P., R. Chevallier, and P.-Y. Balut

1982 *La Laurentine e l'invention de la Villa romaine*. Paris: Institut Français d'Architecture.

Pirson, F.

1996 Mietwohnungen in Pompeji und Herkulaneum: Untersuchungen zur Architektur, zum Wohnen und zur Sozial-und Wirtschaftsgeschichte der Vesuvstädte. Ph.D. dissertation, Ludwig-Maximilians-Universität, Munich.

1997   Rented accommodation at Pompeii: The evidence of the Insula Arriana Polliana VI 6. In *Domestic space in the Roman world: Pompeii and beyond,* edited by R. Laurence and A. F. Wallace-Hadrill, 165–81. Supplementary series no. 22. Portsmouth, RI: Journal of Roman Archaeology.

Plautus
        Mostellaria. Edited by E. A. Sonnenschein, 1996. Oxford: Clarendon Press.

Pliny the Elder
        Naturalis Historiae. Translated by H. Rackham, 1938-63. London: William Heineman; Cambridge, Mass.: Harvard University Press.

Pliny the Younger
        Epistulae. Translated by W. Melmoth, 1931. London: William Heineman; Cambridge, Mass.: Harvard University Press.

Plutarch
        Moralia. Translated by F. C. Babbit, 1962. London: William Heineman; Cambridge, Mass.: Harvard University Press.

Pompeii: Vesuvius AD 79
1999/2000 Semestrale di informazione e di cultura. Pompeii: Soprintendenza Archaeologica di Pompei.

Purcell, N.
1995   Forum Roman (the Republican period). In *Lexicon Topographicum Urbis Romae* II, edited by E.M. Steinby, 325–336. Rome: Quasar.

Ragozzino, A.M.
1987–88 Il larario della Casa di C. Guilio Polibio in Pompei (IX, 13, 1–3). *Rendiconti della Accademia di Archeologi, Lettere e Belle Arti* 60:69–86.

Raper, R. A.
1977   The analysis of the urban structure of Pompeii: A sociological examination of land use. In *Spatial archaeology,* edited by D. L. Clarke, 189–221. London and New York: Academic Press.

Rapoport, A.
1990   Systems of activities and systems of settings. In *Domestic architecture and the use of space,* edited by S. Kent, 9–20. Cambridge: Cambridge University Press.

Rapp Jr., G.
1989   Tracce di giofisica. In *I terramoti prima del Mille in Italia e nell'area mediterranea,* edited by E. Guidaboni, 398–403. Bologna: SGA Storia–Geofisica –Ambiente.

Rawson, B.
1997   The iconography of Roman childhood. In *The Roman family in Italy: Status, sentiment and space,* edited by B. Rawson and P. Weaver, 205–232. Oxford: Clarendon Press.

Reese, D.
2002   Marine invertebrates, freshwater shells, and land snails. In *The natural history of Pompeii,* edited by W. Jashemski and F. G. Meyer, 292–314. Cambridge: Cambridge University Press.

Renfrew, C., J. R. Cann, and J. E. Dixon
1965   Obsidian in the Aegean. *The Annual of the British School at Athens* 60:223–247.

Ricci, A.
1985   *Settefinistre: Una villa schiavistica nell'Etruria romana 2: La villa e i suoi reperti.* Modena: Panini.

Richardson Jr., L.
1983   A contribution to the study of Pompeian dining-rooms. *Pompeii Herculaneum Stabiae* 1:61–71.

1988a   *Pompeii: An architectural history.* Baltimore and London: John Hopkins Press.

1988b   Water Triclinia and Biclinia in Pompeii. In *Studia Pompeiana & Classica in honour of Wilhelmina F. Jashemski,* edited by R. Curtius, 305–312. New York: Caratzas.

Riggsby, A. M.
1997   'Private' and 'public' in Roman culture: The case of the *cubiculum. Journal of Roman Archaeology* 10:36–56.

Roaf, M.
1989   Ubaid social organization and social activities as seen from Tell Madhhur. In *Upon this Foundation-The Ubaid Reconsidered,* edited by E. F. Henrickson and I. Thuesen, 91–146. Copenhagen: Museum Tusculanum Press.

239

Rosaldo, M. Z.

1980   The use and abuse of anthropology: Reflections on feminism and cross-understanding. *Signs* 5, 3:389–417.

Rosaldo, M. Z., and L. Lamphere, eds.

1974   *Woman, culture, and society.* Stanford: Stanford University Press.

Ross, A.

1982   Absence of evidence: Reply to Keryn Kefous. *Archaeology in Oceania* 17:99.

Sacket, L. H., et al.

1992   *Knossos from Greek city to Roman colony: Excavations at the unexplored mansion II.* British School of Archaeology at Athens. Oxford: Thames and Hudson.

Salza Prina Ricotti, E.

1978/1980 Cucine e quartieri servili in epoca romana. *Rendiconti. Atti della Pontificia accademia romana di archeologia* 51–2:237–294.

Scarfoglio, A., ed.

1988   *Il tesoro di Boscoreale: Una collezione di argenti da mensa tra cultura ellenistica e mondo romano.* Milano: Franco Maria Ricci.

Scatozza Höricht, L. A.

1986   *I vetri romani di Ercolano.* Soprintendenze archeologica di Pompei cataloghi 1. Rome: L'Erma di Bretschneider.

Schefold, K.

1952   *Pompejanische Malerei. Sinn und Ideengeschichte.* Basel: Benno Schwabe and Co.

1957a   *Die Wände pompejis.* Berlin: De Gruyter.

1957b   Zur Chronologie der Dekorationen im Haus der Vettier. *Mitteilungen des Deutschen Archäologischen Instituts, Römische Abteilung* 64:149–153.

1962   *Vergessenes Pompeji.* Bern and Munich: Francke.

1990   Die Bedeutung der Malerei Pompejis. In *Pompejanische Wandmalerei,* by G. Cerulli Irelli et al. Zurich: Belser Verlag.

1995   Pompei, terramoto e storia degli stili. In *Archäologie und seismologie: La regione vesuviana dal 62 al 79 d.C., problemi archeologici e sismologici,* edited by T. Fröhlich and L. Jacobelli. Deutsches Archäologisches Institut Rom, Soprintendenza Archeologica di Pompei, Osservatorio Vesuviano, 15–16. Munich: Biering and Brinkmann.

Schiffer, M. B.

1985   Is there a Pompeii Premise? *Journal of Anthropological Research* 41:18–41.

1987   *Formation processes of the archaeological record.* Albuquerque: University of New Mexico Press (republished 1996, Salt Lake City: University of Utah Press).

Seiler, F.

1992   *Casa degli Amorini Dorati,* Häuser in Pompeji 5. Munich: Hirmer.

1995   Zur Lage der Erdbebenforschungen in der Vesuvregion aus der Sicht der Archäologie. In *Archäologie und seismologie: La regione vesuviana dal 62 al 79 d.C., problemi archeologici e sismologici,* edited by T. Fröhlich and L. Jacobelli. Deutsches Archäologisches Institut Rom, Soprintendenza Archeologica di Pompei, Osservatorio Vesuviano, 23–28. Munich: Biering and Brinkmann.

Seneca

        Epistulae morales. Translated by R. M. Gummere, 1979. London: William Heinemann; Cambridge, Mass.: Harvard University Press.
        Naturales Quaestiones. Translated by T. H. Corcoran, 1972. London: William Heineman; Cambridge, Mass.: Harvard University Press.

Servius

        Ad Aeneid. Edited by G. Thilo and H. Hagen, 1961. Hildesheim: Georg Olms.

Shanks, M.

1997   Archaeological theory: What's on the agenda? *American Journal of Archaeology* 101.2:395–399.

Shanks, M., and C. Tilley

1987   *Reconstructing archaeology.* Cambridge: Cambridge University Press.

Sheets, P. D., and D. K. Grayson

1979   Volcanic disasters and the archaeological record. In *Volcanic activity and human ecology,* edited by P. D. Sheets, and D. K. Grayson, 623–632. New York: Academic Press.

Shelton, J.-A.

1988   *As the Romans did: A sourcebook in Roman social history.* Oxford: Oxford University Press.

Sigurdsson, H., S. Cashdollar, and S. R. J. Sparks
1982   The eruption of Vesuvius in AD 79: Reconstruction from historical and volcanological evidence. *American Journal of Archaeology* 86:39–51.

Skeates, R.
1991   Triton's trumpet: A neolithic symbol in Italy. *Oxford Journal of Archaeology* 10:1, 17–31.

Smith, M.
1992   Braudel's temporal rhythms and chronology theory in archaeology. In *Archaeology, annales and ethnohistory*, edited by A. B. Knapp, 23–34. Cambridge: Cambridge University Press.

Sogliano, A.
1886   Pompei. *Notizie degli Scavi di Antichità:* 132–133, 166–169.

1887   Pompei. *Notizie degli Scavi di Antichità:* 33–41, 241–243, 411–415.

1888   Pompei—Degli edifici recentemente scoperti, e degli oggetti raccolti negli scavi dal dicembre 1887 al guigno 1888. *Notizie degli Scavi di Antichità:* 509–530.

1893   Pompei—2. Degli edifici disterrati nell'Isola 2a, Regione VIII. *Notizie degli Scavi di Antichità:* 35–51.

1895   Pompei—Giornale degli Scavi redatto dagli assissenti. *Notizie degli Scavi di Antichità:* 326, 438–440, 474.

1896   Pompei—Edifici scoperti nell'Isola 2a, Regione V. *Notizie degli Scavi di Antichità:* 418–441.

1897   Pompei—Degli edifizi scoperti nell'Isola XI, Regione VI. *Notizie degli Scavi di Antichità,* Series 5, No. 5:14–40, 105–109, 150–157, 198–200, 340–342.

1898a   *La Casa dei Vetti in Pompei Monumenti Antichi* 8:234–387.

1898b   Pompei—Relazione degli scavi fatti durante 1898. *Notizie degli Scavi di Antichità:* 125–127, 503–504.

1899   Pompei—Relazione degli scavi fatti durante 1899. *Notizie degli Scavi di Antichità:* 17–24, 62–63, 141–146.

1900   Pompei—Relazione degli scavi fatti durante i mese di 1900. *Notizie degli Scavi di Antichità:* Series 5, No. 8:146–148, 199–203, 236–240, 409–410, 584–603, 639–641.

1901   Pompei—Relazioni degli scavi fatti durante il meso di febbraio 1991. *Notizie degli Scavi di Antichità:* Series 5, No. 9: 145–170.

1904   Gli scavi di Pompei dal 1873–1900. *Atti del Congresso Internazionale di Scienza Storiche* V:295–349.

1906   Pompei—Relazione degli scavi fatti dal dicembre 1902 a tutto marzo 1905. *Notizie degli Scavi di Antichità,* Series 5, No. 3:374–383.

1907   Pompei—Relazione degli scavi fatti dal dicembre 1902 a tutto marzo 1905. *Notizie degli Scavi di Antichità,* Series 5, No. 4:549–593.

1908   Pompei—Relazione degli scavi esegueti dal dicembre 1902 a tutto marzo 1905. *Notizie degli Scavi di Antichità,* Series 5, No. 5:26–43, 53–84, 180–192.

Soprano, P.
1950   I triclini all'aperto di Pompei, *Pompeiana. Raccolta di studi per il secondo centenario degli Scavi di Pompei,* 288–310. Naples: Bibliotheca della Parola del passato, No. 4.

Spano, G.
1910   Relazione degli scavi eseguiti nell'anno 1907. *Notizie degli Scavi di Antichità,* Series 5, No. 7:315–332.

1911   Pompei—Scavi eseguiti durante il mese di ottobre 1911. *Notizie degli Scavi di Antichità,* Series 5, No. 8:372–377.

1915   Pompei—Scavi sulla Via dell'Abbondanza durante il mese di giugno. *Notizie degli Scavi di Antichità,* Series 5, No. 12:336–341, 416–419, 425–429.

1916   Pompei—Continuazione dello scavo della Via dell'Abbondanza. *Notizie degli Scavi di Antichità,* Series 5, No. 13:117–122, 231–235.

Spinazzola, V.
1916   Pompei rinvenimento di quattro sepolti dal lapillo nel peristilio della Casa di Trebio Valente. *Notizie degli Scavi di Antichità,* Series 5, No. 13:87–90; Continuazione degli scavi in Via dell'Abbondanza. *Notizie degli Scavi di Antichità,* Series 5, No. 13:148–151.

1917   Continuazione degli scavi in Via dell'Abbondanza. *Notizie degli Scavi di Antichità,* Series 5, No. 14:247–264.

1953   *Pompei alla luce degli scavi nuovi di Via dell'Abbondanza (anni 1910–1923)* I–II. Rome: La Libreria dello Stato.

Staub Gierow, M.

1994   *Casa del Granduca und Casa dei Capitelli Figurati,* Häuser in Pompeji 7. Munich: Hirmer.

Stemmer, K.

1992   *Casa dell'Ara Massima,* Häuser in Pompeji 6. Munich: Hirmer.

Stenning, D. J.

1969   Household viability among pastoral Fulani. In *Developmental cycles in domestic groups,* edited by J. Goody, 92–119. Cambridge Papers in Social Anthropology no. 1. Cambridge: Cambridge University Press.

Strabo

     The geography of Strabo. Edited by T. E. Page, 1949. London: William Heineman; Cambridge, Mass.: Harvard University Press.

Strocka, V. M.

1975   Pompejanische Nebenzimmer. In *Neue Forschungen in Pompeji,* edited by B. Andreae and H. Kyrieleis, 101–114. Recklinghausen: Aurel Bongers.

1981   Römische Bibliotheken. *Gymnasium* 88:298–329.

1984a   *Casa del Principe di Napoli,* Häuser in Pompeji 1. Tübingen: Wasmuth.

1984b   Ein missverstandener Terminus des vierten Stils: die Casa del Sacello Iliaco in Pompeji (I 6,4). *Mitteilungen des Deutschen Archäologischen Instituts, Römische Abteilung* 91:125–140.

1991   *Casa del Labirinto,* Häuser in Pompeji 4. Munich: Hirmer.

1995   Die Chronologie des Vierten Stils, von keinem Erdbeben erschüttet. In *Archäologie und seismologie: La regione vesuviana dal 62 al 79 d.C., problemi archeologici e sismologici,* edited by T. Fröhlich and L. Jacobelli. Deutsches Archäologisches Institut Rom, Soprintendenza Archeologica di Pompei,

Osservatorio Vesuviano, 175–180. Munich: Biering and Brinkmann.

Suetonius

     De Vita Caesarum. Translated by J. C. Rolfe, 1924. London: William Heineman; Cambridge, Mass.: Harvard University Press.

Sutherland, I.

1990   Colonnaded cenacula in Pompeian domestic architecture. Ph.D. dissertation, Duke University. Ann Arbor: University Microfilms 9100108.

Tacitus

     Annales. Translated by J. Jackson, 1962. London: William Heineman; Cambridge, Mass.: Harvard University Press.

Tamm, B.

1963   *Auditorium and Palatium: A study on assembly-rooms in Roman palaces during the 1st century BC and the 1st century AD. Stockholm Studies in Classical Archaeology.* Stockholm: Almqvist and Wikseil.

1973   Some notes on Roman houses. *Opuscula romana* 9:53–60.

Tannahill, R.

1968   *The fine art of food.* London: Folio Society.

Tarbell, F. B.

1909   *Catalogue of bronze etc. in Field Museum of Natural History, Chicago, reproduced from originals in the National Museum of Naples.* Anthropology Series vol. 7 no. 3 (June). Chicago: Field Museum of Natural History 30.

Tassinari, S.

1975   *La vaisselle de bronze romaine et provinciale au Musée des antiquité nationales.* 29th supplément à Gallia. Paris: CNRS.

1979   Il vasellame di bronzo. In *Pompei 79,* edited by F. Zevi, 229–240. Naples: Gaitano Macchiaroli.

1993   *Il vasellame bronzeo di Pompei* I–II. Soprintendenza archeologica di Pompei cataloghi 5. Rome: L'Erma di Bretschneider.

Thébert, Y.

1987   Private life and domestic architecture in Roman North Africa. In *A history of private life: From pagan Rome to Byzantium,* translated by A. Goldhammer, edited by P.

Veyne, 313–409. London and Cambridge, Mass.: Harvard University Press.

Thérasse, J.

1979   Le 19e centenaire de l'ensevelissement de Pompéi. *Les études classiques* 47:297–305.

Thomas, R.

1995   Zur Bedeutung der Erdbebenschäden für eine Untersuchung der Stilistischen Entwicklung der Neronischen bis Flavischen Pompejanischen Wandmalerei. In *Archäologie und seismologie: La regione vesuviana dal 62 al 79 d.C., problemi archeologici e sismologici,* edited by T. Fröhlich and L. Jacobelli. Deutsches Archäologisches Institut Rom, Soprintendenza Archeologica di Pompei, Osservatorio Vesuviano, 169–174. Munich: Biering and Brinkmann.

Tilley, C.

1998   Archaeology: The loss of isolation. *Antiquity* 72:691–693.

Torrence, R., et al.

1990   Pompeiis in the Pacific. *Australian Natural History* 23:3–16.

Tran Tam Tinh, V.

1989   *La Casa dei Cervi a Herculaneum.* Rome: Georgio Bretschneider.

Trevelyan, R.

1976   *The Shadow of Vesuvius: Pompeii AD 79.* London: The Folio Society.

Trigger, B. G.

1989   *A history of archaeological thought.* Cambridge: Cambridge University Press.

Ulbert, G.

1969   *Das frührömische Kastell Rheingönheim.* Berlin: Mann.

Van Binneke, M. C.

1991   Some remarks on the functions of houses and rooms in the Insula V at Herculaneum. *Mededelingen van het Nederlands Instituut te Rome, Antiquity* 50:136–144.

Van der Poel, H. B.

1977–86 *Corpus Topographicum Pompeianum,* Pts. 1–5. Rome: H. Van der Poel.

Varone, A.

1988   Pompei Attività dell'Ufficio Scavi: 1987–1988. *Rivista di Studi Pompeiani* 2:142–154.

1989   Pompei Attività dell'Ufficio Scavi: 1989. *Rivista di Studi Pompeiani* 3:225–238.

1995   Più terramoti a Pompei? I nuovi dati degli scavi di Via dell'Abbondanza. In *Archäologie und seismologie: La regione vesuviana dal 62 al 79 d.C., problemi archeologici e sismologici,* edited by T. Fröhlich and L. Jacobelli. Deutsches Archäologisches Institut Rom, Soprintendenza Archeologica di Pompei, Osservatorio Vesuviano, 29–35. Munich: Biering and Brinkmann.

Varro

De Lingua Latina. Translated by R. G. Kent, 1958. Cambridge, Mass.: Harvard University Press.

Rerum rusticarum. Translated by W. D. Hopper and H. B. Ash, 1967. London: William Heinemann; Cambridge, Mass.: Harvard University Press.

Vickery, A.

1993   Historiographical review: Golden age of separate spheres? A review of the categories and chronology of English women's history. *The Historical Journal* 36.2:383–414.

Virgil

Ad Aeneid. Books 7–8, edited by J. D. Christie, 1977. Oxford: Oxford University Press.

Vitruvius

De Architectura. Books 1–10. Translated by F. Granger, 1983. Cambridge, Mass.: Harvard University Press.

Volcano World

<http://www.volcano.und.nodak.edu/vw.html>

Wallace-Hadrill, A.

1986   Review. *Antiquaries Journal* 66:433–434.

1989   Patronage in Roman society: From republic to empire. In *Patronage in ancient society,* edited by Wallace–Hadrill, 63–87. London and New York: Routledge.

1994   *Houses and society in Pompeii and Herculaneum.* Princeton, New Jersey: Princeton University Press.

1997   Rethinking the Roman atrium house. In *Domestic space in the Roman world: Pompeii and beyond,* edited by R. Laurence and A. F. Wallace-Hadrill, 219–240. Supplementary series no. 22. Portsmouth, RI: Journal of Roman Archaeology.

Ward-Perkins, B.

1989   Archeologia e terramoti perdute. In *I terramoti prima del Mille in Italia e nell'area mediterranea*, edited by E. Guidaboni, 409–413. Bologna: SGA Storia–Geofisica–Ambiente.

Ward-Perkins, J. B., and A. Claridge

1980   *Pompeii AD 79*. Sydney: Australian Gallery Directors Council.

Warscher, T.

1948   I Marmi di Pompei. Unpublished manuscript. Rome: Swedish Institute in Rome.

White, K. D.

1975   *Farm equipment of the Roman world*. Cambridge. Cambridge: Cambridge University Press.

Whitley, J.

1992/93 The explanation of form: Towards a reconciliation of archaeological and art historical approaches. *Hephaistos* 11/12:7–33.

Wiedemann, T.

1989   *Adults and children in the Roman Empire*. London: Routledge.

Wikander, O.

1989   A Roman bronze lamp in Stockholm. *Medelhausmuseet* 24:31–34.

Wild, J. P.

1970   *Textile manufacture in the northern Roman provinces*. Cambridge: Cambridge University Press.

Wilkins, A. S.

1907   *The epistle of Horace*. London and New York: MacMillan and Co. Ltd.

Will, E. L.

1979   Women in Pompeii. *Archaeology* 32.5:34–43.

Wilsdorf, H.

1979   Antike Theorien über der Vulkanismus, In *Pompeji 79–1979, Beiträge zum Vesuvbruch und seiner Nachwirkung*, edited by K. Munze, 4–53. Beiträge der Winckelmann Gesellschaft 11. Stendal.

Wiseman, T. P.

1982   *Pete nobiles amicos*: Poets and patrons in Late Republican Rome. In *Literary and artistic patronage in Ancient Rome*, edited by B. K. Gold, 28–49. Austin: University of Texas Press.

Wright, R. V.

1989   *Doing multivariate analysis in archaeology and prehistory: Handling large data sets in MV–Arch*. Sydney: University of Sydney.

Wyke, M.

1994   Woman in the mirror. In *Women in ancient societies: An illusion of the night*, edited by L. J. Archer, S. Fischler, and M. Wyke, 134–151. London: MacMillan Press.

Wylie, A.

1991   Gender theory and the archaeological record: Why is there no archaeology of gender? In *Engendering archaeology: Women and prehistory*, edited by J. M. Gero and M. W. Conkey, 31-56. Oxford: Basil Blackwell.

Wynia, S. L.

1982   The excavations in and around the House of M. Lucretius Fronto. In *La regione sotterata dal Vesuvio. Studi e prospettive, Atti del convegno internazionale 11–15 novembre 1979*, edited by S. L. Wynia, 329–340. Naples: Università degli Studi di Napoli.

Zanker, P.

1988   *Pompeji: Stadtbilder als Spiegel von Gesellschaft und Herrschaftsform*. Mainz am Rhien: Philipp von Zabern.

1995   *Pompeji: Stadtbilder und Wohngeschmack*. Mainz am Rhein: Philipp von Zabern.

Zimmer, G.

1982   *Römische Berufdarstellungen*. Deutsches Archäologisches Institut, Archäologische Forschungen 12. Berlin: Mann.

Glossary

This glossary includes French (Fr), German (Gr), Greek (Gk), Italian (It), Latin (La), and technical terms used in the text. Non-English words are set in italics. Brief definitions, as they occur in the relevant dictionaries, are provided. Where pertinent, an indication of each term's use in Pompeian studies, particularly in the inventories and excavation reports, is included. Further discussion of the use of terms for room types can be found in chapter 7 (see also table 5.a).

abbeveratoio   Drinking trough; refers to small, ceramic, conical vessel with narrow mouth and presumed to have been for birds (see chapter 4; Allison 1999b:67–68) (It)

aedicula   Small structure used as shrine

ala   Wing; refers to open-fronted room off one side of *atrium* (see chapter 7) (La)

ambulatio   Place for walking (see chapter 7) (La)

amphora   Two-handled vessel; usually refers to large conical or ovoid jar used for transporting wine and oil

andron   Men's room in Greek house (Gk)

apodyterium   Used for dressing room in bath complex (La)

apotheca   Storeroom (Gk)

arca   Chest, box, or safe (see Allison 1999b:60–61) (La)

atrium   Forecourt, hall, or principal room; used for front hall with central opening in roof (see chapter 7) (La)

balineum/balnearia/balneum   Bath, baths, bathing-place (see chapter 7) (La)

Bedienstetenatrium   Service *atrium* (Gr)

caldarium   Generally refers to hot room in bath complex (La)

calida piscina   Heated swimming pool (La)

cartibulum   Oblong stone table on pedestal (Varro *De ling. lat.* 5, 125); refers to marble table found in front hall (see Allison 1999b:61–62) (La)

casseruola   Saucepan; refers to bronze, hemispherical pan with long, horizontal handle from lip (see chapter 4; Allison 1999b:67) (It)

cavaedium/cavum aedium   Inner court of house (see chapter 7) (La)

cella   Storeroom, cell (see chapter 7) (La)

cellae familiaricae   Refers to servants' rooms (see chapter 7) (La)

cella ostiaria   Refers to room inside entranceway, reputedly for *ostiarius* (doorman or porter) (see chapter 7) (La)

cella penaria   Room for provisions or storeroom (see chapter 7) (La)

cella vinaria   Wine cellar or room (La)

cenaculum   Upper story, originally a dining room (see chapter 7) (La)

cenatio   Dining room (La)

cisternola   Diminutive of cistern (It)

cliens   Personal dependent or client (La)

compluvium   Opening in center of roof through which rainwater was collected in *impluvium* (see Mau 1899:244; McKay 1977:17, 22) (La)

cortile   Courtyard (It)

cortiletto   Diminutive of *cortile* (It)

cryptoporticus   Enclosed gallery or subterranean passage (La)

cubiculo diurno   Refers to daytime bedroom; room for siesta (It from La)

cubiculum   Used for sleeping room (see chapter 7) (La)

culina   Kitchen (see chapter 7) (La)

dente   Tooth or tusk (It)

dispensa   Pantry or larder (It)

dolio   Italianization of *dolium* (It)

dolium   Large, wide-mouthed globular jar; refers to very large ceramic jar (La)

dormitorii servili   Slaves' bedrooms (see chapter 7) (La)

Efebo   Italianization of *Ephebus* (It)

Ephebus   Greek youth, strictly between ages of sixteen and twenty (La)

exedra   Hall (see chapter 7) (La)

fauces   Throat, jaws, entrance; refers to house entrance or corridor (see chapter 7) (La)

focolare   Hearth or furnace (It)

forma di pasticceria   Pastry mold; refers to both shell-shaped and elliptical bronze vessel (see chapter 4; Allison 1999b:66–67) (It)

fornello   Object or cavity that contained combustible material; refers to open-fronted, semicircular masonry structure, sometimes plastered (It) *frigidarium*   Cold area in bath complex (see chapter 7) (La)

fritillus   Dice box; refers to small ceramic vase assumed to have been a dice thrower (see chapter 4; Allison 1999b: 62–63) (La)

fruttiera   Fruit stand or fruit bowl; refers to large, shallow, quasi-elliptical (or figure–eight–shaped), basket-like bronze dish with upright articulated handles (It)

genius   Tutelary or attendant spirit assigned to person at birth, or place (La)

guardispigolo   Corner guard; refers to L- or U-shaped metal fitting with eyelet for attachment with nails or screws, reputedly corner guard for furniture (but see chapter 4) (It)

hortus   Garden, park (see chapter 7) La)

hortulus   Small garden (see chapter 7) (La)

impluvium   Water-catchment area in center of *atrium*, beneath *compluvium* (see Mau 1899:244; McKay 1977:17) (La)

insula   Island or isle; refers to area of buildings surrounded by streets (that is, a city block) (La)

labrum   Basin, tub, or vat associated with washing; refers to large, relatively flat marble or bronze basin (La)

laconicum   Sweating room in bath complex (see chapter 7) (La)

lapillo   Small stone or pebble of volcanic ash (It)

lararium   Shrine to household gods, Lares; refers to aedicula or painting depicting Lares (see Mau 1899:262–267) (La)

Lares   Domestic deities; protecting deities of household or city (La)

lectus   Bed or couch (La)

Lichthof   Light well (Gr)

oecus   Hall or salon (see chapter 7) (La)

ostiarius   see *cella ostiaria* (La)

ostium   Door, entrance (La)

patera   Low bowl or flattened dish, saucer, libation dish; refers to bronze shallow-bowled vessel with central boss and horizontal, cylindrical handle, often terminating in ram's head (for example, Borriello et al. 1986:176, Nos. 19–20; 178. Nos. 46–47) (La)

paterfamilias   Father of family, head of household (La)

penaria   See *cella penaria* (La)

Penates   Guardian gods of the family (La)

peristylum   Open court or garden surrounded by colonnade (see chapter 7) (La)

pinacotheca   Picture gallery (see chapter 7) (Gk)

podium   Raised platform

porticus   Covered walkway between columns (La)

posticum   Back door (see chapter 7) (La)

procoeton   Antechamber (Gk)

pseudo-peristyle   Partially colonnaded

puteal   Refers to stone or terra-cotta cylinder protecting cistern head

repositorium   Used for storeroom (La)

salutatio   Greeting, salutation, formal morning reception between patron and clients (La)

scalae   Flight of steps, stairs (La)

scodella   Bowl or deep plate (It)

stabulum   Standing place, stall, or stable (La)

strigil   Instrument with curved blade used to scrape sweat and dirt from skin before bath

taberna   Hut, cabin, shop, place of business (La)

tablinum   Balcony, terrace, or room open to air; room where archives were kept; picture gallery; used for open room at end of front hall (La)

tabulinum   Balcony, terrace, or other floored space in open air; place where family records are kept; picture gallery; see *tablinum* (see chapter 7) (La)

tegame   Frying pan (It)

tepidarium   Warm bath or warm room in bath complex (see chapter 7) (La)

terra sigillata   Particular type of red, burnished pottery from Roman period, with stamped or relief decoration, often with maker's stamp at base (It)

unctorium   Used for anointing room (see chapter 7) (La)

vestibulum   Enclosed space at front of house; refers to entranceway to Pompeian house (see chapter 7) (La)

viridarium   Pleasure garden, plantation of trees; refers to garden area of house (see chapter 7) (La)

xystus   Colonnade, garden terrace, shaded walk (see chapter 7) (La)

zotheca   Little private chamber, closet, cabinet, recess, or niche (see chapter 7) (Gk)

Index

Page numbers in *italic* type in this index refer to figures and figure captions. References to specific houses noted in the tables are not included here.